MARGARET BURKE SHERIDAN
1889 — 1958

'Deeply sensitive and intelligent, with a brilliant wit, outspoken, almost
to a dangerous degree, she faced the world alone from babyhood with a
bright, clear courage that never failed her.'

Mary d'Ardia Caracciolo,
Ireland

'I remember, a turquoise-blue hat on golden hair, ropes of pearls on a
bosom that could only belong to a prima donna . . . A musical speaking-
voice with, to English ears, the fascinating hint of a brogue. Small,
exquisitely-shaped hands, dramatically used in conversation . . .
a golden voice, golden hair . . . Maggie.'

Nancy Towle,
England

'La Sheridan was a beautiful woman, an intelligent and sensitive
interpreter, a gifted actress; her voice was that of an authentic lyrical
soprano, with a very individual timbre, penetrating, sweet, fluid and
(with) vivid and spontaneous phraseology.'

L. Riemens,
Enciclopedia Spettocolo, Vol. VIII
Italy

Margaret Sheridan by Sean O'Sullivan, RHA.
(Courtesy: The National Gallery of Ireland)
BACKGROUND: Interior of Teatro Alla Scala, Milan.

La Sheridan
Adorable Diva

Margaret Burke Sheridan
Irish Prima-Donna
1889-1958

Anne Chambers

WOLFHOUND PRESS

© 1989 Anne Chambers
Discography © Alan Kelly

First published 1989 by
WOLFHOUND PRESS,
68 Mountjoy Square,
Dublin 1.

A 1989 RTE film documentary based on this book by Anne Chambers was made on location in Ireland, England, Italy and America.

A record annd tape has been produced by EMI Ireland: *Margaret Sheridan – Centenary LP.* (MBS1 annd TCMBS1)

British Library Cataloguing in Publication Data
Chambers, Anne
   La Sheridan-adorable diva : the biography of Margaret
   Burke Sheridan, Irish Prima Donna, 1889–1958.
   1. Opera. Singing. Sheridan, Margaret Burke, 1889–1958
   I. Title
   782.1'0924

   ISBN 0-86327-230-4 HB
   ISBN 0-86327-231-2 PB

Cover design: Jan de Fouw
Typesetting: Redsetter Ltd., Dublin.
Printed by The Leinster Leader, Naas

Contents

To the memory of my father
A fellow townsman and admirer of
Margaret Burke Sheridan

Acknowledgements

Acknowledgement by name of people who helped me with information and personal reminiscences of Margaret Burke Sheridan is given on page seven, with apologies to any person I may have inadvertently omitted.

In addition I wish especially to acknowledge the following:

The Honourable Garech Browne who kindly placed the Sheridan papers and operatic memorabilia at my disposal and to also thank him and his father, Lord Oranmore and Browne for having the foresight to rescue same from possible dispersal or destruction.

GPA Group Ltd., Shannon, for their generous and timely assistance which enabled me to complete essential outstanding research.

Nora T. Kelly, Milano, for her unstinting research endeavours in Italy, for her acute and sensitive insights into Italian life and for her hospitality.

John Gualini, Milano, for his perceptive knowledge of the history of Italian opera.

Dr. T. K. Whitaker for his helpful comments and observations on the text.

Joan Fanning for her efficient secretarial assistance.

My husband, Tony, for his unfailing encouragement and assistance through-out the duration of the research and writing of this biography.

IRELAND

R. W. Lightbody, Belfast; Kathleen Joy-Evans, Dublin; Pamela Manahan, Dublin; Prince Ferdinando d'Ardia Caracciolo, Dublin (deceased); Dr. Veronica Dunne, Dublin; Annie Walsh, Castlebar (deceased); Norris Davidson, Wicklow; Dr. Cyril Cusack, Dublin; Mildred O'Brien, Dublin; Oliver O'Brien, Columba O'Brien, Dublin; Gwladys McCabe, Dublin; Louise O'Brien, Dublin; Joan Smith, Dublin; Liam Breen, Dublin; Maura Sweeney, Dublin; Joe Lynch, Dublin; Noel Sheehan, Dublin; Padraic O'Hara, Ballina; Michael Cuneen, Dublin; Sister Ignatius, Castlebar; Anne Coyle, Dublin; Sister Cajetan, Dublin; Ester Weldon, Dublin; Derek Walshe, Dublin; Charles Horan, Dublin; Sister Kathleen Power, Dublin; Nancy Cahir, Limerick; Seamus Kearns, Dublin; Jack Cahill, Castlebar; M. J. Egan, Castlebar, Gordon Ledbetter, Dublin; Liam Bergin, Dublin; Margaret Stuart, Dublin; Eve Rogers, Dublin; Patrick Melville, Dublin; Fr. John Fitzgerald, Westport; The Master Terry De Valera, Dublin; Frank D. Morris, Dublin; Anna Fullam, Naas; Niamh Winklemann, Dublin; Dr. T. Walshe, Wexford (deceased); Niccolo d'Ardia Caracciolo, Dublin; Jeannie Reddin, Dublin; Noreen Thomas, Donegal; Dott. A. Barone, Dublin; Bill Maxwell, Dublin; Kevin Myers, Dublin; Pat Mahon, Castlebar; Hugh Coyle and staff, Renvyle House Hotel, Connemara; Margaret Murphy, Dublin; M. B. Keogh, Dublin; B. P. Flusk, Dublin; Eva White, Dublin; Tony Hanna, Dublin; Margaret Chambers, Westport; Gus Smith, Dublin; Raymond McLarnon, Belfast; Dr. D. Ryan, Castlebar; Cristóir O'Dúinn, Dublin; Phyllis O'Sullivan, Dublin; Pat Carroll, Dublin; Catriona Reid, Dublin; J. D. Coyle, Galway; Mary and Dorothy Cooley, Newport.

ITALY

Dott. Giorgio Gualerzi, Torino; Madame Renata Tebaldi, Milano; Dott. G. Tintori, Milano; Prof. G. Burchielli, Pisa; Dott. Rodolfo Celletti, Milano; Dott. A. Pertile, Padova; Giorgio Cavalari, Milano; Gianni Giorgi, Milano; Anna Fabia, Milano; Margaret De Vito, Milano; Dott. Giusseppe Gattamorta, Bologna; David Tabbat, Milano; Italo Carlucci, Roma; Contessa Allesandra Eula, Roma; Peppino Barbieri, Voghera; Maestro F. Gallini, Milano; Contessa A. Ruscour-Gnecchi, Milano; Franca Confalonieri, Milano; Adriano Orlandini, Cento; Luciano Panena, Cremona; Sergio Fouco, Mestre Venezia; Edoardo Gugliemi, Parma; The Ambassador and staff, Embassy of Ireland, Roma; Azzo Zanghieri, Roma; Elena Parenti, Rimini; Piero Robba, Torino; Rose Kennett, Milano; Mary Brown, Milano; Claire O'Donovan, Milano; Prof. Daniele Rubbolo, Milano; Federico E. Scopinich, Milano; Mario Marini, Milano.

AMERICA

Fr. Leo Clifford, New York; Virginia Zeani-Lemeni, Indiana; Michael Bohane, New York; Hubert Valentine, New York; Evelyn Wyvel, N. Carolina; Dennis J. McGeary, Florida; Richard T. Soper; Axe-Houghton Management, Inc., Tarrytown Castle, New York.

UNITED KINGDOM

Alan Kelly, Sheffield; Francesca Franchi and staff, Royal Opera House, London; Dame Eva Turner, London; Arthur Hammond, London; Lord Howard de Walden, Berkshire; Ruth Edge, Archivist, EMI, Middlesex; B. J. Peters, Archivist, Coutts & Co., London; John Steane, Coventry; Clifford Williams, Port Talbot, Wales; P. Street, London.

PROLOGUE

On the night of April 17, 1958, in the Gaiety Theatre, Dublin, the poignant music of Puccini's *Manon Lescaut* was momentarily stilled. The visiting Italian opera company stood in silence on stage as the Italian ambassador to Ireland addressed the audience which included the Irish Taoiseach (Prime Minister), Eamon De Valera. Signore Mazio was speaking in his official capacity not on diplomatic or government business but about an Irishwoman who had died just a few hours previously in a nursing home on St. Stephen's Green, a short distance from the theatre.

To many in the audience, the Italian diplomat's words of appreciation came as a surprise. Few realised the extent of their fellow-countrywoman's high artistic achievements in Italy. But to members of the Italian opera company present, this tribute to La Sheridan – as they called her – the Irish soprano was no more than her memory and her contribution to Italian opera deserved.

'She was a great friend of my country,' the Ambassador said. 'Italy admired and loved her. She was more than a prima donna. She was literally the first great lady of the opera houses of Rome, Milan and Naples. Toscanini and Puccini will ever be linked with her name. My countrymen cherish the memory of the years she spent with us. She made us the gift not only of her golden voice but of her generous, warm Irish heart. It is fitting,' he concluded, 'that tonight's performance should be of a Puccini opera – Margherita Sheridan was his greatest interpreter.'[1]

CHAPTER I

MAGGIE FROM MAYO
Childhood 1889-1901

Born in Castlebar, the administrative town of the County of Mayo on 15th October 1889, Margaret was the fifth surviving child of the local postmaster, John Burke Sheridan, and his wife, Mary Ellen Cooley. Infant mortality rates in the late eighteen hundreds were high and the Burke Sheridan family had not been immune. Three infants, a three-year old boy, Richard, and a two-year old sister, Ellen, had died of complications from measles and croup. Of the five surviving children, there were three boys and two girls. The eldest, John Charles, was born in 1876, Thomas Henry in 1879, a daughter, Hester in 1879 and Patrick in 1887. Margaret was baptised on 24th October 1889 by the parish priest and family friend, Canon Patrick Lyons. Her brother, John Charles, acted as godfather.

By contemporary standards in Ireland, her background was comfortable if not prosperous. The Sheridan family had been minor landed gentry with an estate comprising some 575 acres at Pheasant Hill between Castlebar and Westport. The family had been in residence here since the late 1700s. Due to the dearth of genealogical documentation, the actual relationship between the various Sheridan branches in Dublin, Meath, Down, Roscommon, Mayo and Kent in England, all originating from the main family, traced to the barony of Tullagh in County Cavan around 1600, remains tenuous. It would appear that the Castlebar branch of the family originated from the line of Edward Sheridan of Capel Street in Dublin in the mid-1700s. He, in turn, was related to Thomas Sheridan, father of Richard Brinsley Sheridan (1751-1816), the eminent statesman and dramatist, and also to Joseph Le Fanu Sheridan, the novelist. It was Edward Sheridan who acquired the Pheasant Hill estate in Castlebar which at the beginning of the nineteenth century was in the possession of Margaret's great-grandfather, Henry Sheridan who married firstly Elizabeth (Isabella) Burke and secondly Elizabeth O'Donel. The Burke name was subsequently adopted by Margaret's father, John Burke Sheridan and later also by Margaret and by her brother, Patrick. Her grandfather, John Martin Sheridan, also claimed relationship with the prominent Martin family of Ballinahinch in County Galway.

John Martin Sheridan was an educated, gregarious man, a good landlord to his tenants, an enthusiastic participant in the national politics of the day and was closely associated with the agrarian reform movement. He was noted for his outspokenness and impulsive manner, particularly on political matters. These characteristics were inherited by his grandchild, Margaret, who, throughout her life, tended to express her opinions, both political and otherwise with similar alarming candour (which caused on at least one occasion, an adverse effect on her career). In 1871, for example a much publicised dispute arose between her grandfather and Hyacinth D'Arcy Esquire, landlord of the New Forest estate in County Galway, over the number of evictions Sheridan alleged to have occurred on D'Arcy's estate. D'Arcy challenged the allegations whereupon Sheridan accosted him at the County Club House in Galway and, as was reported, 'a slight scene took place between the two landlords in which Mr. Sheridan acted, to use his own words, "the only part which as a gentleman" was left open to him under the circumstances and inflicted upon D'Arcy, "though with due gentleness, a mark of displeasure that I am perfectly certain no gentleman in the County of Galway, renowned for its chivalry, could be found to brook with such commendable patience and resignation as he (D'Arcy) had done"'.[1]

Her grandfather's impecunious nature was, sadly, another trait which Margaret was destined to inherit. Pursued by creditors, John Martin Sheridan moved from Mayo, firstly to Dublin and from there to the Isle of Man where he died in 1875. The Pheasant Hill estate was sold and eventually became one of the first Mayo estates purchased by the Congested Districts Board for division among the tenants.

Her father, John Burke Sheridan, was an educated and genial man. As postmaster of the town, he had contact with most of its citizens – whom he is reported to have treated with courtesy and cheerfulness. He was forty-two years old when his last and most beloved child, his 'darling little Maggie',[2] was born. His marriage, at the age of thirty-three, to Mary Ellen Cooley was a harmonious and loving relationship. Socially outgoing, he had a good singing voice and frequently performed at social gatherings and at least on one such occasion was reported 'to have carried off the laurels in the singing department'.[3] He encouraged his children musically and all took music as an optional school subject. A Collard & Collard upright piano occupied a corner of the parlour in the Sheridan household and from her earliest years, Margaret recalled her fascination with the instrument and her attempts to pick out tunes to the amusement of her family. Her mother's life, like that of most Irish mothers at that time, revolved around her home and her family, and although the memory was faint, Margaret, in later life, spoke with an almost awe-filled love of her mother's deep religious faith and her devotion to her children and to her husband.

Margaret's mother was the daughter of Thomas Cooley, a building contractor and property owner in Castlebar. Margaret's father became the town postmaster in 1874 and on 16th June 1875, he married Thomas Cooley's daughter. They purchased an imposing three-storied house overlooking the town Mall which was and still is a pleasant tree-encircled green and a focal point of the town, providing pleasurable walks for the town citizens, a safe playing area for children and a suitable venue for the many public gatherings and demonstrations associated with the political and social agitation of the 1880s and 1890s, in Ireland. Symmetrical Georgian houses bounded the Mall on three sides, interspaced with the imposing façade of the Courthouse on one side, the local hotel on another and the infirmary on the west side. At the western end of the horseshoe sweep stood the Protestant Church of the Holy Trinity and at the eastern end, the newly established Convent of the Sisters of Mercy. In one corner of the Mall was the compact Methodist manse and church where John Wesley had preached. Alongside the Convent was the entrance to the Military Barracks and a side entrance to the Lawn, the estate of the town landlord, Edward Bingham, the Earl of Lucan. A connection existed between the Bingham and Sheridan families through the marriage in c.1706 of John Sheridan with Anne Bingham, niece of Sir Charles Bingham. On the purchase by Margaret's father of the house on the Mall and the re-establishment of the post-office business there, his Lordship had a gravel path constructed across the grassy expanse of the Mall 'for the comfort of the townspeople crossing to the Post Office'.[4]

The town benefited from the efforts of its landlord who, unlike many of his predecessors and contemporaries, was intent on improvements in housing, amenities and employment. Although considered an absentee from his 60,000 acre estate, the Earl and his countess were well liked by the townspeople; the Earl's relationship with his urban tenants being described by the local paper as 'an instance . . . that redeems the gloomy and dismal picture of the relations between landlord and tenant'[5] elsewhere. Outside the town, however, the 'holy warfare that the people were waging against landlords, grabbers and graziers for the right to live on the soil that bore them'[6] continued unabated amid evictions, rack-renting and overflowing workhouses and against the ever-threatening shadow of recurring famine.

Within the town of Castlebar, support for constitutional nationalism was strong and was openly demonstrated on the occasion of visits by members of the Irish Parliamentary party. A garrison town, Castlebar, notwithstanding its support for the nationalist cause, still maintained and displayed many of the social customs and traditions of its mixed Anglo-Irish origins. Cricket was a popular game and was regularly played by the professional and trading classes of the town as well as by the British officers and officials stationed there. Tennis was a much enjoyed summer exercise, while bazaars and sales of work helped raise money for Catholic and Protestant charities and causes alike.

Since the establishment of the Union with Britain in 1800, Ireland was ruled from London through a Viceroy in Dublin. The country was still recovering from the effects of the Great Famine of 1846-47 which had been particularly severe in Mayo. Margaret's parents had been born at the height of the famine which had resulted in the death of one million Irish men, women and children and the enforced emigration of a further million. Out of the tragedy of the famine, a new movement seeking political and agrarian reforms in Ireland emerged. Under the leadership of Charles Stewart Parnell and the Mayo-born Michael Davitt the quest for agrarian reform and Home Rule for Ireland became fused in a great national struggle that caught the imagination and support of most Irishmen and some Englishmen, notably the English Liberal Prime Minister, Gladstone.

During Margaret's childhood in Castlebar, a new spirit of optimism and pride in a national identity was emerging. While Gladstone's ambition and Parnell's vision to attain Home Rule were eventually to be shattered, the sense of national identity which the Home Rule crusade fostered, remained. Irish national identity, while nurtured in constitutional opposition, would during Margaret's girlhood, explode into armed rebellion. Her background ensured that she would subscribe to the ideals of the nationalist movement. Her grandfather's landed background was the acceptable face of Irish landlordism: the Catholic minor gentry, as impoverished as the tenants who held under them, were regarded by the tenants as defenders rather than oppressors. Their education and position in society provided them with the ability and means to champion the cause of their fellow Irishmen and

Her birthplace,
The Mall,
Castlebar,
with the
commemorative
plaque erected
in 1958.
(photos:
Frank Dolan,
Westport)

BIRTHPLACE
OF
MARGARET BURKE-SHERIDAN
PRIMA DONNA
LA SCALA & COVENT GARDEN
MILAN   LONDON
15·10·1889 — 16·4·1958

Patrick Burke Sheridan, wife and sons, David and John, Ottowa, 1923.

Ellen Burke Sheridan
(nee Cooley), her mother.
(Courtesy: Pamela Manahan)

Patrick Burke Sheridan,
her brother, c. 1914.

co-religionists. Her grandfather was a tireless campaigner in the cause of agrarian reform and her father a supporter of constitutional nationalism. Her uncle, George M. Sheridan, a successful businessman in London, witty and urbane, was to establish a periodical entitled *New Ireland* with the optimistic aim 'to unite in a literary chain people of all political views and creeds in Ireland, the Unionist with the Nationalist, the Catholic with the Protestant'.[7] Her family involvement in national politics later led to her own virtual adoption by members of the Irish Nationalist Party at Westminster during her subsequent years as a student in London.

Life in the Sheridan household in the initial years of her life seemed secure and serene. Though hardly opulent, the family, given the appalling social conditions then affecting so many of the population, were extremely comfortable. The household furnishings reflected the affluent social background of her parents. Antique furniture, original paintings, rare books, silver, crystal, rare china, adorned the various rooms in the large five-bedroomed house. At the rear of the house, an enclosed yard contained 'two cars nearly new and a strong trap'.[8] Fishing tackle, rods, reels, nets, an anchor, a telescope and a card table indicated the pastimes and pursuits of the family. The house faced onto the Mall and from the windows, Margaret would have seen great crowds gather to listen to orations from national figures such as Michael Davitt propounding on the crimes of Irish landlordism, or John Dillon, William O'Brien or Maud Gonne McBride on the ill-treatment of Ireland by her English neighbour, or on a bleak December day in 1900, she may have watched the departure of the English Chief Secretary, Mr. Wyndam, seated in an 'outside', an uncovered horse-drawn wagon, as he set off from the hotel to see for himself the extent of the poverty and wretchedness in some of the outlying rural areas.

Margaret was an energetic child with, as one schoolfriend described, 'the bluest eyes and the most golden hair' she had ever seen, and 'a regal pose to her head remarkable even then'.[9] A schoolfriend of her days in Castlebar, the late Miss Annie Walsh, remembered her 'lovely, fair and fresh colouring' and she added 'she had a grand style, you'd know that the breeding was in her'.[10] In a rare reference to her childhood, Margaret later admitted to having been 'a little headstrong and very bold'.[11] She was a pet and favourite of her parents, especially her father and being of a precocious nature and endowed with good looks and a lively temperament, she expected and received attention. Throughout her life, her engaging personality acted as a magnet to draw towards her people who were captivated by her impulsive, warm-hearted nature and by her energy, intelligence, wit and outspokenness which often bordered on the libellous. 'Straight and true'[12] was how one of her music teachers described the foibles of her most famous pupil. Her early childhood in Castlebar was certainly happy and secure within an affectionate family circle.

Her older brothers attended the boys' school at the far end of the town while Margaret, with her sister Hester, then in senior class, had merely a short walk across the Mall to the Convent of Mercy. Her brother Patrick (Paddy), as was customary until the age of seven, also attended the Convent. In May 1893, Margaret was enrolled in the infant class there. Music was an integral part of school life and included basic music theory. Margaret was taught from a copy of *Moore's Irish Melodies* (still extant at the Convent) such favourites as 'O Breathe Not His Name' and 'When He Who Adores Thee', which she was later to render so poignantly on record. In September 1894, the Sisters opened a fine new national school, named 'St. Angela's' and it was here that Margaret was to spend her earliest student years. Later, the world press, seeking to wring every emotive nuance from her childhood beginnings, reported that, on being orphaned at the age of four, she had been whisked off to a Convent in Dublin. The reality, while undoubtedly painful, was not quite so dramatic.

After the required years in infant school, she progressed through the senior grades. Her annual results showed moderate achievement, scoring highest points in handwriting and needlework, while her musical ability at this stage was marked 'average'. Her sweet voice, however, was remarked upon by those who heard her in the school concerts and plays.

While in later years, Margaret's life outwardly resembled a series of exciting episodes straight from the reels of a Hollywood film, inwardly there was a disturbing sense of loss, loneliness and transience, even during her more successful periods. There was a sadness, too, which she endeavoured to hide even from her closest friends. To well-meaning questions about her family and childhood in Castlebar, silence or an off-hand retort was the response. Most of the articles and publicity pieces about her in the foreign media and in Ireland, invariably fail to accurately record her early childhood in Castlebar. Her grandfather's insolvency and later her father's battle with alcohol may have been partly responsible for her later attitude to her birthplace. While it is impossible to determine the trials and tribulations that can deeply affect a family from within and yet remain obscured from public perception, on the surface at least, her family life initially appeared normal and happy.

The first real tragedy in her life occurred on 21st April 1895, when her mother, at the age of forty-two, died at home following complications resulting from an acute attack of influenza. Margaret, then only five, was the youngest of the family and therefore, most attached to and dependent on her mother. The void created by the unexpected loss of her mother was a frightening experience for a child of her age, too young to grasp the finality of death, yet old enough to experience the aching sense of loss. Amazingly, the memory of her mother remained fresh and real to her throughout her life and it was her mother's prayerbook, the one tangible memento still in her possession after so many years, that Margaret requested to be buried with her at her own death in 1958. Later, when the glamour and fame of her career failed to overcome the sense of emptiness and loneliness that enveloped her at the end of her life, Margaret reverted to the deep spiritual faith which the memory of her mother epitomized. 'She was an exemplary wife and mother', the local paper recorded in tribute, 'always solicitous for the welfare of those around her and idolised by her family and friends.'[13]

John Burke Sheridan was left as sole parent to a family whose ages ranged from five to nineteen years. He began to experience parental difficulties with his eldest son, John Charles, which eventually led to complete estrangement. Thomas was eighteen and his eldest daughter Hester, then sixteen, had completed her education at the Convent. At the other end of the scale, there were his youngest son, Paddy, aged eight and his 'darling Maggie', aged five. The loss of his wife to whom he seemed deeply attached, he found difficult to cope with and was very probably the main reason why he turned to alcohol. A widow, Mrs. Anne Kearney, was engaged as a housekeeper to run the house and to care for the two younger children. Margaret continued her education at the Convent. She regularly appeared in school concerts, and received the first public notice of her singing career. 'Miss Maggie Sheridan, daughter of John B. Sheridan Esq., a most interesting and intelligent child, sang in a very pleasing manner "Comin Thru the Rye" and received great applause.'[14]

John Burke Sheridan's health began to deteriorate during 1900. Urged by his friend and medical advisor, Edward Brabazon, he entered the Mater Private Hospital in Dublin in January 1901 where it was established that he had carcinoma of the liver and had but a brief few weeks to live. His last will and testament, which he compiled and wrote in a clear and legible hand, sets out in a thorough and practical way the division of his estate. He appointed his 'dear friend', Reverend Patrick Lyons, P.P., as executor and entrusted him with the welfare of his youngest son and daughter.

Canon Lyons had been a friend since his arrival in Castlebar in 1878. He had officiated at the baptisms of the Sheridan children, at the obsequies of their mother and was a frequent visitor to the house on the Mall. He was one of the outstanding churchmen of his time, both as an administrator and innovator. He was responsible for the planning and erection of many amenities and buildings in the town. But it was his work as a supporter of the agrarian reform movement that his energy and intelligence were most noticeably displayed and rewarded. Through the mutual respect which existed between himself and Lord Lucan, he succeeded in attaining additional acreage at negligible rents from the Lucan estate for redistribution among the tenants. He was well-liked and respected by the Protestant communities in the area, as their tribute in 1911 testified when, upon his death, the Protestant and Roman Catholic church bells tolled in unison. To the care and protection of this prominent churchman, Margaret's future welfare and education was now entrusted. From the sale of his house and contents, her father had directed that the proceeds were 'to be divided equally between Maggie and my youngest son, Paddy to be used for their benefit, education and maintenance'.[15] He bequeathed twenty-five pounds to Thomas and fifty pounds plus some items of jewellery to Hester. To Paddy he left his watch, signet ring and gold chain, and 'to my darling little daughter Maggie . . . my sapphire ring with one stone, another sapphire and pearl brooch in cast and locket . . . Father Lyons to keep up Maggie's jewellery until she is of age'.[16] The sale of the house and contents realised six hundred and thirty pounds, no mean sum in 1901, and provided sufficient security to ensure Margaret's future maintenance and education. The penniless orphan, reliant on the charity of others, so vividly painted by the media of later years, was a fabrication.

Relations between her father and her eldest brother had deteriorated greatly – her father's will is ample testimony to the bitterness between them. Written one month prior to his death, the opening sentence is unambiguous and unequivocal. 'I hereby give and bequeath to my eldest son, John Charles, the sum of one shilling only.'[17] John Charles subsequently emigrated and severed contact with his family. Hester and Thomas left Castlebar to live in England. Hester became a nurse and eventually married Alfred Gaillton, a surgeon commander in the Royal Navy. They had one daughter named Moira. Thomas died in

London in 1919 and is buried with his parents in Castlebar.

John Burke Sheridan died in Dublin on 8th February 1901, aged fifty-six years. He was buried in Castlebar and in accordance with his will there were 'no crape or wreaths'[18] displayed at his funeral. The obituary notices in the local papers were lavish in their praise of the late postmaster and great sorrow was expressed at the passing of 'a general favourite' and, the report continued, 'for a long time to come his genial cheery presence will be missed'.[19] For Margaret, his death was the second tragedy in her short life. Then eleven years old, she could comprehend the enormity of the loss of her only surviving parent and the reality of her orphan status. She had been the centre of her father's affection and the abrupt removal of his love and support left her bereft and created an emotional void which she afterwards sought to fill by looking for a father-figure among her teachers and patrons. Her few years in Castlebar were destined to be the only period in her life in which she was to experience a 'home environment', the only time in which she could claim to have belonged and to have been part of a family. She never later acquired a home of her own, or even a permanent residence, but was destined, despite her success or perhaps because of it, to pursue a nomadic uncertain life – like a butterfly flitting from place to place. Her home on the Mall was purchased by her father's friend, Dr. Brabazon, and in accordance with her father's instructions, Fr. Lyons enrolled his young charge in the Dominican Convent in Dublin where his sister, Mother Reginald, taught. There is no indication that Margaret returned to Castlebar during her school-days. There was perhaps little to warrant her return there. Her brothers and sister had left and her more remote relations maintained little if any contact with her during the course of her school-days in Dublin. Castlebar evoked pleasant if sad memories for her throughout her life and her only return visit to her native town was to result in an unfortunate misunderstanding.

Margaret's move to Dublin had many far-reaching effects on her life. Not only was she transferred from the relative tranquility of a rural town to the hustle and bustle of the city but from a family background to a lengthy spell of institutional living subject to the narrow regulatory system of a convent. During her years at the Dominican Convent, there appeared to have been little or no contact between Margaret and her brothers and sisters. Her correspondence and the many public interviews she gave in later life contain no reference to them. Indeed, it was seldom realised that she was one of a family of five; it was presumed that she was not only an orphan but an only child as well.

The age gap between Margaret and her older sister and brothers and the fact that they left Ireland when she was still a child certainly disrupted a normal family relationship and undoubtedly contributed to her lack of interest in them in later life. By then there was too wide an emotional time-gap to bridge. Her brother, Paddy, however, the brother nearest in age to her, eventually contacted her during her student years in London and she kept a photograph of him (dressed in uniform prior to his departure from England to fight in the Great War) among her personal possessions. From the time of her father's death, Margaret faced the world without family support. Luckily, she was endowed with what a friend described, 'a bright clear courage that never failed her'.[20] The upheavals of her childhood were perhaps responsible for shaping her air of independence and her individuality. An extrovert and humorous personality shielded her from loneliness and protected her against the jibes directed at her orphan status. Lack of family contact was also compensated for by her marked ability to make friends.

The Dominican Convent at Eccles Street on the north side of Dublin was founded in 1882 in what was then a fashionable residential part of the city, containing many fine examples of late Georgian architecture. The Dominican Sisters had acquired the townhouse of Lord Tyrawley and established a school there. The early 1880s witnessed important developments in the education of women in Ireland. A formal system of secondary education was introduced and the establishment of the Royal University provided an additional incentive to women to acquire a higher level of education. The initial aim of the Convent was for the 'maintenance of higher education and the advancement in life of the orphan daughters of the upper and middle classes'.[21] Even when the Sisters expanded into the broader areas of education and admitted parented children to the school, a tradition of special consideration for orphan children entrusted to their care continued to be observed. The school was proud of its academic record and many of the graduates attained notable distinction both in Ireland and abroad. But at Eccles Street, the emphasis was not totally on academic achievement. Debating and dramatic talent was fostered and, under the auspices of the Literary Academy founded in the school, an annual series of public lectures in English, French and Irish were given. A strong but not strident emphasis was placed on the Irish language and culture which, as the new century progressed, received added impetus from the Celtic revival of Yeats, Synge, Martyn, Lady Gregory and, in 1904, the opening of the Abbey Theatre in Dublin. A strong sense of national pride was fostered in the school and many Ecclonians were to become actively involved in succeeding years in the national struggle for independence. Many also were active in the campaign for women's franchise and in trade union activities. Belief in a liberal education, in the treatment of pupils as individuals and the cultivation of individual talent prevailed at Eccles Street.

Life here as a boarder was neither better nor worse than in any other boarding institution for young girls. The initial bewilderment and loneliness yielded, in most cases, to a lively inquisitiveness and a capacity to make the best of things. Already well established in the convent some months prior to the arrival of the other students, Margaret got to know every nook and cranny and by the time the 'new' girls arrived for the commencement of term in late summer 1901, the 'veteran Maggie', as one schoolfriend remembered, 'showed her every inch of the place, emphasising the longest bannisters, where they could manage the most exciting slides. We visited the laboratory where we learned the properties of phosphorus the hard way!'[22] Naturally precocious and somewhat spoiled by her father, she rebelled initially against the strict discipline of convent life. Used to having her own way, she balked at rules which sought to make her conform. Unlike her fellow students, for her, there was little release even at holiday time.

Those who knew her at school later testified to her mischievous sense of humour, her wit and her high spirits – qualities which during her school years, probably got her into as much trouble in later life as did her penchant for devastating mots and acid comments. Her high spirits did not always appeal to her teachers and she received her share of punishment and chastisement for her misdemeanours. One teacher in particular singled her out for humiliating punishments – such as making her wear her boots, tied together by the laces, around her neck. An impish naughtiness remained with her in later life, and she always delighted in debunking affectation and hypocrisy.

Despite her high spirits and camaraderie she *was* different to the rest of the pupils. The sadness of her orphan status she hid from her peers for the most part. But the heart-breaking loneliness of the empty and silent dormitory when her schoolfriends went home for Easter, Christmas and Summer holidays, the occasional sneering references to the 'orphan', the absence of family visits or presents, left their mark. She did make occasional weekend visits to the home of a schoolfriend, brief interludes in a family environment which made her all the more acutely aware of this void in her life. 'There's no place like home when you haven't got one',[23] she remarked tellingly to a friend.

During a particularly lonely vigil in her empty dormitory one Christmas Eve, she had a remarkable dream or vision. She saw herself singing before a silver organ, standing at the top of a long green staircase, banked on either side with flowers. A large gathering of people applauded her warmly. Years later at Seaford House, the London mansion of the wealthy philanthropist, Lord Howard de Walden, her dream became a reality, as she later testified. 'In this wonderful house in Belgrave Square was the entertainment of the season. Everybody was there. The famous green staircase *was* banked with malmaison carnations. There *was* a silver organ at the top just as I'd seen it and a small orchestra and singing to it, with everyone in town listening, was Maggie from Mayo.'[24] But before the days of success and applause, many long nights in Eccles Street and elsewhere stretched before her.

Academically, she progressed satisfactorily through junior, middle and senior grades, passing examinations in French, English, literature and composition, arithmetic, book-keeping, history, geography, physiology and, surprisingly to those who knew in later life of her aversion to cooking and anything that smacked of domesticity, she achieved honours in domestic science. 'One would as soon have trusted her with making a good strong cup of tea or boiling an egg as building an atom-plant,'[25] her friend, Larry Morrow, later recorded. 'She wasn't made that way.' In 1908, she featured among the year's list of prizewinners. She had a flair for languages which later on was ably demonstrated by her proficiency in Italian (including some of its many regional dialects), French and German. Her pronunciation and delivery and the beautifully modulated tones of her speaking voice were much admired and commented upon throughout her life. Her acute ear for accents also found an outlet in mimicry. An American acquaintance, Lydia Kerr Cross, remembered listening enthralled as Margaret discussed the merits or otherwise of certain popular stage and film personalities. The name of Marie Lloyd cropped up in the conversation. 'In a thrice a lock of Margaret's hair was jerked out of place, a wedge of orange peel stuck under her lip to hint at protruding teeth. You were caught in the spell of the famous music hall star as Margaret carolled 'A little of what you fancy does you good' in an enchanting cockney voice. 'She was a wicked mimic with an uncanny ear.'[26]

But her own distinctive talent was clearly her musical ability. And by a happy coincidence, it was in the field of musical education and development that Eccles Street was renowned. Shortly after her arrival, Margaret's voice was brought to the attention of the perceptive and talented singing teacher, Mother Clement Burke. This woman,

ABOVE: Dominican Convent, Eccles Street, Dublin, c. 1900.
BELOW - *clockwise*: parlour; science lab; study; refectory. (Courtesy: The Dominican Convent).

Dr. Vincent O'Brien, her singing master and accompanist. (Courtesy: Oliver O'Brien).

Mother Clement, O.P., Margaret's first singing teacher. (Courtesy: *Capuchin Annual*).

Class of Exhibitioners, Medallists and prizewinners of 1908 in Eccles Street. Margaret is third from left in the second row. (From *The Lanthorn*).

who was to be a major influence on Margaret's life, was herself a 'new girl' at Eccles Street, having recently made her final profession there. She had previously studied music and languages in Germany and France. At Eccles Street she taught music and singing and trained the school choirs. She had a good singing voice and her students remembered her as 'unobtrusive and gentle, her kindliness and simple charm had attracted friends to her at all stages of her life. She was tenderly affectionate and sincere in her relations with her pupils and loyally devoted to them'.[27] She sought to 'create' music in her pupils. After a half an hour spent in 'Mother Clement's Parlour', many who had never realised their musical potential found themselves producing notes far beyond the range of what they had thought themselves capable. Her teaching technique was based on voice production and interpretation, the correct placing of the voice and its subsequent development by 'humming' exercises. As one student recalled, 'not until the pupil had developed a 'hum' that vibrated through the entire frontal bone structure of her face was she permitted to sing'.[28] She placed a strong emphasis on interpretation and in later recordings of Sheridan, particularly of the Irish melodies and love songs, this expressiveness of word and phrase is clearly evident, while reviews of her live operatic performances in Italy constantly applauded her interpretative ability. Mother Clement's criticisms were constructived, never destructive. She sought to make each pupil become her own severest critic. The singing lessons held in what was known to generations of pupils as 'Mother Clement's Parlour' became the highlight of the week for Margaret, a welcome release from the humdrum school life. Among the pupils taught by Mother Clement, who later attained eminence at home and abroad, were Kitty Reddy, Nellie Ryan, Florence Ryan (Hewson), Mollie O'Callaghan, Maud Clancy Hunter, May Piggott and Maggie Lydon from Galway whose voice Margaret later described as 'the most beautiful of any I ever heard'[29] and who eventually, like Margaret, was sent for further training to London. But the star pupil to emerge from Mother Clement's Parlour was undoubtedly Margaret Sheridan.

Margaret found sympathetic and patient understanding in Mother Clement. The outspokenness and flamboyance, evident even then, she accepted as the ingredient that added 'colour' to Margaret's singing voice. The affectionate links forged between teacher and pupil endured long after Margaret's departure from Eccles Street. Over the years, Margaret sent brief, hurried letters from abroad, photos of her operatic triumphs, paid return visits to the Convent, and gave special concerts in the 'Parlour'. These were reciprocated by Mother Clement's concern for Margaret's spiritual and moral welfare in the worldly milieu of operatic society, and her great pride in her pupils' operatic triumphs. She had letters and messages delivered to Margaret by ex-Ecclonians visiting Italy or London, sent telegrams and messages during her performance at Covent Garden and in Italy. The friendship continued until Mother Clement's death in 1946. Margaret readily acknowledged the debt she owed to her first teacher and the quality and soundness of her teaching methods.

The distinctive quality of Margaret's voice was evident at Eccles Street and attested to by schoolfriends who themselves won prominence in the music world. The late May Piggott, lecturer in Music at University College Dublin, recalled her first day at Eccles Street in the convent chapel. 'I was feeling cold and sorry for myself . . . when I became conscious of a sound that warmed and excited me, the sound of an exquisite voice singing the *Adoro Te*. I looked around and saw a face which matched the voice in loveliness.'[30] The Dominican Community also listened and were moved as the only pupil remaining during the Christmas holidays at the convent, the warm timbre of Margaret's young voice filled the chapel with melody on Christmas Eve.

Dr. Vincent O'Brien, a prominent Dublin singing master, conductor, composer and arranger, was soon to note the potential of the young schoolgirl. 'A charming, kind teacher',[31] O'Brien had 'discovered' and trained John McCormack, then at the beginning of his operatic career, and had also taught James Joyce, who despite possessing a fine tenor voice, was destined instead to find fame as one of the world's greatest writers and novelists. Vincent O'Brien became acquainted with the third of his most famous pupils in his capacity as conductor to the Eccles Street choir. He agreed to give her additional tuition in more advanced singing techniques and he also chose her to perform in a public recital of *The Messiah* in 1906 at the Gaiety Theatre in Dublin. His son recalled the schoolgirl pranks Margaret played on his father when he visited the Convent, putting flower petals into his tall black hat as it lay on a chair, and the explosion of mirth from her schoolfriends when the petals cascaded down his frock coat as he placed the hat on his head. She became somewhat dependent also on his musical accompaniment. 'I must tell you,' she wrote to him, 'you've spoiled me a little, I cannot sing with everybody any longer.'[32] Like many of the people who contributed to her musical development, Margaret became emotionally attached to her new teacher. Denied the usual family environment and outlet for her affections, it is not surprising that her emotional allegiance tended towards the people with whom she had formed a relationship which gave exclusive attention to her as in a teacher-pupil capacity. With Dr. O'Brien, as with Mother Clement, she later maintained contact, albeit irregular, writing with familiarity, humour coupled with an underlying loneliness, appreciative of encouragement he gave to her occasionally faltering ego, and of his belief in her abilities. To him, Margaret poured out her hopes and despairs: 'I feel as if I've nothing to say to anyone', she confided in one of her more depressed moods. 'Did you ever get that "dried up" sort of feeling . . . tell me what's the cause of it,' and in a more enthusiastic moment, 'What a gamble life is, one never knows, does one and when one does one never can be sure, can one? I *love* not being sure.'[33]

Margaret's school days were drawing to a close. The money from her father's estate had seen her through her formal education; she must soon begin to earn her living in the world outside the convent. Relatively happy and content within that sheltered environment, she briefly considered entering the religious life. But the yearning to sing and realise her childhood vision was stronger. If her dream was to come true however, her rich mezzo voice required further development and training. This was a costly and lengthy process. Mother Clement and Vincent O'Brien had established her as the most promising voice at Eccles Street. But who had heard her in Dublin, in London, in the rest of the world? A young girl's ambitions could be exaggerated and her expectations great but unfounded. Margaret was determined to test her potential. In March 1908, Vincent O'Brien introduced her as a solo artiste to the Dublin public in a charity concert which he conducted in the Rotunda Rooms in the presence of the English Lord Lieutenant of Ireland and his wife, the Earl and Countess of Aberdeen. Heading the bill, fresh from his triumphs at the Royal Opera House, Covent Garden, was the star of the O'Brien school, John McCormack; last on the bill was the untried beginner, Margaret Sheridan. This was to be the only time that Ireland's most famous singers were to share the same concert platform. Not unnaturally, McCormack received the lion's share of the acclaim and the notices, with cursory mention of the supporting recitalists; Margaret received no mention at all.

A chance invitation by a schoolfriend to Rush, Co. Dublin set the next cycle of her career in motion. She was asked to sing in a local parish fund-raising concert. In the audience was Lady Millicent Palmer, wife of Sir Roger Palmer, owner of the nearby Kenure house and estate. Lady Palmer was much taken with both the voice and personality of the young singer. Shortly after this chance encounter, she heard Margaret sing again, this time at nearby Whitestown House, the home of Mrs. Kelly, a wealthy landowner and business woman in the area. Lady Palmer subsequently invited Margaret to sing at Kenure, one of the great historical houses of Ireland. Today, nothing remains of the stately mansion except its great portico, incongruous and forlorn, a monument to official vandalism. The imposing main entrance gate has been preserved, from which a long, tree-lined avenue led to the house. The pillored entrance hall was covered in marble and a great mahogany staircase ascended towards a glass canopy in the roof. The house was furnished with Sheraton, Chippendale and Regency furniture, ornate plaster covered the ceilings and the walls were hung with fine paintings. Kenure was Margaret's first entrée to the splendour of aristocratic life. It was also a milestone in her career: it was the efforts and influence of Lady Palmer on her behalf that enabled her to take another and a most important step forward.

In late Spring, Margaret took her final examinations at Eccles Street. As her friends and school-mates packed their bags for the last time and excitedly discussed their future plans and careers, Margaret's lack of direction and, more acutely, her lack of finance, became more apparent and worrying. Girls with less promising voices but wealthy parents who were willing to spend more than their daughters' talents justified, boasted of their plans for further vocal training. Stung by a deprecatory remark about her financial circumstances and her singing ability, Margaret reacted decisively. The premier competition for young Irish singers and musicians was the annual Feis Ceoil. By then in its twelfth year, it had produced such talent as John McCormack, a gold medal winner in 1903 and Lily Foley, the winning soprano in the same year, later to become McCormack's wife. In 1904, James Joyce had been denied gold in the tenor section because he refused to attempt the compulsory sight-reading exercise. In 1908, at the age of 19, Margaret Sheridan entered the competition, significantly in the mezzo-soprano section, and out of nineteen competitors, duly won the gold medal award, singing the recitative 'Ye Verdant Plains', the aria 'Hush Ye Pretty Warbling Choir' by Handel and the Irish air 'By Avon's Tide'. There was great rejoicing in Eccles Street and Margaret later loved to relate how, decked out in a mix of the best curtains of the Convent and a most expensive necklace, borrowed from a wealthy benefactor, she won the first gold of her career.

Now the Dublin concert scene was opened to 'this talented young lady'.[34] Music recitals were an important part of Dublin social life and for many young hopefuls, the recitals, particularly the charity benefit concerts which attracted the wealthy and influential, were the launching pads to a musical career. Dublin was also a prestigious venue on the international music circuit and attracted the leading performers of the day. Nellie Melba, by then the highest paid and most famous diva, had returned to the Dublin stage that year and played to packed houses at the Gaiety Theatre. The world's leading tenor, Enrico Caruso, also received an enthusiastic reception. Every year Dublin hosted international seasons of opera and the Carl Rosa opera company, billed 'the oldest opera company in the world' regularly performed here. In June 1908, Margaret was invited to participate in the Thomas Moore Memorial Concert at the Theatre Royal. Sharing the stage with more established recitalists such as Agnes Tierney, May Durkin and J. C. Coyle, she opened the concert, singing 'Go Where Glory Awaits Thee'. Despite her apparent initial nervousness, the critics were enthusiastic. 'Her voice is of a rich moulded quality. Her phrasing and enunciation are both exceptionally good in so young a singer . . . Her style is most graceful.'[35] Amid an outbreak of typhoid fever in the city, on 15th October, again accompanied by Vincent O'Brien, she sang at another charity concert at the Catholic Commercial Club Hall in O'Connell Street. The critics were accurate in their assessment of her vocal potential. 'Her voice is divinely sweet and possesses extraordinary power; the range is high and the tendency is still upward.'[36] In November, she appeared at the Rotunda and received a standing ovation for her rendition of Tosti's "Goodbye". In December, in the Aberdeen Hall of the Gresham Hotel, before the Lord Lieutenant and Lady Aberdeen, 'the treat of the evening was 'Stances' (A. F. Flegier) sung by Margaret Sheridan with violin obligato by Nora O'Hea.'[37]

As the new year approached, Margaret had good reason to feel pleased with herself. She had conquered the concert platform of Dublin and had earned both general and critical acclaim. The cheers and plaudits were a welcome and uplifting experience. But there was a limit to what the Dublin concert stage could provide. Now aged nineteen, she realised that, despite the success of her public appearances, she had much more to learn in order to extend and perfect her art. Her friends and patrons agreed and arranged to match their friendship with practical assistance. Lady Millicent Palmer and the Jesuit fathers John Sullivan and Thomas Finlay started to make arrangements to ensure Margaret's further training. Accepted as a pupil by the Royal Academy of Music in London, her friends in Dublin organised a benefit concert in the Theatre Royal on 20th May

1909. There was an over-flowing attendance and such was the popular-
ity of the beneficiary that the audience burst into spontaneous applause
when Margaret appeared on stage. 'She sang Orditi's well known
"L'Ardita" with quite remarkable power and skill', the critics
reported, 'and displayed uncommon effectiveness in her mastery of its
many difficulties. Needless to add, she was cheered and encored.'[38]
Financially, the concert was a success and a purse of £600 was
collected.

With the cheers of the Dublin audiences ringing in her ears and her
financial position secured for a two-year period in London, Margaret
bade farewell to Eccles Street, to which she would return during the
holiday breaks from her study. Leaving Ireland also about this time,
following a holiday in Galway, was *the* man of the time, Guglielmo
Marconi, the Irish-Italian inventor of the wireless telegraph and by
then an international celebrity. He was destined to play a major role in
furthering the aspirations of the young Irish singer.

TOP LEFT: Lady Millicent Palmer, Kenure House, Rush, Co. Dublin, Margaret's first patron. (Courtesy: Ann Coyle).
ABOVE: Lord and Lady Howard De Walden. (Courtesy: Lord Howard De Walden).
BELOW: The Salon, Chirk Castle. (Courtesy: The National Trust).
BOTTOM LEFT: Margaret in London, *circa* 1912 – a romantic image. (Courtesy: *Capuchin Annual*).

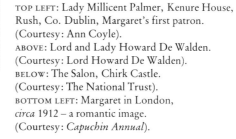

CHAPTER II

PEG O' MY HEART
London 1910-1916

Margaret arrived in London towards the middle of September. The summer of 1909 had been warm and sunny and London enjoyed heatwave temperatures. Her benefactors in Dublin, with the approval of her guardian, Canon Lyons, reserved a place for her in the Convent of Les Filles de Marie, at Vicarage Gate, Kensington. The Convent provided hostel accommodation for young Catholic women alone in London and was to become Margaret's new home for the following two years.

London was a vibrant and wealthy city, basking in the mellow glow of the last year of the Edwardian age. It was a good time to be there, particularly for the wealthy and privileged classes. An air of well-being and contentment prevailed and the pace of life was leisurely; society was quietly assured, dignified and elegant. The Empire was still intact and Britannia, Kaiser Wilhelm's claims notwithstanding, considered that she still ruled the waves. Despite the sinister growth of two armed camps on the continent and the deepening diplomatic international crisis, London as yet appeared uninterested and unaffected by political tensions abroad. Domestic events, such as the more spectacular incidents associated with the suffragette movement, seemed more important or tiresome, depending on one's viewpoint, while the unending question of Home Rule for Ireland continued to be debated.

Margaret adapted to her new surroundings. She enrolled at the Royal Academy of Music, then situated at Tenterden Street and commenced her studies there on 16th September 1909. Founded in 1822, the Academy was the premier school of music in Britain. Its directors included Henry V. Higgins, Chairman of the Grand Opera Syndicate at Covent Garden, the financier and music patron, Alfred de Rothschild, and Sir John Murray Scott, the patron and friend of John McCormack. Her new teacher was singer, pianist, composer and Mendelssohn scholar, William Shakespeare, the Professor of Singing at the Academy. Walking or taking a tram or horse-drawn omnibus from her Convent in Kensington, Margaret attended the Academy and, under the tutelage of her professor, improved her singing technique, developed her repertoire and, in addition, studied the piano.

During breaks in her daily routine, she loved to stroll among the flowers, trees and shrubs in Regent's Park and in later life, during her many sojourns in London, this, and in particular the Queen Mary rose garden, continued to be her favourite promenade. Other than occasional visits from her patron, Lady Millicent Palmer, she had little contact with Ireland. There is no evidence to suggest that she renewed any significant contact with her sister Hester, then living near London or with any of her brothers. Her time was fully taken up by her studies at the Academy and the regulated hours at the Convent at Vicarage Gate. The accommodation at the Convent was spartan but adequate. Each student enjoyed the privacy of a cubicle and the food was plain but wholesome. She experienced a great sense of home-sickness and longed for Ireland or the 'Green Isle' as she referred to it in letters to Mother Clement and Vincent O'Brien whom she besieged for tidings in her own inimitable style. 'Is there any news from Dublin', she wrote him, 'if so tell me the worst!'[1] She returned for holidays to Eccles Street where she enthusiastically shared her newly-gained knowledge with the younger students. The eminent contralto, Maud Clancy Hunter, then a student in the school, recalled 'the amazing colour and beauty of tone she possessed. There was an underlying sadness especially in the lower voice, which would wring the listener's heart, while in the upper voice was a quality that soared like the ecstatic flight and song of a skylark'.[2]

Margaret's rehearsals at the Convent invariably produced drama and high spirits. She practised regularly each evening at half-past seven with the young May Piggott in the front parlour of the Convent.

Margaret kept a watchful eye on the street outside to see if their rendering of her current favourite 'Has Sorrow Thy Young Days Shaded' had been heard by the passers-by. Soon they succeeded in attracting a large crowd nightly, who applauded loudly and at length, much to Margaret's delight. But not to the delight of the Sisters. During one performance, Mother Clement discovered the reason for the commotion outside and promptly banished the two nightingales to a room at the back of the Convent. And yet, while her ambition to sing burned more brightly than ever, a canker of self-doubt that would eventually consume that ambition surfaced. 'Do you really want me to sing *The Messiah*', she wrote to Vincent O'Brien in reply to his invitation to perform again at a Christmas concert. 'If the committee are anxious to have any one else, do not consider me as I am rather frightened of the undertaking. I don't want to sing in Dublin until I feel sure you will be very pleased with me.'[3]

But her musical ability and dedication to her studies at the RAM were vindicated by her examination results, passing at bronze level in 1910 and at silver level in 1911. As her period of training at the Academy drew to a close, uncertainty once again surrounded her future. The money from the bursary which had financed her tuition and maintenance in London was exhausted. Again her patron, Lady Millicent Palmer, provided the financial assistance to enable her to enroll for an additional term at the Academy which by then had moved to Marylebone Road. 'I sang for Lady Palmer . . . here in London,' she wrote to Vincent O'Brien, 'and she sent me a cheque for £100 that will secure me for another while.'[4] And it was to be through Lady Palmer's influence that Margaret moved another step towards her dream.

In addition to Kenure in Rush, Co. Dublin, the Palmers owned the Cefn estate near Wrexham in North Wales. There, Margaret was invited for a holiday and during her stay sang at a dinner party. Among the guests were the newly-married, wealthy, philanthropic couple, Lord and Lady Howard de Walden, then resident at nearby Chirk Castle. Margherita (Margot), Lady Howard de Walden, daughter of Charles van Raalte, of Dutch extraction, had a special interest in singing and possessed a fine voice, having studied for a short period with the famous tenor, Jean de Reske, in Paris. Her husband, Thomas, the eighth Lord Howard de Walden, descendant of the Dukes of Norfolk, was said to be a 'shy and somewhat eccentric millionaire . . . He was an authority on heraldry, armour and horses, and loved to indulge in sports like fencing and hawking'.[5] A friend of the Irish writer, George Moore, he was involved with Moore in the Celtic revival movement and wrote plays in Welsh and translated plays from Welsh to English. Both he and his wife were active and generous patrons of music. Enraptured by the natural beauty and quality of the voice of the young Irish singer, Lady Howard invited Margaret to sing at Chirk. This massive pile, built about 1300, was one of a chain of border castles constructed to protect the conquests of Edward I in Wales. Built by Roger Mortimer, one of the King's war-lords, the castle changed hands on many occasions throughout its turbulent history. In 1595, the castle was bought by a prominent merchant adventurer, Thomas Myddleton, whose descendants still live at Chirk to this day. In 1911, the castle was leased to Lord Howard de Walden for thirty-five years. As her friendship with the family, particularly with Lady Howard de Walden, grew over the succeeding years, Margaret was to spend many holidays at Chirk with its beautiful landscaped parklands and frequently sang at house parties given there for guests who included royalty, statesmen and many of the literary and artistic notables of the day.

Lady Howard de Walden sent Margaret for further study and training to her own singing teacher, Olga Lowenthal. Of Russian-German extraction, Madame Lowenthal, or Olga Lynn as she was later to become known, was a major influence on Margaret's career. Described as 'one of the smallest, plumpest little people, with large, reddish-brown eyes',[6] Olga (Oggie to her friends) had been trained by Jean de Reske especially to teach. (She did however, perform in opera at Covent Garden.) She conducted her singing lessons in a room in Hanover Square and occasionally had access to Aeolian Hall, a small concert hall in Bond Street where she could instruct her pupils in stage craft. 'She was a fiery, orange-eyed little female and shouted at one,' Margherita Howard de Walden recalled in her memoirs, 'and on occasions deliberately reduced people to tears which she said was good for the voice.'[7]

At musical soirées at Olga's home, Margaret was introduced to the aristocratic and artistic 'flappers' of London society; Lady Diana Manners and her future husband, Duff Cooper, Basil Hallam, Denise Orme, Phyllis Neilson Terry, Mollie Miller Mundy, Iris Tree, Gabriel Ray, who gathered to chat and to sing, to discuss poetry and politics, to gossip and to drink champagne into the early hours. As the clouds darkened over Europe, they sought to snatch moments of pleasure from the jaws of the fast approaching disaster. Margaret was to remember that set of irrepressible hopefuls as much for their charm as for their intelligence.

She moved from Vicarage Gate to a boarding house in Bayswater and commenced her studies under Olga's direction. For the first time she savoured the freedom and the reality of life on her own, without the influence and support of a convent environment that had been her 'home' for the previous twelve years. She had little means to continue her studies in London, she was mainly dependent on the generosity of her society friends. Margaret's temperamental behaviour led to occasional explosive rows with her strict but understanding teacher who seemed much taken by her extrovert Irish pupil. As quickly as they flashed, Margaret's threats to abandon her studies with Olga

Margaret during the years of study in London.

would pass. 'I've been in hot water lately,' she confided to Vincent O'Brien. 'I had such a fight with Olga, but I couldn't help it. I just told her what I thought of her and made my exit.'[8] But Lady Howard de Walden invariably made peace and Margaret resumed her studies. Under Olga's direction, she struggled to come to terms with the subtleties of opera. The complexities of the character of Manon in Puccini's *Manon Lescaut* proved particularly difficult. 'I hate the opera,' she wrote of the part for which she would become famous, 'but Olga says I can do it better than anyone else has ever done it, if I make up my mind.'[9] And making her mind up was always her greatest problem. But she did make progress despite initial outbursts and setbacks and her tendency to enjoy the partying and good life of her new-found 'freedom'. 'I've got the hang of things much more now,' she wrote to Vincent O'Brien. 'Lady Howard was so pleased she said she must give me something at once so I've been out all day buying everything I liked. I'll show you them all, or *nearly all* when we meet again!'[10]

In 1912, Margaret saw her first opera at Covent Garden. It was, prophetically, *Madama Butterfly*. The Czech soprano, Emmy Destin, one of the finest interpreters of the part, was in the title role with John McCormack as Pinkerton. Covent Garden was nearing the end of a golden period in its operatic history. The crystal clear voice of Nellie Melba, who reigned over the theatre as *prima donna assoluta* from 1888 to 1914 (missing only one season) had kept all rivals at bay until the arrival of one of the best loved sopranos of all time, Luisa Tetrazzini. The rivalry between them, both on and off the stage, ensured full houses for their respective performances. Among the outstanding male performers of the era was the great Enrico Caruso, together with Antonio Scotti, Giovanni Martinelli, Mario Sammarco and John McCormack. From her first experience of grand opera, Margaret never wavered in her ambition to reach the operatic stage and once there, her allegiance to her chosen medium never faltered. Even when self-doubt and uncertainty beset her career, when concert and recital promoters waved contracts and financial inducements to entice her from the operatic stage, she remained firm, perhaps not wisely, in her loyalty and in her conviction that, for her, singing could only mean grand opera.

The road to her ambition however, was paved with many obstacles which, without good friends and not a little luck, might have proven insurmountable. Now almost twenty-five years old, she had yet to earn her first income. A short stint in the chorus of the Quinlan opera company provided some experience and a little money. Again, Lady Howard's intervention assured a more lucrative career. It was the age of the musical soirées in the Belgravia and Mayfair mansions. The soirées and salons of this incredibly wealthy society 'were multifarious occasions at which not only cabinet ministers and bankers, but poets, ballet-struck subalterns, shipbuilders, concert pianists and guests of a score of other vocations jostled and bewildered each other'.[11] Margaret, who became part of this extravagant society, graphically described the atmosphere in an interview later. 'Nothing has been known like the society and entertainment of those days . . . There was a brilliance, an utter disregard for money, a richness and at the same time the highest possible level of intelligence and wit. You get it all in Wilde and if you don't understand what I mean, well then I never can explain it to you. But it will never be the same again. Two world wars brought it to an end. Luxury living is over'.[12]

Through Lady Howard, Margaret was introduced as the new musical prodigy of the season and immediately became the darling of the wealthy and sophisticated London set. Her rich voice soared at evening soirées and her intelligence and witty repartee all found favour with the wealthy, aristocratic set and she in turn was totally at ease in their company. The only knowledge these English lords and ladies, dukes and earls had hitherto of the Irish was probably through contact with their Irish domestics. Margaret learned to cope with the standard retort on being introduced to a soprano who was also Irish: 'Oh how quaint, my cook, maid-servant, is Irish too.' Soon Margaret would anticipate and quickly interject, 'and before you tell me, I bet your cook is Irish too!'[13] They had never before seen or heard anyone like her from the dark troublesome land of Ireland and they adored her. A story against herself which she later related with pleasure concerned this period of her life. Singing at a society house in London, she was introduced as 'the wonderful young soprano from Ireland'. She elected to sing something ethnic, 'The Irish Emigrant'. The guests were delighted with the sincerity of her interpretation, and one lady in particular warmly congratulated her: 'Your singing of that song, with your lovely Irish accent brought me many memories,' she said. Acting the young girl fresh from Ireland, Margaret replied in a most pronounced Irish accent 'and what would you be knowing about "The Irish Emigrant"?' 'Well,' came the diffident reply, 'you see my mother wrote the words.'[14]

She was inundated with invitations to sing Moore's Melodies, Tosti's fashionable drawingroom songs, or popular arias from the operas. From the Cavendish Square mansion of the leading society 'queen', Lady Emerald Cunard (friend of George Moore) to the Belgrave Square town house of Howard de Walden, to Londonderry House, the stately home of the foremost society hostess, the Marchioness of Londonderry, she was fêted and applauded. Mingling with many of the famous names of the day, among them Churchills, Asquiths and Balfours, she more than held her own. 'I am singing at a big party at the Duchess of Marlboroughs . . . pray for me,'[15] Her humour, carefree style, ease and adaptability ensured success.

For another Eccles Street-educated student who had arrived in London for further study and who had been invited to perform with Margaret on one such occasion, the experience was to prove far too daunting. Seated opposite her companion at a lavish dinner-table prior to their performance, Margaret noticed that, despite the attempts of guests to engage her in conversation throughout the course of the lengthy dinner, the young student refused to respond and, with downcast eyes, partook of none of the sumptuous meal after the fish course. After dinner, as they prepared in the powder room for their recital, Margaret tackled her about her silence at dinner. From her mouth, the young student removed numerous fish bones which, through fear and embarrassment, she had stoically retained in her mouth throughout the meal rather than be thought unmannerly by depositing them on her plate!

Soon Margaret's success as society entertainer came to the notice of members of the Irish Parliamentary Party. As politicians, regardless of philosophy, gravitate towards the wealthy and influential, the presence of the Irish members in the salons of the English aristocracy was not unusual or uncommon. Margaret was soon 'adopted' by such redoubtable political war-horses as Joe Devlin from Ulster and, more particularly, the revered member, T. P. O'Connor, who was to become her mentor and father-figure. T.P., or 'Tay Pay', as she affectionately referred to him in an exaggerated west of Ireland brogue, was born in Athlone in 1848 and had known her grandfather and her family background. A journalist, he had been elected Parnellite M.P. for Galway in 1880 and in 1885 had won the Scottish Division of Liverpool which he represented for almost forty-five years. A good orator, a prolific author, and a newspaper proprietor, he was a much respected figure in the House of Commons. His commitment to the ideal of Home Rule for Ireland was unequivocal and he was president of the United Irish League of Great Britain since 1883. 'As a champion of Ireland's rights', a contemporary report testified, 'in Great Britain and

America, he has won countless staunch friends for Home Rule in the House of Commons where he is in the foremost rank of orators and debators'.[16] Attracted by the personality of his young countrywoman and proud of her artistic abilities, T.P. became her unofficial guardian and remained her moral and financial advisor until his death in 1929. Through him, she became acquainted with many of the leading political figures of the day, including David Balfour, Lloyd George, Mr. Asquith, Lord Beaverbrook, Winston Churchill and Earl Grey of Falloden.

Caught up in this quickening social whirlpool of parties and entertainment, Margaret did not fail to realise that, where her career was concerned, she was simply going nowhere. She saw beyond the glitter and the glamour and longed for something more. 'I had an easy success,' she recalled. 'I was at the top of everything as far as singing to fashionable audiences went. That wasn't enough. I knew that I was at a dead-end. I started at the top and could go no further in these surroundings.'[17] She had drifted from the training and study through which she had hoped to find her way to the operatic stage. Covent Garden was still the mecca of opera in Britain. While the golden era of Melba, Caruso, Destinn, and Tetrazzina was drawing to a close, Thomas Beecham, a name that became synonymous with Covent Garden, came forward to produce operas with British artists and encourage opera in English. Son of the wealthy industrialist Sir Joseph Beecham, the manufacturer of the popular Beecham's Pills, had the means to indulge his passion for opera. A musical amateur and conductor, intolerant and headstrong, Thomas Beecham had a charming personality which some women, most noticeably Lady Emerald Cunard, found irresistible. Small, dapper and impeccably groomed, with a short beard 'as trim and elegant as that of an Arabian Night court jeweller',[18] his ambitious operatic plans for Covent Garden set him on a certain collision course with the old guard, the Grand Opera Syndicate who had long dictated policy at the Royal Opera House and who, in turn, had been dictated to by the leading singers, particularly Melba. Margaret sought an audition with Beecham and he was sufficiently impressed by her voice to give her a contract to sing in a season of opera he was planning at Covent Garden. But it never materialised. 'I'm very disappointed over Beecham,' she wrote to Vincent O'Brien in Ireland. 'You may have heard he engaged me for *Butterfly* and *Bohème* . . . and now he has fallen out with the Company and will let none of his own artistes appear. If I sing I will make an enemy of Beecham and as the season is not long, Olga does not think it worthwhile to sing at all.'[19]

Soon however, both the untried and the established artists alike were to be without prospects at Covent Garden for many years. Britain entered the war that was to utterly change the political and social framework of Europe. Earlier, Melba had sung in what was to be her last gala performance for five years at Covent Garden. In the packed audience were seven kings and queens, many of whose sceptres, crowns and kingdoms were swept away in the impending conflagration. As Britain prepared for war, Margaret enjoyed her last summer in Ireland for many years. After a stay at Eccles Street and some brief tuition from Vincent O'Brien, she journeyed to Limerick and Clare to stay with the O'Gormans, a landed family with an estate and fine house called Cahercalla. 'It's glorious to be back,' she enthused to Vincent O'Brien. 'I am enjoying the country more than I can tell you. I'm just "running wild" with the three children who are here, we just go mad together and', she added, referring to her rounded figure. 'I've got quite respectable looking from all the exercise I take playing with them.'[20] She was reluctant to leave Ireland despite letters from Olga Lynn urging her to resume her studies in London. Margaret delayed her return further to comfort a friend who had lost a son in action. 'You can imagine how sad everything is here', she wrote. 'I feel very sad myself too.'[21]

Back in London, much had changed. Many of the bright young hopefuls who had tried to dance, sing and joke away the idea of war had bowed to the inevitable with similar good humour and high spirits and gone to face their personal nightmares in the muddy fields of France and Flanders, most of them never to return. Their female contemporaries joined the Red Cross, wrote cheery letters and endured their own nightmare, dreading the fateful telegram. The war altered everything and opera was not immune. Covent Garden was requisitioned by the British government as a furniture repository and until Thomas Beecham later determined that, war or no war, the public would not be denied opera and formed his own British company, scores of singers and musicians were redundant. Margaret was becoming desperate. The war appeared to have shattered her hopes of reaching the British opera stage. The success of her compatriot, John McCormack, at the Metropolitan Opera in New York and the apparent craze among the American public for opera made her contemplate the possibility of achieving her ambition there. She approached T.P. who, with Joe Devlin and John Redmond, M.P., had returned from a tour of America where they had collected funds for the nationalist cause. T.P. recalled 'the ignorant, timid, little flapper asking seriously to go to America . . . a little lamb asking to be sent to a tiger cage.'[22] T.P.'s answer on that occasion was an emphatic 'No'.

But while her future musical prospects remained clouded, a silver lining emerged in the form of her first serious romance. It was within T.P.'s political circle that she met the handsome nationalist M.P. for North County Galway, Richard Hazelton. The thirty-five year old parliamentarian from Blackrock, County Dublin, represented the North Galway constituency for the Nationalist Party at Westminster since 1906. In the 1910 general election, he successfully contested a seat in County Louth as well as retaining his seat in North Galway but, on petition, he was unseated in Louth.

Despite mixing in the sophisticated and urbane company of the London artistic and society set, Margaret, in her relationships with men, still retained much of the naivety of her convent upbringing. Throughout her life there continued to be an air of immaturity in her relationships with friends, often manifested by her directness and outspokenness, childish pranks and temperamental outbursts. She often expressed her feelings with such lack of inhibition that they could be easily misconstrued. Yet with her outward displays of emotion went a certain inner reserve, even fastidiousness. She, more than most, craved love and attention. Her feelings for Richard Hazelton were sincere and were obviously reciprocated. 'Peg o' my heart'[23] he lovingly referred to her, and on a return visit to Eccles Street she excitedly informed Mother Clement that they were to become engaged. But before she could make a commitment to Richard Hazelton and perhaps forever shelve her operatic ambition, fate once more intervened.

The dream-vision she had had in Eccles Street on that Christmas Eve so long ago, was realised in the Belgrave Square house of her benefactor, Lady Howard de Walden. As Margaret descended the great double onyx staircase and accepted the by now familiar applause of the fashionable audience, a dark-haired man rushed up to her, kissed her hand and exclaimed, 'This is the voice I have been waiting to hear all my life'.[24] It was the great inventor, Giuglielmo Marconi, partly Irish and married to an Irishwoman, Beatrice O'Brien, daughter of Lord Inchiquin and friend of her hosts and patrons. Every nation had heaped honours on the inventor of the wireless telegraph and Nobel prize-winner and both sides were using his remarkable invention in the great conflict that was tearing Europe apart. Marconi told Margaret what she already knew; that she had fulfilled her potential in England and that only in Italy, the land of *bel canto*, could her ambition be

Surgeon Commander Alfred Gaillton, R.N. married to her sister, Hester.

Richard Hazelton, M.P., Margaret's first romance.

Sir Thomas Beecham, Bart. (Courtesy: Royal Opera House).

T. P. O'Connor, M.P. 'Father of the House of Commons', Margaret's mentor.

Guglielmo Marconi. 'Yours is the voice I have waited to hear all my life.' A portrait she treasured signed 'To Peggy Sheridan, Guglielmo Marconi Rome 1918'. (Courtesy: *Capuchin Annual*).

realised. Marconi offered her the chance to go to Italy under his patronage and protection. Margaret found herself in a quandary, torn between the love she needed and the career she desired. She told a former schoolfriend from Dublin who visited her in London 'of the desperate struggle' she was going through to decide 'between love and ambition and how her advisers had prevailed upon her to leave love and follow ambition.'[25]

Eventually, Margaret made her painful decision, one which in retrospect she may have regretted. A picture of Richard Hazelton and his telegram of congratulations on the occasion of her subsequent London operatic debut were found among her personal papers at her death. Early in 1916, in the midst of the war, she made her perilous way, with Marconi, to Italy. The journey was slow and eventful. Their ship was dogged by German submarines in the Channel. Through the chaos of France, after many weeks, they reached Milan. As the train emerged from the darkness of a railway tunnel, Margaret's first and abiding impression of the country she was to love, was of a vivid blue sky and warm sunshine. At the Stazione Centrale di Milano, the arrival of Marconi was greeted by a multitude of cheering admirers. Acknowledging the cheers of the crowd, Marconi turned to his Irish charge and said, 'It's nice to be famous, Margherita, some day you must be famous too.'[26]

CHAPTER III

'UNA MIMI DELIZIOSA'
Operatic Début - Rome 1917-1918

Since the outbreak of the war, for almost an entire year Italy had chosen to remain neutral. Nonetheless, the country suffered much internal political and social upheaval. Despite fifty years of nationhood status, there was little central cohesion, direction or purpose. Unified in theory, Italy contained and nurtured diversities of language, education and affiliations. The role of central government continued to be thwarted by powerful self-interest groups and by a distinct lack of national identity among the masses. Most Italians spoke only dialect. Almost forty percent of adults were illiterate. The social and economic gap between the industrial north and the rural south was painfully evident; a similar chasm existed between town and country. There was no centrally controlled social welfare system; governmental provisions tended to benefit particular influential groups of workers. Communications were rudimentary; a popular press was but in its infancy and, although Marconi had invented the wireless in 1896, Italy as yet had no central broadcasting system.

Politically, the country mirrored its demographic diversities. The shrewd liberal leader, Giolitti, Prime Minister from 1900 to 1914, by a policy of integration and compromise, had managed to manipulate the many vociferous pressure groups, Socialists, Radicals, Catholics, and Nationalists: he had contrived to reconcile Italians generally with the idea of national government and had attempted to push forward a programme of social reforms and economic progress. But his policy was fraught with pitfalls. Forced to concede concessions to one group, he automatically fell foul of another. In any event, his conciliatory methods of government became obsolete after the introduction of male suffrage in 1912 and the emergence of mass political parties with fervent patriotism as their overt motivation and ideology.

In its foreign policy, Italy, a member of the Triple Alliance with Austria and Hungary, had dithered in its allegiance and adopted a neutral position in the war. While internally racked by a year-long series of riots, demonstrations and strikes, as anti-war Socialists and pro-war Nationalists clashed in open confrontation on the streets, externally, Italy's plight was unenviable. Her neutrality risked being regarded as an act of betrayal by her former allies. On the other hand, if the Entente comprised of Britain, France and Russia, won the war, it would hardly be disposed to grant an enemy the territories she most coveted, the Austrian-controlled areas of Trieste and Trent. Throughout the latter part of 1914 and during the spring of 1915, Italy bartered with both sides. In the event, the Entente held out the promise of greater concessions and by the end of May, despite the violent opposition of the Socialists and the total apathy of a great number of the population, Italy, expecting a brief offensive campaign leading to quick territorial gain, had entered the war with high hopes.

Marconi brought Margaret on to Rome, where he installed his protégée in the Hotel Excelsior on the famed Via Veneto. In the opulent ambience of Rome's premier hotel, Margaret's lifestyle continued more or less as it had been among her London aristocratic friends and patrons. Marconi introduced his new musical discovery to his circle of wealthy and influential Italian friends. Margaret's head reeled at the frenetic pace of the Roman social life which, for sheer splendour, made London seem dull in comparison; 'It was almost like a fairyland,'[1] she later recalled. In the great palazzi and in the villas of princes, dukes and counts, her voice was heard and applauded and her vivacious personality and blonde, blue-eyed good looks drew extravagant and passionate compliments from the dark Latins. The Duce Uberto Visconti di Madrone, president of the Teatro alla Scala, came from Como to listen and prophetically acclaimed her as the new 'Wally' of Catalani's difficult opera of the same name. But in a society which, despite its overtly permissive and amorous atmosphere, adhered to a strict public code of social morality, particularly towards women, whose only acceptable and respectable status was that of wedlock, Margaret's lone and unmarried state could well be open to misinterpretation and exploitation, particularly in the worldly circles in which she mingled. The patronage of one as powerful as Marconi and her own upbringing and background assured her reputation. She enjoyed the high life, the luxury, the compliments and the gifts, but soon realised that she had merely exchanged a gilded cage in London for a golden one in Rome. Her serious musical ambitions were, in effect, being thwarted by sheer luxury. 'The best hotel in Rome, perhaps in the world', she later remembered, 'the greatest names in the country but that was all. I had arrived in a way as a sort of musical toy. To start serious study would mean breaking with all these people and they didn't want me to do that.'[2]

Within Marconi's social circle she did, however, encounter men of music; the elderly librettist and composer of *Mefistofele*, Arrigo Boito, and Umberto Giordano, the jolly composer of *Andrea Chénier*, given to playing practical jokes and eating voraciously. But two men in particular were indirectly to become major influences. Giacomo Puccini, like Marconi, then an idol of the Italian masses, met the lovely Irlandese in Rome. A distinguished sixty year-old, with an eye for a beautiful woman, Puccini was to know her only as 'Peggy from Ireland',[3] a friend of Marconi. By then, the creator of *Manon Lescaut*, *La Bohème*, *Tosca*, *Madama Butterfly*, *Fanciulla del West*, Puccini had just completed *La Rondine* (*The Swallow*) which was to have its première at Monte Carlo the following year. Conscious of his advancing years and the imminent end of his artistic cycle, the great composer, melancholic, unhappy and reserved, was perhaps momentarily touched by the vivacity of the lovely young Irishwoman. In the exotic social setting which inwardly he loathed and generally avoided in preference to the solitude of his home at Torre del Lago, his good nature and boyishness responded to her candour, her wit and joie de vivre. He did not at this time hear her sing. Knowing full well that every woman with half a voice who came within earshot of the famous maestro imagined herself as an ideal Mimi or Butterfly, Margaret, on her initial brief encounter with Puccini, determined not to enlighten him about her frustrated operatic ambition. She did not reveal how she had struggled with the complexities and colours of his Manon in London; nor did she reveal how her own melancholic sensibility found an identity in the pathos and unfulfilled longing of his compositions. To describe and to interpret these emotions one must experience self-doubt and self-awareness, and undergo the endless, unfulfilled searching and intensity of desire which Puccini's music portrays. Both creator and would-be interpreter had a shared understanding and experience, but, for the moment, they outwardly shared little except the conviviality and superficiality of the social scene.

Sir Francesco Paolo Tosti, however, did hear her sing his own composition, 'Goodbye' at a fashionable party; since the early days of her singing career in Dublin, it had been an established song in her repertoire. One time music teacher, to the Queen of Italy and later to the English Royal Family, Tosti had also been a member of the Committee of Management at the Royal Academy of Music during

Margaret's student days. Having come from Italy in 1880, he settled in England, became a British subject in 1906 and was knighted in 1908 for his services to music. In 1912, he retired to Italy and resided with his wife Berthe at the Hotel Excelsior where he became acquainted with the young Irishwoman. A prolific composer in Italian, French and English, his ballads such as 'Forever', 'Goodbye', 'Amore', 'Ideale', 'Marechiare', 'Mother', 'That Day', were enormously popular. They were essential items in the repertoire of soirée and drawingroom singers. Impressed by her interpretation of his song, her personality and circumstances, Tosti arranged to coach Margaret personally. To this elderly composer, she poured out her anxiety about the lack of musical direction and development in her career, and the unrealised operatic ambition which had induced her to come to Italy in the first place. Tosti was sympathetic. He spoke with Marconi. Neither was overly anxious to lose the star of their social circle. But Margaret appealed and eventually got her way.

It was decided that she should see the much respected operatic coach, Alfredo Martino, who would pronounce on her voice. Martino was an operatic coach and assistant conductor at Rome's premier opera house, the Costanzi, and was regarded by the renowned tenor, Alessandro Bonci, as 'perhaps the greatest singing teacher alive today'.[4] Flanked by Marconi and Tosti, Margaret arrived at Martino's studio in the narrow Via Sistina. There Margaret and her powerful and influential friends quickly discovered that, where Martino was concerned, art preceded wealth and influence. Margaret later recalled their first meeting: 'Martino kept us waiting for 15 minutes. Kept Marconi waiting. Of course you'd need to have been in Rome in those days, in that atmosphere, to realise what that meant . . . to keep Marconi waiting! There we sat in a little room while Martino finished with his previous pupil'.[5]

Eventually they were admitted to the Maestro's studio and there, in the room where some of the greatest Italian operatic singers had rehearsed – Gigli, Toti del Monte, Lauri Volpi, Supervia, Franci and others – Margaret Sheridan auditioned. When she had finished there was, as she described it, 'a shrieking silence'. Marconi was forced to speak. 'Isn't it the most amazingly beautiful voice, a real discovery?' Martino's reply was unexpected. 'It depends on what Signorina Sheridan has come to Rome to do,' he said, 'to sing or to learn to sing. If she had come to learn, then perhaps he would agree with Marchese Marconi – when she had learned.'[6] Her patrons were indignant at Martino's response and departed in a huff to the Excelsior where they had arranged a surprise party for what was to be a celebration of the wonderful future predicted for Margherita. But there was no party. When her patrons had gone, disappointed and hurt, Margaret, dream in tatters, retired to bed. Shortly after, the telephone rang beside her. It was Martino. In broken French, (for Margaret as yet had little Italian) Martino put his proposal to her, bluntly. She had a voice, he conceded, but she did not know how to use it properly. If she was prepared to begin to study all over again, abandon totally her extravagant social lifestyle, move out of the pampered opulence of the Excelsior, he would accept her as his pupil. Margaret did not hesitate. The door of the golden cage in which she was suffocating had opened and, gratefully, she escaped into the bracing air. Marconi approved of her decision, remained in contact with his protegée and followed her career with interest and admiration. Tosti did not live to see the outcome of his intervention; he died in Rome in December 1916.

Now in her late twenties, Margaret became a student again. Clearly financially subvented still by Marconi, she took up residence in the Hotel Quirinale on the Via Nazionale, a short walk from Martino's studio on the Via Sistina. Her room overlooked the gardens which adjoined Rome's premier opera house, the Costanzi (now the Teatro dell' Opera di Roma). Returning to the rudiments of singing scales, exercises, breathing, placing, shading and colouring of each individual note, Martino began the process of raising her voice from the mezzo it had been to full soprano.. It would take time and patience to develop her technique and ensure that the elevation in pitch was built on a secure foundation. Study was not confined to vocal technique. She became familiar with the literature and background history of the operas she studied. Dante, D'Annunzio, Leopardi and Shakespeare became as much a part of her study as Verdi, Puccini or Donizetti. She began to experience for the first time the spirit of Italy, and of Rome and readily succumbed to its unique charms. 'Beauty everywhere,' she remembered, 'beauty jutting out of the walls, beauty of line, exquisite colours wherever you go. The people are beautiful and there's something . . . oh I can only describe it as loving your surroundings and being loved by them in return and if you cannot react to all that you'd better go back and forget it all.'' The great city, one-time capital of the world, was an international melting pot, attracting foreigner and national, student and teacher, pilgrim and poet alike to its antique streets and unique atmosphere. Through the jostling crowds on the Via Nazionale, down the narrow, cool Via Sistina where Martino had his studio, on to the opening above the great downward sweep of the

Spanish Steps, Margaret would linger to watch children playing or to observe artists sketching and swapping comments with young girls who waited their turn as models. Along the great avenue leading to elegant Pincio garden, from the high terrace she had an unforgettable view of the city, with St. Peter's in the distance crowned by the famous cupola of Michelangelo, ochre domes, spires, roofs. It was easy to study, to sacrifice, to cast off the rich trappings of society life, in such glorious surroundings. But it was not all hard work. It could never be with Margaret around and she soon became the centre of a coterie of students and bohemians. The life of the artist suited her temperament. She was in love with life and life seemed to love her in return. But practice and study were not in themselves sufficient. 'It isn't what you learn in the studio or how many scales and exercises you do,' she later advised. 'It is very good for you to learn scales and exercises but it is not in the studio that you learn the real secrets in opera.'[8] To Margaret, 'success in opera could not be taught in a studio', but as she believed, 'in the communal life of the artist. In becoming absorbed in music, in thinking music, exchanging ideas, hating, loving, feeling . . . living completely.'[9] Rome released the emotions she had locked away inside herself. Her love embraced the city, her surroundings, her work, her fellow students.

In that excitable atmosphere of her artistic circle, her natural warmth, sincerity and good natured authority drew to her the fears, self-doubts and infatuations of her fellow artistes, men and women who sought comfort and support from her seemingly endless resources of love, affection and advice. Her own indecision and self-doubt, in turn, seemed to evaporate. As in Eccles Street and at the RAM, she had re-entered a structured world with, at least in the short-term, a definable purpose. Although nearing her thirtieth year, her carefree sense of mischief and fun thrived just as it had in her schooldays at Eccles Street. 'I had a glorious life,' she later recalled. 'In the mornings we used to go to the Villa Borghese and breakfast under the trees, then back to a lesson; and in the afternoon we lunched just outside Rome at places like Tivoli and Ostia; then we came back for another lesson. The opera started at eight o'clock and after supper, somewhere at the back of the theatre, with delicious food and what fun – we often prolonged the evening by having a rendezvous with our friends to sing songs and duets by moonlight in the Colosseum.'[10]

The opera house (which her room overlooked) drew her like a magnet. Unable to afford a ticket, she profited from her friendship with Maestro Martino. Sneaking backstage each evening, she hid among dusty rolled-up curtains and listened and learned from many of the great performers during that season. Rosina Storchio, Nazareno de Angelis, the exciting new tenor, Beniamino Gigli, Gilda Dalla Rizza, and many others. Crouched in her musty backstage hideaway well might she fear detection. The Costanzi was ruled by an intimidating directrice, Emma Carelli. An acclaimed soprano in her day in Italy, Spain, Portugal and South America, Carelli married the impressario, Walter Mocchi, and succeeded him as manager of the opera house in 1912. A tough, uncompromising woman, she attracted the leading operatic stars to the Costanzi and she had a reputation for searching out new talent. Margaret had often observed her in the balcony of her apartment in the opera house as she watered her flowers, fed the pigeons or talked to her dog, 'Bello'. Margaret did not realise that her voice was already known to Carelli. For, whether by accident or design, Margaret practiced daily with the windows of her room wide open, and within earshot of Carelli's office in the Costanzi. One morning in late January 1918, Carelli wrestled with a major but not uncommon problem for a theatre manager. Alice Zepelli, who had sung the role of Mimi in the first performance of Puccini's *La Bohème*, had fallen ill. A replacement for the subsequent performance due to be staged in four days time had not been found. The advance ticket sales indicated a full house. Remembering the beautiful voice from the Quirinale Hotel, Carelli decided to take a chance. She sent a summons to the hotel for the student who sang with her windows open to come immediately to her office. Terrified at first that Carelli had discovered her trespassing backstage, Margaret was assured by the hotel manager that Carelli had also asked about her nationality and where she had been singing. Margaret felt a thrill of fear and excitement but her instant concern was what she should wear to impress the great Carelli. 'I did my best to doll myself up,' she remembered, 'and the chief thing I had recourse to was a lovely pair of long white kid boots which someone had sent me from Paris. I started to lace up these boots and I felt as if they had about 150 eyes. I puffed and blew and struggled with them and finally got them laced. After all, I was depending on these boots to make an impression.'[11] At the theatre, Margaret was ushered into 'the Presence'. Carelli, with a curt 'sit down', ignored her and continued writing at her desk. Casually she asked, 'Tell me what you are doing here in Rome?' Margaret told her she was studing to sing in opera. Carelli derided her presumption, that like the rest of the English, she could sing opera. Stung by this, Margaret responded that she was Irish. To Carelli it was all the same, only that the Irish were

LEFT: Back of the Costanzi Opera House, photograph taken from the window of Margaret's room in the Quirinale Hotel.
BELOW: Margaret with young friends in Rome, 1917.

LEFT: Maestro Alfredo Martino.
BELOW: Umberto Giordano, composer
of *Andrea Chénier*.
BOTTOM LEFT: Giacomo Puccini.

more troublesome and temperamental. Looking at the white boots, she observed that if Margaret could afford to pay a maid to lace them, then she had too much money for a student. Margaret replied that she had no maid and Carelli retorted that, in that case, she must not have much intelligence to waste time on such a ridiculous fashion. She then asked how many operas she knew. Demoralised but determined, Margaret replied, 'several', and began to list off *Manon Lescaut, Mefistofele, Butterfly, Bohème* . . . Carelli cut her short. 'That's a lie. You know two arias from *Bohéme* and I'm sick to death of listening to them. In any case,' she continued, 'if you did know these operas you would not have the courage to sing them in a big theatre. No, you would say, your Maestro would not allow you to sing yet, your top "C" was not quite perfect.'[12] Margaret hotly denied that she would be afraid. There was silence. Carelli then told her the real purpose of the interview. The day was Wednesday; Carelli offered to teach her the role of Mimi and in four days she would make her debut before the Roman public on Sunday night at the Costanzi. While Margaret absorbed this wonderful offer, her teacher, Martino, entered Carelli's room and angry words flew between the directrice and the coach. His pupil's voice, which he had raised to soprano, was not yet prepared for operatic roles, her technique, her training were incomplete. It would be disastrous for her future to undertake such a demanding role. He begged Margaret not to accept Carelli's offer but to wait until her technique was perfected. There would be other offers. Now was too soon. But Margaret did not consider it a minute too soon. Carelli offered her the breakthrough she needed and in Italy in 1918 it was exceptionally difficult to obtain a foothold on the operatic stage. There were some 150 lyric sopranos on the agency books at any one time and of those, there were as many as sixty Mimis, many established interpreters of the role, such as Storchio, Farneti, Caracciolo, Muzio, Dalla Rizza, Agostinelli, Spani, Zamboni, Melis, etc. Competition was fierce and standards were very high.

For the following four days, Margaret hardly left Carelli's side as she learned to impersonate Mimi. Puccini's *La Bohème*, 'in which the infinitely subtle changes in volume, orchestral colour and tempo suggest the depth and the transience of youthful emotions' seemed an appropriate choice for her debut. Carelli, herself once a superb Mimi, now coached Margaret in every entrance, every movement and every phrase. Word by word, note by note, she inspired her, not only to sing Mimi but to become Mimi. There was no time for a rehearsal with the orchestra but then Carelli merely required the student for one performance – until she could find somebody more suitable. Posters proclaiming the appearance of an unknown foreigner were hastily plastered in public places. 'Margherita Sheridan as Mimi in *La Bohème*',[13] they announced. Unlike many foreign singers seeking success on the Italian opera stage (including her compatriot John McCormack, who, in his early appearances in Italy was billed as Giovanni Foli, (an Italian version of his wife's surname Foley), Margaret refused to Italianise her surname. When the fateful night arrived, Margaret later remembered, she was more excited about her make-up and costumes than about singing!

On Sunday, 3rd February 1918, as a distinguished and critical Roman audience filled the splendour of the Costanzi, as Marconi and her grand society friends (whom she had not seen for almost eighteen months) took their boxes and the diminutive figure of King Vittorio Emanuele III entered the royal box, there, in the wings, waiting to fulfil a life's dream, was 'Maggie from Mayo'. In the best Hollywood tradition, her debut was a success. With the tenor, Salvatore Paoli, as her Rodolfo, Arturo Romboli as Marcello, under the baton of the eminent conductor, Teofilo de Angelis, the Roman audience rose to the Irish pupil of Maestro Martino, whose fresh beautiful voice so sympathetically interpreted the tragic role of Mimi. They proclaimed her 'Una Mimi Deliziosa'. To Italian audiences, long used to more matronly figures singing about young love while dying of consumption, the attractive and youthful appearance of the Irish Mimi was an agreeable change. The Italian critics, often hostile to foreign singers, were also enthusiastic in their praise. 'A young artist blessed with a wonderful voice who gave an unforgettable performance as Mimi', *Il Messaggero* stated. 'the public gave her a thunderous reception."[14] 'She sang the entire opera with a sweet, most moving voice, with delicate toning and accentuation',[15] the *Rassegna Melodrammatica* reported. Shouts of 'brava' greeted her second act aria, 'Mi Chiamano Mimi', but the critics observed, 'her real moment of glory was in the last act, in the death scene which she rendered with emotive sweetness of voice'.[16] 'Tiny hands, whiter than those of the Goddess of Ease', the words seemed to have been written especially for her as she used her own finely shaped hands to great effect both on and off the stage.

The applause was loud and long as she came forward again and again to receive the acclaim of the Roman audience. Laden with floral tributes, as she curtsied low, her eye was caught by a figure in the prompter's box by the footlights. It was Maestro Martino, with tears streaming down his face. Amid the applause, he alone perhaps realised

ABOVE: Margaret at her début in 1918.
RIGHT: Poster of Margaret's operatic
début, 3rd February 1918.

that the premature acclaim his pupil now enjoyed might well one day spell a premature ending. Margaret happily acknowledged the cheers.

With Marconi in the audience that night were the English admirals, Jellico and Beatty, and from Jellico's flag ship, the Iron Duke, news of Margaret's success was telegraphed among the more urgent war news and carried by English and Irish newspapers. The London papers searched frantically for a photograph of the unknown new soprano. Finally a schoolfriend produced a 'stickyback' photo of Margaret during her schooldays at Eccles Street. It was, as she later explained, 'one of the twelve for 6d variety. I had a big blob where my teeth should have been and my eyes looked crooked. It was not at all flattering.'[17] It adorned the front page of the *Daily Mirror*: 'Fame at a bound'. Papers in Ireland proudly proclaimed the success of an Irish girl in the competitive world of Italian opera and drew an analogy with the famous Irish soprano, Catherine Hayes from Limerick who, over seventy years previously, had had a successful Italian career with many appearances at La Scala in Milan. Margaret had a long road to travel before she could emulate the success of her compatriot but she had made a great start.

Instead of one intended performance, Margaret, or Margherita as she was now billed, was retained at the Costanzi until the end of May and gave six performances as the 'new' Mimi. Among her co-performers was Benvenuto Franci, considered one of the greatest baritones of the century, together with Gilda Dalla Rizza and one of the finest lyric sopranos of the day, Rosina Storchio, who was performing in *La Traviata* and Ambroise Thomas's *Mignon*. Storchio, the original *Butterfly* was impressed with the young Irishwoman's expressive interpretation of Mimi. She urged her to study *Butterfly* and gave her the benefit of her own great experience in the role. In May, Margaret performed at a gala performance of *Bohème* held in honour of the Prince of Wales who was on a state visit to Rome. Later in the month, she sang in a special performance of the opera to commemorate the third anniversary of Italy's entry to the war.

At the end of the opera season, she celebrated her success with her student friends, and despite Maestro Martino's initial opposition to her performance, it is obvious from her correspondence that she returned for further study and training with him later that year. In August she went for a short holiday to the countryside and returned to the Quirinale in the autumn. As the summer drew to a close, the war also lurched into its final trail of slaughter and destruction. Italy's involvement, despite the high hopes originally entertained, had been long, bloody and expensive with high casualties and an undermining air of national stability and unity. The disastrous defeat of Caporetto, when the Austrian forces routed the Italian army, forced the Italians for the remainder of the war, to fight a defensive and demoralising campaign on their own soil. But as the Allies launched a major offensive against the Axis in June, Italy, with the assistance of England and France routed the Austrians. On 11th November, after an unconditional capitulation to the Allies, Germany signed the Armistice agreement. For Margaret, peace meant a return journey to England and Ireland could be contemplated in safety if she wished. But, she realised, for the moment she must continue her study with Martino, enlarge her repertoire and hope that when the war clouds evaporated, Italy and the rest of Europe might return to a normal musical existence, favourable to her budding operatic career.

Cho Cho San – *Madama Butterfly* – Dal Verme, 13 December, 1919.

CHAPTER IV
BUTTERFLY INSUPERABILE
Praise from Puccini 1919-1921

Margaret bided her time in Rome as the numerous opera houses around Italy tried to reassemble their resources and personnel for the post-war resumption of normal operatic schedules. In England, opera had experienced mixed fortunes during the war years. The Beecham Company of English artists had, however, under the direction of Sir Thomas Beecham (knighted for his services to opera in 1915) kept opera alive during the war when international artists were unable to visit Britain. Based firstly at the Shaftesbury Theatre, then at the Aldwych and finally at Drury Lane, Beecham's company provided almost continuous seasons of opera throughout the war years. Towards the end of the war, Beecham became involved in the purchase of the entire Covent Garden estate, including the markets area, the opera house and the Drury Lane Theatre. But the Grand Opera Syndicate still controlled the lease of the opera house which had twenty years to run. In early 1919, an alliance was formed between the Syndicate and the Beecham Company and plans for the first season of international opera since the war were hastily announced.

Henry Higgins, the Chairman of the Syndicate, issued an invitation to Margaret to appear in the new international season. Margaret left the negotiation of her contract with Covent Garden in the capable hands of her friend and former teacher, Olga Lynn. The fee agreed was seventy-five pounds per performance and the contract was to be renewable for five years. Higgins had not heard her sing and explained in a letter 'as a rule I never engage Artists whom I have not heard; but Sir Thomas Beecham, with whom I am collaborating in the organisation of this Season, has spoken to me in enthusiastic terms of your voice and Miss Lynn assures me that she was quite satisfied that you have every qualification for making a great success here'.[1]

Initially, it was intended that she would make her debut in the Covent Garden premiere of Puccini's latest creations, *Suor Angelica* and *Gianni Schicchi*, two of three short operas comprising *Il Trittico (The Tryptych)*. But Margaret requested that her all-important debut at Covent Garden might be in the more familiar role of Mimi in *La Bohème* or as Cho Cho San in *Madama Butterfly*. Higgins agreed but also decided to cast her as Iris in the Covent Garden première of the Mascagni opera of the same name. He urged her to study the difficult role and to be in London by the 20th April so as to avail of the assistance of the *metteur en scene*, Monsieur Almanz, who, he assured her, 'is extremely good at assisting those like yourself who have not had a long experience on the stage'.[2]

Much was promised by the organisers as details of the new season were outlined to the public in the Spring. The preliminary announcements hinted that the great conductor, Arturo Toscanini, would conduct the Italian operas, including the proposed première of *Il Trittico*. Neither Toscanini nor *Il Trittico* materialised, however, because of a quarrel between the composer and the conductor. Puccini protested bluntly in a letter to Ricordi, the powerful publisher in Milan who held the performance rights, 'I do not want that pig of a Toscanini',[3] because, he alleged, he had denigrated his work. Administratively an uneasy truce existed at Covent Garden between the old Syndicate and the 'new boy', Beecham. Beecham believed that, in order to survive, opera could no longer remain the preserve of the wealthy but should be open to the new opera audiences who had flocked to his seasons during the war. Many of the established, dictatorial artistes, like Dame Nellie Melba, also disagreed with Beecham's assertion that conductors should dictate musical policy, not the singers. Beecham's attitude, both on and off the podium infuriated Melba. On her return to Covent Garden, the diva exploded in anger on discovering that the dressing room, long regarded as her personal domain, had, on Beecham's instructions, been repainted without her permission. Her temper was not assuaged by Beecham's response to her tirade. 'I pretended not to remember who she was,' he recalled in his memoirs, 'and asked what the deuce she meant by entering my private office unannounced, adding that I knew nothing of private ownership of rooms in this building'.[4] But the attitude of the new régime at the Opera House merely mirrored the changes wrought by the war on society in general. The old order had collapsed and the remaining survivors found it almost impossible to conform. Well might Melba declare that on her return to Covent Garden, which she long regarded as her private 'artistic home', that she was 'singing to an audience of ghosts'.[5] Margaret made the journey from Rome to London in advance of the

Italian party and arrived in late April to finalise preparations, especially for the demanding première of *Iris*. The composer, Mascagni, was on hand and coached her personally, teaching her to play the Japanese samisen as required for the part. The celebrated Italian conductor, friend of Verdi and Caruso, Leopoldo Mugnone (whom she had met in Rome and with whom she was to appear in many later performances) also coached her during the course of the London season. Their shared sense of humour made for an ideal working relationship. On one occasion, seated together at the piano as he rehearsed her *Iris*, Mugnone at a particularly beautiful phrase in the opera gave a sudden finger and thumb squeeze to her thigh saying, 'And that, Cara Margherita, is how it should go.' 'But Maestro,' she countered, 'that is not in the score.' 'I know, I know,' he replied, 'but that is life!'[6]

During a full rehearsal at which she was singing particularly well, Mugnone stopped the orchestra and asked,

'Margherita, where did you say you came from?'

'From Ireland, I'm Irish,' she explained.

'No, mai, è impossibile, no Irish or any other foreigner ever sang like that.'

'I assure you Maestro, I am Irish', Margaret insisted.

'All right, all right, have it your own way,' Mugnone replied and, to the loud laughter of those present, continued, 'but let me tell you something you don't know: your mother one day paid a flying visit to Naples and you are the result.'[7]

Her friends, Olga Lynn and T. P. O'Connor, welcomed her back and awaited expectantly her London debut. It was to be on the 24th May as Cho Cho San in *Madama Butterfly*. As the opening date of the season drew near, it became apparent that the remainder of the Italian cast would not arrive in time for rehearsals. Henry Higgins then decided that she would replace Melba as Mimi in *La Bohème* after the diva had opened the season in her favourite role. Margaret protested that as a newcomer she could hardly be expected to hold her own against the reputation of the famous and much admired prima donna. But Higgins was adamant that she could do it. 'Never mind comparisons in this case,' he consoled her, 'if the lady who is to sing the premiere was really at her zenith it would be a different matter.' He reminded Margaret that Melba had not been singing for two years, and added, 'I am by no means certain in my own mind that she will sing this time . . . I should like you to be ready for the première in case.'[8]

In the event, the Australian diva did sing and the opening night of the

International Season on 12th May turned out to be a glittering, emotional occasion. 'The scene was amazing,' the *Daily Telegraph* reported. 'The decoration was as before but it seemed to shine with a new brilliance, the gold to be more golden, the magnificent crimson more crimson than ever before.'' The war was over. Britain and her allies were victorious. A great ovation greeted the arrival of the King and Queen. That the young consumptive Mimi should be sung by the fifty-eight-year old, rather large, diva, mattered not at all. The voice of the indestructible Melba sounded as silver-toned and as clear as ever. Nostalgia ruled. It was a hard act to have to follow. Margaret was nervous, very nervous. Her first scheduled appearance as Mimi was cancelled and it was not until the 27th May that she felt sufficiently secure in herself to replace Melba. With her on stage, perhaps to bolster her courage, was her former teacher and friend, Olga Lynn, in the role of Musetta. There was a full house. All her aristocratic and political friends and patrons waited expectantly in their plush crimson and gold boxes: Lady Howard de Walden, Lady Randolph Churchill, Mrs. Asquith, Lady Diana Manners, Lady Cowdray, Lady Palmer, Mrs. Miller Mundy, T. P. O'Connor, Richard Hazelton, and a large contingent of Irish friends and well-wishers anxious for an opportunity to celebrate another Irish success at Covent Garden since the appearance of John McCormack there prior to the war; anxious too for an Irish victory to counteract the reports of violence and destruction that emanated daily from Ireland, then in the throes of armed unrest. Telegrams and flowers from friends and well-wishers in Ireland, England and Italy filled her dressing-room. There were telegrams, too, from family members she hardly remembered; one from her brother Paddy, recovering from the war in a hospital in Glasgow, another from her sister Hester, then living in Sandown and another which read, 'Three cheers for Auntie Peggy',[10] from Hester's only daughter, Moira.

With Thomas Burke as Rodolfo, Alfred Maguenat as Marcello, Gustave Huberdeau as Colline and conducted by Percy Pitt, Margaret regained her composure after a nervous start and the audience was treated to the true potential of the new lyric soprano. Despite an enforced forty-minute interval due to the sudden illness of the tenor, Thomas Burke, she cast aside the nervousness displayed in the first act and sang uninhibitedly. An enthusiastic final ovation recalled her six times before the curtain came down on this most exciting debut.

British press reviews were fair and objective. While noting her obvious nervousness in the opening act, which led to a little 'pinching'

Milan, c. 1920.

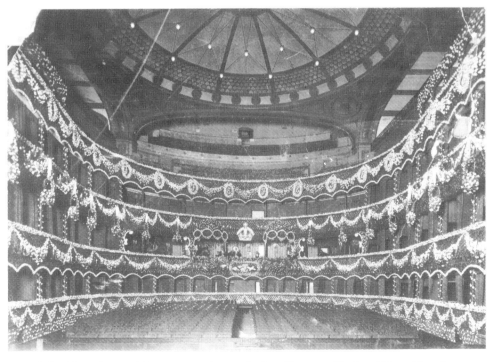

Gala night at the Royal Opera House, Covent Garden. (Courtesy: The Royal Opera House).

Dame Nellie Melba, whom Margaret replaced as Mimi in *La Bohème*, Covent Garden, 1919. (Courtesy: The Royal Opera House).

in her upper register, and her lack of stage craft, the critics were other-wise enthusiastic. 'Hers is a lyric soprano voice of beautifully sympathetic quality,' reported *The Daily Chronicle*, 'with an unusu-ally even quality of tone throughout.'[11] 'She represents the ideal Mimi,' *The Morning Post* enthused. 'Miss Sheridan has an exceedingly beaut-iful soprano voice which she uses well, intelligently and with convic-tion. Thus in her is found the long-looked for Mimi, who shall embody the true conception of the character, its grace and pathos and human-ity.'[12] Melba, not overly given to imparting generous compliments to upcoming rivals, must have agreed to some extent with the assessment of the new Mimi. However, although she publicly presented Margaret with a fan as a tribute, privately she contacted the offices of the newspapers who had written most effusively about the new Irish soprano to ask, 'had their reporters been drunk while reporting on the performance of the new-comer?'[13] While Melba, even at fifty-eight, might not fear vocal competitors, there could be no denying that the silhouette of the young, attractive, blonde soprano emphatically scored over the ageing, statuesque diva. On succeeding performances, on the 5th, 11th and 28th of June, partnered by such eminent artists as Martinelli, Dinh Gilly and Sammarco, Margaret's voice grew in confi-dence and she drew sustained applause each night. Her London friends rejoiced in her success and parties and suppers were arranged in her honour. The journalist, Larry Morrow, recalled first meeting her 'at a supper party at Pagani's in Great Portland Street, where she was implored by the manager in a cascade of Italian to write her name on the wall alongside a self-caricature by Caruso.'[14]

But ahead lay an ordeal even more demanding than her debut, the creation of the title role of 'Iris'. On the 8th July, under the baton of Leopoldo Mugnone, this strange, allegorical Japanese tale of the battle between good and evil was presented for the first time to an English audience. It was a demanding role vocally and physically. During rehearsals, Mugnone drily remarked, 'Iris was the greatest imbecile in the world, Margherita, the part suits you to perfection.'[15] To the press, Mugnone expressed the opinion that 'in Miss Margaret Sheridan we possess the ideal personality for the representation of the title role.'[16] Leading a well-seasoned cast of Huberdeau (Il Cieco), Couzinou (Kyoto) and Lapuzzo (Osaka), she emerged with her reputation further enhanced. 'Miss Margaret Sheridan made her mark as Iris,' *The Daily Mail* reported, 'It was an achievement that brings her to the front.'[17] 'As Iris, Miss M. Sheridan achieved a great success auguring well for her career as a singer and actress,'[18] the critic from *The Times* observed. Some reviews were more explicit. 'The vocal honours of the evening fell to Margaret Sheridan who as the heroine sang very finely. She had some difficult work which she overcame with apparent ease.'[19] All agreed that by her performance in this historic première she had taken a significant step forward.

When the curtain fell on the 1919 International Season at Covent Garden in early August, Margaret had every reason to feel pleased. Despite offers from music agents and promoters in Britain to perform concerts in London, Liverpool and Glasgow, she knew that she had found her medium in grand opera. Italy was the place in which to perfect her art if she was to reach the top. In Italy, reports of her performances in *Bohème* and *Iris* were carried in the press. 'Margherita Sheridan ha avuto un grande successo come Mimi'[20] (Margaret Sheridan has had a big success as Mimi) the prestigious *Corrière della Sera* announced and operatic impresarios and theatre managers wondered that an unknown foreigner should represent Italian opera abroad.

On her return to Italy in early Autumn, she moved to Milan which was to become her 'home' for the following fourteen years. Staying at the centre city, modestly-priced Palace Hotel, frequented by musicians and singers, she set about establishing herself on the operatic scene, no easy task as her compatriot, John McCormack, had discovered a few years earlier. Italy could prove a difficult and inhospitable arena for foreign artists.

In the aftermath of the war, political unrest continued, but Milan remained the centre of Italy's musical life 'and the capital of the world empire of Italian opera'.[21] Business, industry, finance, as well as culture, flourished amid Milan's solid monumental-style architecture, broad streets and pulsating piazze. Long dominated by a wealthy, pragmatic bourgeoisie, it sought both commercial and cultural leadership. Musically, its supremacy was unquestionable, with La Scala, the accepted world shrine of opera, presiding over the city's social and musical life. The Milan Conservatory was the most illustrious and prestigious in Italy. The influential publishing house of Ricordi sat in autocratic judgement over singers, musicians, composers and theatres alike by virtue of its precious copyright monopoly of old Verdi and Puccini works. Its power extended to every other opera house within Italy and throughout the world. Ricordi could promote or hinder a career and its proprietor, Tito Ricordi, was much courted by artists and composers alike. The influence and control of the company had also spread to the rapidly developing gramophone industry. The Galleria Vittorio Emanuele – uniting the wide Piazza Duomo, on which Milan's multi-spired, richly embellished cathedral is situated, with the small Piazza della Scala – was the principal meeting place and promenade for the Milanese. There, daily, from 9 a.m. until 11 p.m., the great names in finance and industry, the intellectuals and the artists, converged to see and be seen. Cultural life centred around the high vaulted spans of the long galleries. A few decades earlier, Puccini had sauntered with the rest to catch a glimpse of the greats of his day: the venerable Verdi, chaperoned by his publisher, Giulio Ricordi. Now they came to look at him. At midday in the Galleria everyone gathered in the halls of the concourse. Successful singers, composers and the influential impresarios met to be seen, to chat and sip coffee or an aperitif in the expensive coffee houses like Savinis or Biffis. Aspiring singers and students loitered outside, hoping for an introduction to an impresario or a maestro. 'Students of singing and maestri de canto who battened on them, campremari (small-part artists) and coristi went to make up this clearing house of the opera world.'[22]

Margaret promenaded with the rest and eventually made contact with the most influential theatrical impresario in the musical world, Giusseppe Lusardi, who agreed to promote her. A lawyer by profession, Lusardi had been editor of *Lanterna*, a bi-monthly newspaper of the theatrical agency of Gustavo Agenti. On Agenti's death, Lusardi assumed control of the agency and renamed the paper *Il Corriere dei Teatri*. His influence in Italy and abroad was immense. He had a monopoly on many of the greatest singers and conductors and both Italian and foreign opera houses depended on him for artists. Like other agents, he assisted unknown singers of ability by paying their upkeep and tuition, being amply rewarded if they proved successful. Unlike many aspiring singers, Margaret had a track record, albeit a short one, having proved her potential in *Bohème* and *Iris*. But she felt she was capable of more and suggested *Madama Butterfly* to the agent. Lusardi was reluctant. A foreigner in the premier role, the preserve of Italian sopranos? It was unthinkable. How could a foreigner from such a cold, reserved, unemotional country such as England, even if she had the voice, interpret the drama of betrayed love with the sensitivity, the pathos and the passion, the combination of strength and delicacy which the score required? Margaret reminded Lusardi that she was Irish, not English, and that there was a passionate difference in temperament. 'It was my description of Ireland and the sorrows of Ireland that finally convinced my impressario that I had the right temperament to sing Butterfly.'[23] she later recalled.

While the mecca of opera was La Scala, Margaret had to prove herself elsewhere. La Scala was the Olympian home of the Gods and Goddesses, she had but commenced her novitiate. Moreover, La Scala had lain dormant for some time with the exception of a performance of *Mefistofele* in remembrance of the deceased composer, Boito. The great opera house remained silent and shut, the paintwork peeling, the machinery rusting and the dust silently settling over its splendour like a shroud. The privately owned Dal Verme theatre was Milan's second most prestigious opera house and since the closure of La Scala had assumed even greater importance. On 13th November, Margaret signed a contract to sing *Butterfly* at the commencement of the autumn carnival season there, with Mascagni's *Lodoletta* as an option. She was booked to sing a minimum of three performances at an overall fee of 5,000 lira, of which her agent received a commission of five per cent. Romeo Endrigo was to be her Pinkerton. Advance publicity in the Milanese press introduced her as 'una cantante Irlandese' (an Irish singer) and Milan waited to see what the foreigner could do. During rehearsals her unique interpretation of the psychological development of the character that is Butterfly became evident. 'You are a born artist,'[24] the theatre manager, Oreste Poli, told her.

On 13th December 1919, she faced the Milanese opera fanatics and conquered their hearts and fulfilled their testing standards. In a review of her performance, the *Corrière della Sera* sought to put some Italian flavour on the success of the foreigner. 'Miss Sheridan is Irish,' it conceded, 'but either by luck or instinct she sings as an Italian . . . only the colour of her lower notes revealed her different origin . . . ' 'Her clear steady range and smooth phrasing'[25] was highly praised. Her interpretation of Butterfly was different, the critics thought, to past interpretations (a view that the creator of Butterfly would later confirm in person to her)

> 'but this only emphasised more the individuality of Miss Sheridan who with her excellent qualities as a singer and an actress completely conquered the audience which accorded her rapturous applause at the end of each act and at the beginning of each scene and demanded, constant encores.'[26]

The new 'foreign' singer was found to have the qualities that appeal to Italian operatic taste, vocal power, a dramatic temperament and a sensuousness of interpretation. 'La Sheridan has a most beautiful voice,' Carlo D'Ormeville, director of the reputable weekly artistic magazine *La Gazzetta dei Teatri* reported, and 'is very well educated in the Italian school of singing, possesses also a most suitable stage appearance, pronounced our language most remarkably and shows an uncommon talent.'[27] From now on, Margherita Sheridan would become adopted by the Italian public as one of their own.

She played to packed houses and gave eight instead of the three performances expected. Drawn by the extravagant reviews of the foreign Butterfly, Puccini's son attended and promptly urged his father to hear this different Butterfly. Puccini, who detested hearing his operas distorted, at first refused. But on reading that the new Butterfly was Irish and had studied in Rome, he remembered his brief encounter with the blonde Peggy Sheridan there and decided to see and hear her for himself. 'After the second act,' she later related in an interview, 'he came around to my dressing room, pulled back my heavy Japanese wig to satisfy himself that I was his blonde friend from Rome.' 'May God bless you, Peggy, why did you never tell me you were a singer,' he asked her. Margaret explained that she wanted to get into opera on her own without embarrassing him by seeking his patronage. Then she asked for his verdict on her performance. 'First of all there is not a dry eye in the theatre,' he told her:

'. . . even the toughest types are in tears. It's an interpretation that is completely new to me – yours not mine. It's full of dramatic intensity and childlike appeal. This could never have been learned from anyone. It's the instinct that comes from an old race like the Irish, full of dramatic temperament and spiritual vision and have often a tear in their voice.'[28]

Puccini recognised Margaret's instinctive empathy with his character and with his music which, as the music of human emotion, transcended culture, language and nationality like no other. His music was a language understood by all, reflecting his own inner self-doubt, his desire for perfection, his vain quest for love. Small wonder that the sensitive and emotionally responsive Margaret Sheridan, also seeking love and self-confidence, should become a faithful interpreter of the Maestro's work. Later, he would coach her personally for Manon in his opera, *Manon Lescaut*, a work for which she was also to receive great critical acclaim.

Her contract at the Dal Verme was promptly extended and she was engaged to sing *Bohème* which opened on the 21st February with a cast which again included Endrigo and the bass, Fernando Autori, who was to become a good friend and who appeared in many other productions with her. He eventually became almost as famous a caricaturist as an opera singer and published drawings of the operatic greats of the day, including Sheridan. In *Bohème*, Margaret scored, as one Italian paper described 'una nuova brillante vittoria'. 'As in Butterfly, Signorina Sheridan was in splendid voice, singing confidently and genuinely impressive in her dramatic interpretation. She received the most frequent and warmest applause of the entire evening.'[29] It was a triumph as the *Corrière della Sera* correspondent noted. 'Fra i quali, a vero dire, emerse solo la Sheridan, che interproto la parte di Mimi assai bene, con voce fresca e graziosa, ottimo metodo di canto, e grande efficacia di azione drammatica.'[30] (Among them all, to tell the truth, only La Sheridan distinguished herself, she interpreted the part of Mimi extremely well, with a fresh and pretty voice, excellent singing and with effective dramatic action.) She gave seven performances of *Bohème* and remained at the Dal Verme until the close of the season in April.

Hers had been an important Milan debut and in media reviews of the 1919/1920 Italian opera season, she featured prominently. The fabled conductor, Arturo Toscanini, who, like Puccini, had been drawn by the reviews to hear the new Butterfly was to consider her in his future plans at La Scala. But others wanted to engage her services more urgently. Mascagni urged her to come to Palermo to perform Iris there. Lusardi negotiated a contract for her to sing Marguerite in Faust in Turin. But further south, Naples had heard reports of the 'find' of the season and the impresario, Lagana, arrived in Milan with an invitation for her to sing Butterfly at the famous San Carlo theatre there. Margaret's preference was immediate and she wrote her reasons to Lusardi, anxious not to give offence to one so influential. 'Pay is better in the Naples contract', she assured him, 'and I do not have to sing consecutive recitals. I also like the repertoire. I do not know Faust and have not the time to study it and would not wish to sing an opera for the first time before an important audience like the Turin one.' And she added, rather lamely, 'my health would not allow for singing in a cold climate either.'[31] She signed the contract to appear at the San Carlo for the season beginning on 25th January 1921 in an opera from her repertoire. But prior to her departure to the city of sun and song, she fulfilled an additional and final engagement at the Dal Verme in December, singing the parts of Margherita and Elena in Boito's *Mefistofele*. Singing with her on that occasion was Nazareno de Angelis, considered the finest Mefistofele for over thirty years.

She spent Christmas 1920 within the coterie of fellow artists at the Palace Hotel. In the aftermath of the war, the political and social unrest which had erupted throughout Italy manifested itself most clearly in the north and particularly in Milan. As the new fascist dogma asserted itself publicly and violently, it was a difficult time for a foreigner in Italy. Margaret was additionally vulnerable to other more personal pressures. Her position, personality and looks attracted exaggerated avowals of friendship and offers of unstable relationships from men and women in the close-knit circle. They vied for her attention and affection with promises of material assistance, protestations of undying devotion and the inflated words and compliments that come easily to the Latin temperament. 'Why do I see you before my eyes all the time,' one female companion wrote to her, 'You have bewitched me.'[32] Another rehearsed at her piano with Margaret's photograph before her, while a potential lover wrote of his desire to kiss her hands and eyes (no vulgar intercourse between these select Muses!). Their common theatrical background bound them together and embellished their everyday life and relationships. The most mundane incidents, comments and stories became dramatised and it is during these years in Milan that Margaret's health problems, which as time went on, were to interfere with her career, together with damaging doubts about her artistic ability, became more apparent. By now one of the 'regulars' at the Palace she had her own designated room, number 101, and had become a favourite with both management and guests. The 1920 New Year's Eve dinner menu at the hotel offered 'Macedoine de Fruits a la Sheridan'.[33]

The New Year got off to an inauspicious start when, due to illness, Margaret sought to be released from the remaining performances of *Mefistofele* at the Dal Verme. One of her friends at the Palace advised her on the drafting of her letter to the theatre manager; she had to be cautious to avoid any repercussions on her career – 'Keep yourself in a neutral position (like Switzerland),' her friend warned, 'without any compromise and without any risk of having to pay costs'.[34] But there was no hesitancy in commencing her contract in February with the San Carlo in Naples. In the many interviews she gave throughout her life, Margaret's love of Naples and its people was always apparent. Perhaps her flamboyancy, good nature, humour and outspokenness appealed to the extrovert Neapolitans. The warm, rich timbre of her voice, not to mention her blonde, blue-eyed looks, also found favour with the Neapolitan ear and eye. She eventually became fluent in the local dialect and often recalled how she had the 'cheek' (as she called it) to sing 'Santa Lucia' in Neapolitanese at an impromptu recital shortly after her arrival there.

Enjoying a reputation second only to La Scala, the San Carlo, lavishly appointed with a seating capacity of three thousand five hundred, also enjoyed the dubious reputation of attracting volatile and vociferous audiences who were not averse to whistling and shouting their disapproval. Under the baton of Vincenzo Bellezza, who became a close friend and with whom she was to work on numerous occasions in Italy and in London, Margaret gave her first performance in Naples on 28th February 1921. Interpretation, her great forte, held her responsive and admiring audience enthralled from her Butterfly entrance. The atmosphere generated by her appearance and her singing was electric. A compatriot and fellow artist, Walter McNally, baritone at the San Carlo, was in the audience:

> 'I shall never forget her *Madama Butterfly*. It was thrilling; it made one lose oneself to be in the audience and hear a great mighty host of thousands of people standing up on the seats shouting "Brava, Brava" and crying aloud "Sheridan, Sheridan".'[35]

The singer remembered the occasion as one of the most thrilling first nights of her career: 'After the first act I heard the whole audience shouting "Viva l'Irlanda! Viva l'Irlanda! – I was overcome and very delighted.'[36]

The critics were impressed: 'La Sheridan is a rare artist', *Il Mattino* reported the following day.

> 'A spontaneous and instinctive performance, intimate and varied combined with a passionate rendering of the music . . . she interpreted the role with intelligence and feeling. With these qualities . . . rare even among our own singers . . . La Sheridan received last night at the San Carlo a warm, full, instant and, for her own career, important success.'[37]

It seemed in Naples she could do no wrong. Even when in one performance a blonde curl carelessly appeared from under her black Butterfly wig, the critics' reaction merely referred, poetically, to the 'fugitive golden lock of hair of La Sheridan'.[38] Her conductor, Vincenzo Bellezza, perhaps most accurately assessed the reason for her great success in Naples: 'Her musical temperament was typically southern rather than Nordic.'[39] To commemorate her Butterfly success at San

Carlo, a bronze bust was presented to her by the directors of the opera house, with the inscription – *A Margherita Sheridan, Butterfly Insuperabile*[40] Naples was reluctant to allow her to depart and offered her a contract 'in bianco' if she would remain on as prima donna at the theatre. It was a tempting offer but, in the summer of 1921, other, more exciting possibilities beckoned.

In London, her old mentor, T. P. O'Connor, through his influence and journalistic contacts, especially at *The Daily Telegraph*, ensured that the story of Margaret's success in Italy was recorded in the British and Irish papers. T.P. now urged her to consider extending her career to America where John McCormack had already discovered the seemingly insatiable musical appetite of Americans. Many of her Italian operatic friends and acquaintances enjoyed renown and lucrative earnings at the Metropolitan Opera in New York and at the Chicago Opera in particular. T.P. consulted with Leon and Gertrude De Sousa, friends of Marconi, who had befriended Margaret during her stay at the Excelsior in Rome and who were anxious to assist her career. They agreed that it was impractical for her even to consider America without first acquiring the services of a reputable agent, and they recommended Denis F. McSweeney, then associate manager of John McCormack, later to be in sole charge of the tenor's business affairs. An engaging personality and amazingly energetic man, McSweeney had introduced himself to McCormack in 1912 with the words, 'I'm an Irishman from the kingdom of Kerry, who wants to welcome you to New York.'[41] Initially an impresario for charity concerts and functions in New York, McSweeney soon became an indispensable companion and advisor to McCormack. T.P. was impressed by the Kerryman's ability and business acumen. 'I have formed myself a very favourable impression of McSweeney,' he wrote to Margaret in Italy. 'He is certainly a hustler but that is all to the good for you and', he added, 'I am quite sure you would be safer in the hands of an Irishman and a Catholic than anybody else.'[42] Of McCormack, T.P. wrote that 'with a little attention (he) would also be a warm help. He has some difficult qualities in his character, but at bottom he is a good fellow and' – an essential in T.P.'s book – 'is a thoroughly good Irishman.'[43] Margaret dithered. Though the applause and tributes of the Italians were generous, the financial rewards were small. In any event, she was hopeless where money matters were concerned. Her life-long inability to manage her financial affairs may have stemmed from her dependent upbringing. Until the age of twenty-nine, her finances and material well-being were administered by others. But now she was on her own. 'While I rejoice at the splendid success you have made in Naples, I do not think Italy offers any real future for you,' T.P. advised. 'What you want to do in the next ten years is to make all the money you can while your voice is still in all its freshness and big money is not to be got, as I understand, in Italy.'[44] Despite T.P.'s insistence that America held the key to her future success and financial security, fate again intervened in the person of the legendary conductor and musical genius, Arturo Toscanini, and T.P.'s advice, America and money (about which in any event she cared little) faded into oblivion.

Teatro Dal Verme, Milan. (Courtesy: Castello Sforzesco, Milan)

Teatro di San Carlo, Naples. (Courtesy: San Carlo, Naples)

Teatro Comunale Giuseppe Verdi, Trieste.

Teatro Comunale, Cento.

Teatro Ponchielli, Cremona.

CHAPTER V
LA WALLY
La Scala Début 1922-1923

To most operatic singers, Milan signified one thing – the Teatro alla
Scala. Regardless of the success an artiste might achieve elsewhere in
Italy, Europe, America or in any part of the world, every triumph
appeared petty if one had not conquered La Scala. Its unpretentious
exterior belied the allure and prestige it undeniably held. To the
Milanese La Scala was sacrosanct: 'No other theatre anywhere ever
meant anything to the Scala clique . . . For the most part we disliked
newcomers on the boards of our hallowed stage and we disliked foreigners.' 'In a word', a Scala patron recalled, 'We were the biggest, most
bigoted opera snobs that ever existed. Opera was part of life and everybody in Milan, from the boxholders to the people who scraped
together their lira for a back seat in the gallery were born and bred in
opera and knew a good deal more than the most professional critics.'[1]
A campaign, spearheaded by the *Corriere della Sera*, to re-open the
fabled theatre, existed since 1920. Protest meetings and press agitation
finally provoked the municipal authorities to agree to re-open the
theatre, provided it would henceforth serve all the citizens and no
longer be dominated by wealthy, aristocratic patrons as in the past. A
new political dawn was breaking over Italy ands even the sacred La
Scala would have to conform to the new thinking and changing times
if it were to survive. A new administrative body, the 'Ente Autonomo
del Teatro alla Scala', was formed. The hereditary box-holders relin-
quished their proprietary interests; a campaign for voluntary contribu-
tions was inaugurated among the citizens and a tax was levied on all
amusement enterprises in the city, such as cinemas, sports events and
other theatres, the money to be spent on the total reformation of the
opera house. In July 1920, the Municipal Administration appointed
Arturo Toscanini as director of La Scala 'with complete and absolute
authority'.[2]

The conductor's previous associations with the theatre from 1898 to

1903 and from 1907 to 1908 were best described 'as a series of melodramatic arrivals and stormy departures, of angry ruptures and reconciliations'.[3] In his determination to reform all aspects of opera, both artistic and administrative, Toscanini had encountered much resistance. But the iron will of this remarkable genius was unshaken. As the resentment grew, he abandoned La Scala in disgust for the Metropolitan Opera House in New York. It endured his reforming zeal from 1908 until 1915. No-one was spared. Even the once all-powerful prime donne were forced to comply with the Maestro's demands. Some resisted. 'Maestro you must follow me, I am the star,' one of the Metropolitan divas rebuked him from the stage during rehearsals, as the conductor insisted on following the tempo ordained by the composer and not that decided on by the 'star'. 'Madam,' came the icy reply from the podium, 'the stars are in heaven. Here on earth there are only good and bad artists and you are a bad artist.'[4] Now in 1920, it was La Scala's turn again to experience the maestro's fanatical lust for perfection.

With the financial position of La Scala secured, Toscanini set about implementing the reforms he considered essential to his plans. Under his supervision, major renovation was carried out to the physical structure of the theatre: the roof was raised seven metres, the stage was widened, extra lighting and stage equipment were installed. A chorus of some seventy male and fifty female performers and a permanent orchestra, individually selected by Toscanini, were established. A galaxy of operatic stars, drawn by the spell of La Scala, were assembled, including Aureliano Pertile (the Maestro's favourite tenor), Toti Dal Monte, Mariano Stabile, Ezio Pinza, Gilda Dalla Rizza, Juanita Caracciolo, Zaleski, Rosa Raisa, Francesco Merli, Galeffi, Claudia Muzio, Fanny Heldy, Elvira Cosazza, Nazareno De Angelis, Rosetta Pampanini and Margherita Sheridan. Margaret was not the first Irishwoman to tread the famous Scala stage. In 1846, the Limerick-born soprano, Catherine Hayes, had made her debut there in the role of Linda di Chamounix by Donizetti. For many years, La Hayes had enjoyed great success in Italy prior to her departure on an extended tour of North and South America and Australia.

To retain one's position at the new-look Scala, one had to submit to being directed and dictated to by Toscanini. Some could not take the bullying and departed. Most endured the regime for a time at least to learn from the greatest operatic innovator of all time. A new process of re-education for singers was introduced. Singers, chorus, stage presentation, orchestra, all were but part of an integrated work of art; music and dramatic components all fused into a unique, integral concept. Toscanini insisted that the principal singers, regardless of vocal ability, must not merely stand on stage and sing, they must act and interpret through voice and action; they must look the part they acted. He aimed to make opera conform to modern-day expectations and be realistic. As Margaret later recalled, 'he realised that the days of the old singer, perfect though her singing might be, were gone, unless the lines of her figure were harmonious as well. So he got rid of all the over-forties from La Scala. He refused to have 'old women with three chins and four tummies singing about their fatal beauty'.[5] Toscanini's single-minded quest for perfection, his uncanny musical memory, his dominating personality and his intolerance of anything less than first-rate, both intimidated and inspired his artistes. One of the younger singers, Malfada Favero, later described her ordeal. 'The whole thing was a dream. I remember that I sang and that I acted but it wasn't I. It was the spirit of Toscanini which made me sing, with two deep eyes, always fixed on me, eyes which were so eloquent that one had to become excellent even if one was not.'[6] Margaret was more forthright in her assessment of the Maestro. 'I think Toscanini was the greatest dictator ever known in the world of opera. He always knew what he wanteds and always insisted on getting it. It might not be what you wanted and always insisted on getting it. It might not be what you realised her good fortune to have been chosen to be part of the innova-tive crusade being waged by the Maestro within the operatic world. 'I was very fortunate,' she recalled:

'When I went to Milan (La Scala) Toscanini had revolutionised the whole art of opera. He had watched the rise of the ballet and the cinema and all that they meant in the way of technique and realism. In future, he decided, Manon must look like Manon. He acted as a sort of Svengali. He compelled us to do things. He educated us. He made us read and study in detail the period of the opera we were rehearsing.'[8]

By then fifty-four, the dapper, balding conductor-director, still shed a personal radiance and magnetism that was highly attractive to most women. His eyes, deep-set and dark, were framed by heavy eyebrows which, when drawn together, signalled the oncoming storm. Married to the beautiful Carla de Martini at thirty, his extra-marital philandering was common knowledge both within and outside opera-tic circles and increased rather than diminished as he grew older.

Margaret jocosely remembered being authoritatively directed by Toscanini as to how she should sing an aria expressing the state of mind of a girl who had been seduced. 'He seemed to know all about it,'[9] she mischieviously remarked. The blue-eyed, blonde Botticelli looks of the Irlandese were doubtless not lost on the Maestro but the temper and outspokenness that simmered beneath her doll-like complexion he had yet to experience. He had heard her Butterfly at the Dal Verme and later at the San Carlo and had been impressed. But La Scala was sacred, only the very best would be admitted through its portals and there were many who clamoured for admission. Influence could help to obtain an introduction but once on the stage, you were on your own and no amount of influence could camouflage an inadequate voice. For a foreigner, influence was essential but difficult to come by. But Margaret's engaging personality had attracted people who could be helpful. Ferrucio Calusio, principal music arranger at La Scala, then working on an arrangement of Romeo and Juliet by Zondonai, a close confidant of Toscanini, had been smitten by the personality of his Irish friend. Her directness, her honesty, her unwillingness to tolerate the insincerity of Italian 'small talk', as she called it attracted him. While his initial romantic overtures, which she regarded as being no more than fleeting trifles, did not succeed, a friendship developed between them which Calusio effusively referred to as being like a 'journey of light, lighting my spiritual life'.[10] When she eventually received the summons from Toscanini, it was Calusio who coached her in the difficult part chosen by the Maestro for her debut at La Scala. Angelo Scandiani, the administrator at La Scala, on occasions used his influence, to patch up her many subsequent disagreements and arguments with Toscanini.

Toscanini drove both himself and his artistes relentlessly. In fear and in dread, the great names spoke of the 'red' rehearsal room where he put his charges through their vocal paces, as 'the room of the heart attack'. 'Every time we went in there', Toti Dal Monte recalled, 'it was like mounting the guillotine'.[11] Margaret was not spared. At a dress rehearsal, she inadvertently wore velvet slippers instead of the required shoes, thinking that it would neither be noticed nor considered important. But Toscanini noticed, stopped the rehearsal and before the entire company, ordered her off the stage to change into the regulation footwear. According to Margaret, 'it was the prime donne who were the bane of the maestro's life at La Scala. If they had lovely voices they had no brains and when they had brains, good looks and voices then they were almost impossible to put up with.'[12] As Margaret undoubtedly belonged to the latter group, a collision between herself and Toscanini was inevitable.

Initially she towed the line, elated to be among the Scala elite. Toscanini had her in mind to fulfill a special undertaking, the revival of the opera of his deceased friend, Catalani, *La Wally*. This production was to commemorate the thirtieth anniversary of the opera's world premiere at La Scala in 1892. Before Margaret commenced the rigours of rehearsals, Toscanini arranged for the eminent soprano, Maria Farneti, to coach her. Farneti took a great interest in Margaret and they became good friends. Farneti presented her with the magnificent gold kimono that she had worn in *Butterfly* and which had been given to him by the Emperor of Japan. The role of Wally was exacting, both vocally and physically as Margaret recalled:

'One had to be a peasant girl and proud as a queen . . . I had to run down a precipice, built high at the back of the stage, dance, wearing about ten petticoats, carrying the tenor on my shoulder (he was heavy), die with him in an avalanche, and remember my singing and all Maestro Toscanini had taught me.'[13]

While Toscanini was not to conduct the opera, Margaret did piano rehearsals under his direction and he was present at the orchestral rehearsals for the important revival of *La Wally*.

As a further part of her preparation, Toscanini sent her every night for a week to the performance of the great Italian actress, Elenora La Duse, to absorb her stage craft and presence. It was decided that *La Wally* should be first presented at the San Carlo in Naples. On 7th January 1922, heading a cast which included the young tenor, Franco Lo Giudici, baritone, Baratto, and bass, Percy Costa, under the baton of Mascheroni, the celebrated conductor of the original performance in 1892, she faced her favourite audience. Because of the special qualities she had shown in *Butterfly* the previous season, there was a sense of expectation among the Neapolitans that La Sheridan's Wally would be something special. 'The expection was realised', the *Corrière Della Sera* reported, 'because La Sheridan, from her first aria, confirmed her excellent artistic qualities – the success was complete'[14] Once more the applause was warm and long for 'La Sheridan, suggestiva e mirabile protagonista'.[15] There were many messages of praise. 'Congratulations without end, Catalani's spirit happy at last',[16] read one of the many telegrams. Messages from her former teacher in Rome, Maestro Martino, from Denis McSweeney, then in France, from Herbert

Hughes, the music critic of *The Daily Telegraph* and from the ever-faithful Olga Lynn who had been informed by a friend who had attended the performance that 'she had never heard anything so beautiful, your voice a mixture of Melba and Destinn'.[17] High praise indeed, but Margaret had yet to face her sternest test, her La Scala debut.

Having performed *La Wally* six times at the San Carlo, she returned to Milan to prepare for its opening there. La Scala had reopened its doors to an expectant and excited public on the traditional night of 26th December. In the midst of the social and political violence that continued to divide the community, as fascist clashed with socialist and pro- and anti-war protestors continued their out-of-date battles on the streets, the re-opening of the Teatro alla Scala was regarded as a beacon of hope towards the building of a new and harmonious society out of the ruins of despair and division. Toscanini had limited the season to ten works, five of which he chose to conduct himself, the remaining five, including *La Wally*, he assigned to his assistant, Ettore Panizza.

On 6th April 1922, the myriad lights dimmed in the great crystal chandelier, high over the packed stalls; the lights over the six-tiered rows of crimson and gold boxes that rise upwards from the ground to merge high above with the raised ceiling, faded gradually, leaving a pink after-glow within the boxes to contrast with the black darkness of the horseshoe pit in front. Margaret Sheridan waited silently, fearfully, in the wings of the greatest opera house in the world. Flanked by de Voltri, Bertana, Di Lelio, Marini and Noto, the young Irishwoman faced her first La Scala audience. The Marchese Malacrida who later came to live in Ireland, vividly recalled the scene:

'For the first night of *Wally* with the new singer, the theatre was full of professional and unprofessional critics in an extremely critical mood. The opera begins with Wally running down a precipitous mountain path, bare armed and barefooted with her blonde hair flying in the wind. When she (Sheridan) appeared we remained speechless, he recalled. 'She was agile, she was lovely but above all she was young, young, young. Well, the physique was certainly there. But how would she manage the great aria that murderously – even for an experienced singer – takes place a few minutes after her entrance. It is by that Wally stands or falls and for one or another reason no one had ever managed it since the great Darclée (1892). But Margherita sang throughout the piece with freshness, an air of effortless ease, a dramatic power, a charm that took the whole theatre by storm. She had a terrific ovation.'[18]

Mimi in *La Bohème*. (Courtesy: Derek Walshe).

Cho Cho San in *Madama Butterfly*.

Desdemona in *Othello*.

Manon in *Manon Lescaut*.
(Courtesy: Anne Chambers)

Candida in the world première of *Belfagor*.

Maddalena in *Andrea Chènier*.

While audience reaction to her Wally was tremendous and she played to packed houses on each of her seven performances, earning spontaneous applause for her arias (much to the displeasure of Toscanini who frowned on such outbursts), the Milanese critics considered that she had not done full justice to the savagery and passion of the first act. In the lyrical arias, however, they praised her warm, clear, delicate interpretation. Critics aside however, the Scala audiences applauded warmly and Toscanini was pleased enough to sign her on for the next season.

On the closing of the Scala season in May, Margaret returned to England to spend the summer months with her friends there. They had kept abreast of her triumphs which had been well-documented in the British papers, particularly in *The Daily Telegraph*. During her stay in London, she received an invitation to make a gramophone test at the HMV studios. Fred Gaisberg, the pioneer of the recording industry, had heard her sing in Milan and was impressed. A man of infinite enthusiasm for the industry and with a special and essential understanding of the artistic temperament, Gaisberg's initial invitation to the Irish prima donna was eventually to bear fruit. Sound recording at this time was still a mixture of the old cylinder and newer disc recording methods. The trumpet-like projectory was still in use as the microphone did not become widespread until after 1925 when enormous developments occurred in the recording industry generally.

Margaret was eventually signed by HMV in 1926 and 'was one of the few English-speaking singers to be awarded celebrity status (red label) by HMV'.[19] Her association with HMV was, however, to prove both temperamentally and financially unrewarding. She found it difficult to adapt to the demands of recording techniques. Cancellations, accusations and histrionic outbursts marked her tempestuous association with the company. While her output was relatively small, she made several memorable recordings, including the first complete electrical recording of *Madama Butterfly*, excerpts from *Bohème*, *Manon Lescaut*, *Othello* and *Andrea Chénier*, and many Irish melodies. She sang memorable duets with her favourite tenor, Aureliano Pertile, and with the Chilean tenor, Renato Zanelli. She had a strong, even powerful, recording voice and delighted in telling how the technicians would make her stand some feet away from the microphone and behind her tenor! Her recording with Pertile of the love duet from *Madama Butterfly* is, perhaps, the most emotive of all renderings, with two expressive voices soaring to a majestic climax. This duet led the Irish politician, James Dillon, noted for his witty and often caustic comments, to enquire of Sheridan, 'Don't tell me you both went your separate ways after singing that?'[20] Arthur Hammond, the English conductor and arranger considers the duet 'one of the most beautiful opera records ever made'.[21] Tributes through the years have been paid to the Sheridan recordings, many of which were unfortunately removed from the HMV lists, lost or destroyed. The few that survive, despite their age and the technical shortcomings of the day, capture some of the rich, expressive timbre of her voice and are, for later generations, the only legacy of her voice. The eminent Italian critic, Dottore Giorgio Gualerzi, considers that the Sheridan recordings reveal:

> 'a voice of a great authentic lyric soprano of the old school which unfortunately no longer exists today. Her distinctive timbre and a particular expressiveness which is evident in her recordings assured her a place of great merit in operatic history. Together with Rosetta Pampanini, but with more careful taste, she made a gradual transition from the old style Puccini interpretation towards a more modern stylistic approach partially acceptable even today.'[22]

To a modern-day diva, Renata Tebaldi, Sheridan's recordings are proof of her outstanding interpretative artistry. La Tebaldi recalled that it was La Sheridan's Puccini recordings which were considered the definitive examples; it was these she studied during the course of her operatic training in Italy. La Tebaldi wrote: 'Recording my admiration for that great interpreter of verismo roles, I believe that her recording of Manon Lescaut is a memorable rendition of that role, she is in it a superb singing actress combining great artistry with remarkable technique.'[23]

During Margaret's vacation in London in the summer of 1922, the Irish baritone, Walter McNally, invited her to join him in concert at the Theatre Royal in Dublin the following November. She had been absent from Ireland since her departure with Marconi for Italy in 1916 and much had happened in her 'own country' since then. She had followed the traumatic events of the intervening years with anguish from Italian newspaper reports of the 1916 Rising in Dublin and the subsequent executions and imprisonments. She heard of the horrors perpetrated by the infamous Black and Tans in Ireland as England made a final, desperate attempt to subdue the struggle for independence which had by then replaced the Home Rule aspirations of the earlier years. Reading of these events in far-away Italy moved her deeply and her affection and attachment to Ireland had remained strong. Postcards and letters sent to friends in Ireland during the 'troubles' were often bedecked with slogans such as 'God Save Ireland'. She later claimed that, on hearing of the death from hunger strike in prison in England of the republican Mayor of Cork City, Terence MacSwiney, she refused to sing a scheduled performance of *Madama Butterfly* on the night and the performance had to be cancelled. 'His great sacrifice for our national freedom fired the imagination of all Europe far more than those at home ever dreamed of,'[24] she was later to recall. But her pride in her Irish identity never produced bitter or anti-English feelings. 'Perhaps the greatest friends of my life, both artistically and personally, were those who came to hear me in Covent Garden,' she later attested. 'The English public has a fidelity and loyalty to the artist which I can only describe as . . . commovente.'[25] She had many staunch and generous friends in England who had not only provided the means and the opportunity for her success, but were proud of her achievements, loved her for herself and provided her with moral and financial support in her difficult years, friends who expected nothing in return, and, indeed, often endured temperamental, ungrateful outbursts. She never suffered, as many Irish exiles did, an inferiority complex regarding her Irishness. She wore her nationalism confidently and with flair. Neither did her pride in her Irishness prevent her from being outspoken about shortcomings she found in Ireland.

In November 1922, during Ireland's darkest hour of civil war following the British withdrawal, she returned to Eccles Street. Amidst the rattle of Thompson and Lewis machine guns and the sharp crackle of rifle and revolver fire in the streets of Dublin, against the background of reprisals, executions and hunger strikes, she prepared for the only public concert she was ever to give in her own country during her operatic career. Despite the turmoil of the time, her concert, as expected, was a sell-out. Her presence in Dublin overcame, temporarily, tragic and bitter divisions. 'Maybe all roads lead to Rome,' *The Evening Herald* of the 1st December 1922 read;

> 'but certainly all routes led to the Theatre Royal yesterday. All kinds of people comprised the audience – from the wives of the staff of the National Army to the active members of the opposing forces, from constant attenders at the old "Castle drawingrooms" to a "Red" sister imported from Russia'.[26]

For a moment, political differences were abandoned and the shooting appeared to cease as the glorious voice of Margaret Sheridan, accompanied by her former teacher, Dr. Vincent O'Brien, filled the Theatre Royal.

Her programme of operatic arias included the poignant 'Un Bel Di Vedremo', and she sang some Irish melodies. Her voice and stage presence won over the Irish audience who were 'by no means ready to accept Miss Sheridan on her Italian reputation'.[27] The critics also were impressed. 'Miss Sheridan is an interpreter. She lives the part she is acting . . . She has a voice of immense power, of great range and of ravishing beauty.'[28] Her rendition of the Moore's melody 'O Breathe Not His Name' was reported to have 'opened all hearts to her magnetic personality. She sang the song as only an Irishwoman and a lover of Ireland could sing'.[29] But the critics also observed what Margaret herself well realised. 'Miss Sheridan on the platform is out of her element . . . To see her at her best we must see Miss Sheridan in opera.'[30] Margaret concurred with the assessment; opera was her true medium. 'I was very nervous when coming on to the concert platform in Dublin,' she confessed in an interview, 'because I felt as if it was not my real element. I did not feel half as nervous any time when appearing at La Scala. A concert is something necessarily cold and I feel myself that I can best and most completely express myself in opera.'[31] She also expressed the hope that she might return to sing in grand opera in Dublin so that her 'own people' might see and judge her in her 'natural' environment. 'I hope that a first rate company will be organised between Milan and Covent Garden and that grand opera in really fine style will be given in Dublin. I see no reason,' she added, 'why the great musical traditions of Dublin should not be maintained and continued.'[32] Like so many of her hopes and plans, this ambition was never realised. Both the media and her audiences were captivated by her warm smile, sparkling personality and sense of fun. 'A sense of humour', one critic astutely observed, 'is only possessed by those having deep and intense emotional feeling. Miss Sheridan has both.'[33]

Dublin was reluctant to let her depart and an additional concert was arranged in an attempt to satisfy the many who clamoured to hear her.. Reporters haunted the convent in Eccles Street for interviews with the prima donna. She dallied in Dublin, reluctant to move on. She remained at her convent home over the Christmas period and once again delighted her teachers and friends by her impromptu concerts in 'Mother Clement's Parlour'. But she had to move on and by the New Year she was in London. From London, the lure of La Scala and the chance of making operatic history sent her hurrying back to Milan.

Teatro Alla Scala, Milan, interior.

Teatro Alla Scala, Milan, exterior.

CHAPTER VI

THE EMPRESS OF IRELAND and
'THE WHIP' 1924-1926

There had been many significant political developments in Italy during Margaret's absence. On 30th October 1922, Benito Mussolini, former labourer, migrant worker, soldier, journalist and newspaper proprietor had become Italy's new leader. Taking advantage of the post-war social unrest, unemployment and a morbid fear among the middle and upper strata of Italian society that a socialist take-over of Italy was imminent, the one-time socialist and anti-establishment agitator, changed his policy mid-course to become the champion of the right and of a society he had once despised. Following an intimidatory march on Rome by thousands of Mussolini's black-shirted *squadristi* (units), armed units led by the strong-arm *ras* (commanders), the accommodating, nervous king, Vittorio Emanuele III, had little option but to confer complete power on the new leader, *Il Duce*. A fascist regime, to remain in power for over twenty years, was installed. In the initial years, Mussolini enjoyed much support within Italy. The advance of socialism, which had demonstrated its power by the strike weapon over the preceding years, had left much of the population 'frightened of socialist talk and of revolution and ready to look on Mussolini as a lesser evil'.[1] The powerful middle classes, alienated by a series of strikes and a growth in the crime rate, were unwilling to accept their social inferiors, the working classes, as their partners in government. But apart from the aristocracy and the powerful industrialists, who had most to gain by keeping socialism at bay, many people backed the new leader. Even Toscanini had been swayed by the early posturings of Il Duce and considered him the only person of sufficient strength and magnetism to unite the differing Italian political factions. So sure was Toscanini that fascism was the only alternative for Italy that he offered himself for election on the fascist ticket in Milan in 1919. But earlier than most of his compatriots, Toscanini realised Mussolini's real intent and his initial support of the dictator turned into

Milano, 29 Dicembre 1924   (Conto Corrente colla Posta)   Anno XXIV. - N. 1005

RASSEGNA MELODRAMMATICA

Uffici in Milano: Via Carlo Cattaneo 2 — TELEFONO 8-26   Notiziario lirico, Organo dell'Agenzia del Comm. VITTORE DELILIERS   Indirizzo per lettere e giornali   Vittore Deliliers - Milano

ABBONAMENTI   Non si accettano inserzioni e pubblicità   **Esce tre volte al mese**   Un numero cent. 70 — Arretrato Lire Una.   **PAGAMENTO ANTICIPATO**   **ABBONAMENTI**

FRA LE DIVE

MARGHERITA SHERIDAN

Il suo grandioso, ultimo successo personale
al Teatro Comunale di Bologna nell'opera *Andrea Chénier*

Nella "Manon" del Maestro Puccini

Andrea Chénier a Bologna

Star Treatment, 1924. 'Among the Divas'.

uncompromising revulsion. The power Mussolini had secured relatively bloodlessly, he intended to retain by whatever force, political or physical, he thought necessary. During the first two months of his reign, newspapers reported 'an average of five acts of violence a day'.[2] Mussolini knew that the only way to consolidate the power 'bestowed' on him was to terrorise all who sought to oppose him. But, blinded by showmanship and rhetoric that was as much part of fascism as the murders and beatings by the *squadristri*, by the flags, the orchestrated cheers and parades, by the stage-managed mass demonstrations, and most of all by the raw force of Il Duce's oratory and carefully packaged public personality, the majority of Italians roared their approval while those who disagreed remained, for the most part, silent.

As a foreigner Margaret learnt to restrain her opinions. With the obvious exception of Toscanini, most of her friends, her fellow artists and her wealthy and aristocratic patrons supported the fascist regime and readily accepted the honours and promotions that the system bestowed on them. Her position as a foreigner was vulnerable and, as an operatic singer, at times difficult. The nationalist ideology that, to be culturally the best, one must be Italian, which was fostered by fascism, could harm her career prospects. As one of the few non-Italian artistes officially tolerated as residents, it must be assumed that Margaret, like most of her fellow artistes was publicly pro-fascist.

Reinstalled at the Palace Hotel on her return, she was signed by La Scala as primo soprano, at a fee of 2,000 lire per performance, to sing Candida in the world premiere of Ottorino Respighi's comic opera, *Belfagor*. This opera consisted of two acts with a prologue and epilogue and was based on a story by Machiavelli. In the score, the composer managed to reflect the intricacies and perceptions of the story line: 'A thousand musical devilments put their tails into Respighi's music.'[3] Margaret rehearsed under the supervision of Toscanini and Respighi. However, the score itself was considered unmelodic, and was not expected to arouse great public reaction. But it was a world première and therefore the cause of great excitement in Milan. Before a full house, on 26th April 1923, with a distinguished cast comprising Mariano Stabile, Francesco Merli and the bass, Azzolini, it was again Margaret in her beautiful costumes by Caramba of Rome, who received special mention and applause. 'The fully harmonious voice of Margherita Sheridan,' the *Corriére della Sera* reported, 'used so effectively by the famous artist was much appreciated by the audience. Her fresh and most beautiful voice was in full bloom. The many duets she had with Baldo made a remarkable contribution to lyrical expression.'[4] Her vocal agility, particularly in her duets with the tenor, Merli, was also noted. But after her aria in the second act, in which she reiterates her love for Baldo, the audience broke into spontaneous applause. This was the only aria in the opera to be applauded. While the critics found the new opera somewhat exuberant and unequal in quality, Respighi had good reason to be well pleased with the style and performance of his principal interpreters. To Margaret, he autographed his photograph: 'Alla Prima Candida, Milano, Teatro alla Scala, 26 IV 1923'[5] (To the first Candida, Milan, La Scala Theatre, 26 IV 1923). After four performances as Candida, the 1922-23 Scala season ended with a brilliant performance, conducted by Toscanini, of Verdi's *Requiem*. The Mass, composed by Verdi in memory of Manzoni, was revived by Toscanini as a tribute to the great writer's fiftieth anniversary.

In London, her friends, especially T.P., were again somewhat anxious about her future prospects in Italy. Another tempting offer from America, this time from the Chicago Opera company, had materialised. T.P. was in no doubt where her destiny lay. He predicted that there was no financial future for her in Italy, whereas in Chicago 'hundreds of thousands of your own people will see in you a great representative of their race, with the prospect of never being without a big income for many years'.[6] But she immediately became apprehensive at the prospect of leaving the familiar surroundings of Italy to conquer new audiences in a country so far away. She had a deep affection for Italy and the Italian people. She was by now fluent in Italian and had even mastered some of the dialects. The Italians understood her temperament. Italy gave her room to breathe, to be herself; she was secure in the camaraderie of the circle of friends she had attracted. Her finances were frequently stretched because her relaxed attitude to work often meant she was 'unavailable' for performances; but she invariably managed. Within her social circle in Milan, she found the psychological and financial support she needed. 'I almost hugged the customs' officer at Domodossalo,' she once confided to Vincenzo Bellezza after a trip to England. 'I was so happy to be coming back to Italy!'[7] Moreover, she was by now at the height of her fame and her latest success at La Scala augured well for her future. The great English dramatic soprano, Dame Eva Turner, recalled Margaret's success at this time. 'When I went to La Scala in 1924 she was already established there and had made a great success especially in Catalani's *La Wally* . . . She was very good-looking, had a great sense of humour and a very attractive personality.'[8] Her success, gaiety and attractive looks ensured her place among the élite at the Galleria where she enjoyed her fame to the full. Fred Gaisberg, a frequent visitor to Milan on behalf of his recording company, remembered her also at this period as:

'the toast of Milan where her blonde beauty and vivacious tempera-ment endeared her to her colleagues and society alike. She could often be seen, the radiant centre of an adoring crowd, at the Bifi, Savini or Cova restaurants, just as voluble in Italian as the Italians themselves and like them talking with gesticulations and eyes.'[9]

Whenever she required a rest from the intensity of her work and social life, she would retreat to the fashionable resort of Bellagio on Lake Como. She stayed at a hotel which is still owned by the Bucher family with whom she maintained contact since her student days at their other hotel, The Quirinale in Rome, and later at The Palace in Milan. There, at the Grand Hotel Villa Serbelloni, a palatial residence much favoured by Italian and English society, Margaret relaxed and renewed her energy among the splendour of mountains and lake.

Beneath the facade of her gaiety however, lingered self-doubt. To T.P. she confided her reluctance to leave Italy for America; her fears of failure and of the insecurity of unfamiliar territory. T.P. berated her lack of initiative and confidence. 'The prizes of life are worth fighting for,' he admonished. 'Like most of our race, you lack grip, you lack courage, you lack confidence. Do get rid of that form of "other worldliness" which was graven into your soul by your education in your convent.'[10] But her sense of misgiving persisted and as offers of engagements throughout Italy continued to entice her to stay, Margaret's decision on America was once again deferred.

She had been offered a further contract with La Scala for the follow-ing season. Meanwhile, during a visit to Rome early in 1923, she had renewed acquaintance with Puccini who had a new role in mind for her. On a photograph he sent her, Puccini wrote, 'To the most beaut-iful artist, Miss Peggy "Mimi" Sheridan with the affectionate remem-brance of Giacomo Puccini'.[11] In her interpretation of Mimi and Butterfly he was aware of her instinctive response to his characteriza-tion and his music. He decided that she should perform 'Manon' in his opera *Manon Lescaut* and commenced to coach her for the part. 'Puccini referred often to the aristocratic voluptuousness of Manon,' she related later, 'and it is this voluptuousness, this richness, which tells us all about the opera. *Manon Lescaut* is an opera of shading, of texture, of colour. Manon demands more care and thought than any opera I have ever sung . . . Puccini loved his Manon more than any of his heroines – and they say he was in love with each of them. He often said that the fourth act, "Sola, perduta abbandonata", was the finest music he ever wrote.'[12] As she had done in *Butterfly*, Margaret's interpretation brought a new dimension to the character. Arthur Hammond recalled discussing the opera with her in Dublin many years later and 'how she had leaned over and softly sang in my ear the famous aria, "In quelle trine morbide". It was unbelievably beautiful,' he remembered, 'and she sang it in a slightly different tempo to that in which it is usually sung and which I subsequently tried to get my singers to copy.'[13] Dr. Franco Armani, son of the Italian conductor, Giacomo Armani, who had worked with Margaret on many occasions, and the famous soprano Juanita Caracciolo, a noted Puccini artist, observed that 'when she came to that gavotte in *Manon* she did not only sing it but played it and danced it as it had never been done'.[14]

The prestigious Autumn Carnival festival of opera at the seaside town of Rimini was the venue chosen to launch Puccini's 'new' *Manon*. On the night of her first performance, a large parcel was delivered to her dressing room. Inside was a magnificent gown of blue silk and gold lace for her to wear in Act II, a gift from Puccini. Estimated to have then cost a staggering £200, it was a creation of the famous couturier and stage designer, Caramba of Rome. Accompanied by Badini, Bergamaschi, Pedroni, Sampieri and Cilla, her performance was a triumph. 'She has at her disposal,' *L'Avvenire d'Italia* recounted, 'superb resources and a delightful voice of crystal-like purity . . . she has reached the very heart of Puccini's music. Her singing is of the kind that rouses our public to the highest pitch of enthusiasm. It is singing that is at once fresh, sweet, suave. The longer she sings the warmer becomes her timbre. I cannot analyse her performance in detail', the reviewer wrote, 'I can only say that she was magnificent.'[15]

During the Rimini Carnival season, she also performed Maddalena in Umberto Giordano's fiery revolutionary opera in four acts, *Andrea Chénier*. In this, she partnered the 'new Caruso' of Italian opera, Beniamino Gigli. The passionate duets in *Chénier* were given full expression by the voices of the great tenor and his leading lady. Theirs was a partnership that was destined to be renewed.

Immediately after her many performances of both *Manon* and *Chénier* at Rimini, Margaret appeared again in *Manon* at the Teatro Municipale at Cento, near Bologna, where she gave nine performances. Cento was an important venue on the operatic calendar and for the annual season presented artists of the highest calibre. Margaret's performances there are still recalled with pleasure and with pride by the residents of the small town, particularly her triumph there on the night of 23rd September when Puccini came to Cento to hear his protégée. After the performance, surrounded by a huge crowd Margaret with Puccini was cheered from the theatre across to the residence of the local Comune where a reception was held in their honour. Later, flanked by Puccini, and Gatti Casazza, the managing director of the New York Metropolitan, and Italo Balbo, the prominent fascist leader and member of Mussolini's government, they drove in an open carriage in triumph through the streets to the Falzon-Gallerani mansion, home of a prominent aristocratic family, where Puccini with Margaret by his side came onto the balcony to acknowledge the cheers of the excited populace below. Her frequent visits to the little Marian grotto in the local church on her way to daily rehearsal at the theatre are also remembered by some of the older residents of Cento to this day. The local Comune erected a plaque in the town to commemorate the occasion.

Italo Balbo became one of her most ardent admirers, often arriving unexpectedly at her first-night performances or sending her bouquets of flowers when he was unable to be present. An accomplished, if somewhat flamboyant, airman, on one occasion, she often recounted, he actually 'buzzed' a theatre with his plane during her performance. In later life, friends remembered her occasional references to the young, ruthless squadristri leader and future Marshal of the Italian Airforce and her genuine upset on hearing of his death when his plane was shot down in Libya in 1940.

She was booked for further performances of *Manon* at the Teatro Ponchielli in the fascist town of Cremona, noted for its critically vocal audiences. Margaret was warned that she would be lucky to complete one performance there. As the hour of her appearance drew closer, she became increasingly nervous. The audience was particularly difficult and her first act was greeted with catcalls, howls and shouts of 'fuori la straniera' (away with the foreigner) as the fascist leanings of the audience manifested themselves. But she persevered. Dressed in Puccini's gorgeous dress in Act II, she braced herself and defiantly faced the by now hostile crowd. She started to sing the lovely aria 'In quelle trine morbide'. There was a hush and, expecting a further noisy outcry, she became so nervous, that on reaching the high B flat, she could not come off it and held on and on in a state of semi-panic.

Teatro A. Ponchielli - Cremona

Recita N. 16   d'Abbonamento N. 15

STAGIONE LIRICA 1923-1924

Domenica 10 Febbraio 1924 - Ore 21 prec.

SECONDA RAPPRESENTAZIONE dell' Opera in 4 atti

MANON LESCAUT

Musica di G. PUCCINI

Protagonista: **Margherita Scheridan**

ESECUTORI

Manon Lescaut	Margherita Scheridan	Il maestro di ballo	Gastone Vivaldi
Lescaut, sergente delle guardie	Giuseppe Spadarotti	Un musico	Maria Gubbioli
Renato Des Grieux, studente	Piero Menescaldi	Sergente degli Arcieri	Giovanni Novelli
Geronte di Revoir	Oreste Carozzi	Un lampionaio	Antonio Gilardi
Edmondo, studente	Antonio Gilardi	Un comandante di marina	Vincenzo Ferraro
L'oste	Giovanni Novelli	Un parrucchiere	N. N.

Borghesi - Fanciulle - Popolane - Studenti - Arcieri - Marinai ecc.

Maestro Concertatore e Direttore d'Orchestra

FRANCO GHIONE

Maestro sostituto	Maestro dei cori	Maestro suggeritore	Direttore di scena	Coreografo
M. G'ACOPETTI	Cav. O. VERTOVA	A. FRANCIOLINI	R. MAGISTRI	G. CERUTI

Prezzi d'ingresso per questa Sera

Platea e Palchi	L. 15	Poltronoine (oltre l'ingr.)	L. 20
Militari e ragazzi	» 8	Sedie a bracciuoli	» » 15
Galleria	» 10	Posto riservato	» » 8
Loggione	» 6		

Nei prezzi sopraindicati è compresa la tassa erariale

N.B. Il Camerino del Teatro resterà aperto dalle ore 16,30 alle 18.

V. LA DIREZIONE   L'IMPRESA

Manon – *Manon Lescaut* – Cremona, 10 February 1924.

A thunderous applause erupted from the audience. 'Il brono (in quelle trine morbide) La Sheridan procurea una ovazione'[16] (In the passage 'In quelle trine morbide', La Sheridan received an ovation), the *Cremona Nuova* reported. Instead of the scheduled four performances of *Manon* at Cremona, she sang six times and was presented with a gold medal by the *Cremona Comune* to commemorate her performances there. The reviews were loud in their praise. 'La Sheridan is beloved by the people for her marvellous voice and for her intuitive and artistic interpretation.'[17]

After Puccini's untimely death in November 1924, a series of commemorative operas was held throughout Italy. By now recognised as a celebrated Puccini interpreter, Margaret was inunnundated with offers. From Piacenza, Trieste, Brescia, Naples, to Genoa, Modena and Cascina, La Sheridan triumphed in each. The conductor, Vincenzo Bellezza, testified to the high esteem in which Puccini held her. 'He spoke of her,' he later wrote, 'as a great hope for the future, both for the opera world in general and for his own works in particular. He was not mistaken. Peggie was an unparalleled interpreter of the music of Puccini. The humanity of his characters and the lyricism of his music found a subtle echo in her, and thereby "lived".'[18] Renata Tebaldi remembered Puccini's daughter saying that her father considered Margaret 'the outstanding Butterfly of all'.[19]

Following successes at Rimini and Cento, in November 1923, Toscanini chose her to perform Anna Marie in another Scala première, the comic opera *I Compagnacci* by Primo Riccitelli. Preceded by a performance of the one act opera, *Salome*, by Strauss, based on the play by Oscar Wilde, *I Compagnacci* opened the 1923-24 Scala season. With Ernesto Badini singing the buffo role of Bernardo del Nero and with Bovaro, Tedeschi, Alabriso and Nessi, Margaret's 'fresh voice and correct technique'[20] were praised by the media. Six performances of the new work, described as 'fresh, gay and sentimental'[21] were given under the baton of Vittorio Gui.

Margaret's final performance at La Scala, although it seemed an unlikely possibility at the time, was as Maddalena in *Andrea Chénier*, for which she won acclaim both for live and for the recorded performances, particularly for her duets with such tenors as Beniamino Gigli and her own favourite, Aureliano Pertile. For the Scala performance which opened on 14th May 1924, she shared the stage with the outstanding baritone, Benvenuto Franci with whom she had sung in her début in Rome in 1918, her friend, Fernando Autori and Luigi Marini as Chénier. The three performances of the opera received an enthusiastic reception. Margaret was greatly praised for her 'flexible and caressing voice'[22] and especially for 'her lyrical phrasing in the character of Maddalena in the third act'.[23] As she closed the 1923-24 Scala season on the 21st May with the final performance of *Chénier* and listened to the appreciative applause of the Milanese audience, there was no indication that she was taking her final curtain in the theatre with which she ,was most closely associated. Among her personal papers is a contract, dated 2nd May 1927, with La Scala, signed by its director general, Angelo Scandiani, engaging her, at 2,500 lire per performance, to sing *Manon* in the forthcoming carnival season. Her return was widely heralded but did not materialise. Later, in the 1927-28 Scala season, posters announced her return as Dolly in the Wolf-Ferrari opera *Sly*, based on the Shakespearean comedy, *The Taming of the Shrew*. With a cast which included Pertile, Rossi, Morelli, Badini and Baracchi, the opera was to open 26th December 1927. At the last moment, Margaret fell ill and her part was taken by Mercedes Llopart. Although she represented La Scala at the International Seasons at Covent Garden from 1925-1930, she did not sing again at La Scala. Reviews of her performances in other theatres throughout Italy from 1924 to 1930 are, without exception, full of praise and there is not the slightest indication of any shortcomings.

There are some possible explanations for her alienation from La Scala or, more especially, from Toscanini. She was in the mould of prime donne, temperamental and inclined to be headstrong. That she enjoyed the extravagant social dimension of operatic life is clear from her correspondence. Much sought after in the houses of the wealthy and in the fashionable restaurants and coffee houses of the Galleria, she was not an overly industrious artist and her lively social existence was not always conducive to the high level of commitment demanded by Toscanini. Where rehearsal and study were concerned, Toscanini was a strict disciplinarian. 'He dealt sternly, even ruthlessly, with laziness and incompetence,'[24] Gigli recalled in his memoirs. But the combination of two hot artistic temperaments, combined with divergent political views, may have been the main reason for Margaret's alienation from Toscanini, and consequently, from La Scala.

By 1924, fascism was a solidly established dogma under Benito Mussolini as dictator of Italy. Toscanini's initial flirtation with fascism and his admiration of Mussolini had turned to a passionate hatred. He would not acknowledge the legitimacy of the fascist government and refused to allow portraits of either Mussolini or the weak and accommodating Italian King to hang at La Scala. He banned the playing of the

LEFT: Beniamino Gigli. (Courtesy: The Royal Opera House). RIGHT: This portrait is signed: 'To my companion, Margaret Sheridan, with great admiration and affection, Beniamino Gigli 1948').

Ezio Pinza.

Maria Caniglia, a close friend and colleague.

Renato Zanelli.

Eva Turner.

ABOVE: Cia Fornaroli (Prima Ballerina).
LEFT: Aureliano Pertile. (Signed: 'To a
gracious companion and supreme artist . . .
Turin 1930), Sheridan's favourite tenor and
recording colleague.

Giacomo Lauri Volpi.

Ernesto Badini.

Mariano Stabile.

Otorino Respighi. (Signed: To the first Candida, Milan, La Scala Theatre 26.10.1923'. (Courtesy: *Capuchin Annual*).

Arturo Toscanini. (Signed: 'With cordial remembrance of good times in the past'.

Margaret (centre) on tour in Italy.

Galleria Vittorio Emanuele.

fascist anthem, the 'Giovinezza' at Scala performances. Despite threats from the fascist mobs, Toscanini stood firm. Margaret had, during her years at La Scala, earned her measure of Toscanini's vitriolic temper. But while others mutely accepted the Maestro's caustic remarks out of respect for him and in fear for their careers, Margaret's quick temper often flashed back at the dour dictator, to whom she referred as 'The Whip'. 'L'Imperatrice d'Irlanda' – 'The Empress of Ireland', was his sarcastic name for her. They had many clashes during their association at La Scala and the rest of the company knew that Margherita could be relied upon not to let Toscanini off without retort. On one occasion when Toscanini was rehearsing a soprano, who during a difficult passage sang an incorrect note, he stopped the rehearsal and had her repeat the offending note. Nervously, the singer tried again, but on three occasions simply repeated her mistake. 'Get out of this theatre', the angry Maestro shouted at her, 'and into the streets where you belong.' Sheridan, who was listening to the exchange from a seat in the theatre, in her bell-like voice, remarked loudly: 'In Ireland they'd shoot a man for saying that'.[25] As she later recalled, 'Tosti once said to me: "the colour of your voice is lovely Margherita", but then Toscanini spoiled it all by saying "it's only the colour of your voice Margherita that makes people think that you know what you're doing"'.[26]

At the time, rumours abounded that Toscanini had political ambitions to establish a republic, become its first president and rout his avowed enemy, Mussolini. Margaret, on the other hand, as other prime donne, had many fascist admirers. Many of her fellow artistes, like Tito Schipa and Rosina Storchio, had publicly declared their loyalty to the fascist regime in published pledges of solidarity. Gigli, on return visits to Italy from his triumphant success in America, was regularly received by Mussolini, and in his memoirs indifferently protested that to him 'Italy was Italy, no matter who ruled the country'.[27] By this time, foreign media reports accused Italy of being hostile to foreigners and accused the Italians of being chauvinistic and biased against non-Italian residents in every walk of life. Margaret sprang to the defence of her 'adopted' country and wrote a letter to the press. Unfortunately, she chose the fascist paper, founded by Mussolini, *Il Popolo d'Italia*, to illustrate her point. Her letter, published on 7th February 1926 read:

'At this moment when such an unjust anti-Italian campaign is operating abroad with regard to the hospitality of this country towards foreigners, I, as a foreigner feel it my duty to unite my words with those who are protesting against such dishonesty. When some years ago I came to Italy to study singing, I had the good fortune to be received in the school of a Maestro for whom, today, my gratitude to the artist is as great as my respect for the man. After a time I made my debut at the Teatro Costanzi and since then have continued an uninterrupted career, passing from the provincial theatres to the very biggest, like the San Carlo of Naples, the Comunale of Bologna and La Scala of Milan. Everywhere and especially at La Scala, although a beginner and a foreigner, I was conscious of an atmosphere of goodwill. I was helped and encouraged by everyone – by the conductors, by my fellow-artists, by the public and by the Press. I realise all this with gratitude and what's more I wish to declare publicly that I, because a foreigner, have been forgiven weaknesses for which an Italian artist would have been severely reprimanded. Everywhere I go I find nothing but kindness and hospitality from the public and from my fellow-artists. I should like you to publish these few lines which have been prompted by my sincere gratitude towards a country which has received me as it receives every foreigner and for which I have a deep affection and admiration. Grazie! Margherita Sheridan.'[28]

Toscanini was outraged. At a subsequent rehearsal at which Margaret was not in particularly good voice, Toscanini pounced on her. 'Signorina Sheridan,' he hissed across the footlights, 'if you spouted less in political papers you would be a better singer than you are'.[29] Margaret, impulsively strode to the footlights and, in a loud voice, before the assembled company replied, 'Maestro, may I also suggest that if you dabbled less in politics you would be an even greater conductor'.[30] There was an audible gasp from the astonished, but admiring, artists.

But whoever ruled outside La Scala, Toscanini ruled within. While Margaret continued her association with the opera house, she never again appeared on stage there. When Toscanini left La Scala for America in 1929, there were other developments taking place in Margaret's life which precluded her return. In later life, however, Margaret and Toscanini patched up the quarrel and in 1950, when Toscanini stopped over at Shannon Airport en route to the USA, his first question on arrival in Ireland was, 'Dové La Sheridan?'[31] and she was there to meet him. Again, at a subsequent meeting in London in 1952, he was sufficiently moved to present her with a photograph, autographed with the inscription, 'To Margaret Sheridan with cordial

Margaret with Eustace Blois and friends,
Bellagio, c. 1928.

Margaret and the soprano, Carmen Melis, on vacation at Grand Hotel Villa Serbelloni,
Bellagio, c. 1927.

Italo Balbo, on Mussolini's right (with beard), an admirer of Margaret.

Medals bearing the inscription 'A Margherita,
Superba Wally, Alla Scala' and 'A Margherita
Sheridan di Squista Interprete di Manon Lescaut'.

remembrance of good times in the past'.[32]

In May, as she ended her final public appearance at La Scala, Margaret could look back, not only on her successes there, but also at Rimini, Cento, Cremona and Monte Carlo. On 27th and 31st January 1924, under the baton of Victor de Sabata, she had sung *Butterfly* in the beautiful Opera de Monte Carlo in what was to be her only operatic performance outside Italy and England. In June, she returned for the summer to London. During a performance at Hammersmith by the Carl Rosa Operatic Company which she attended, she gave an interview about her career to-date in Italy, particularly at La Scala, where, the newspaper report stated, 'she is due to return for the re-opening of the season'.[33] This was not to be. La Scala – and Italy – still held her artistically but, London now had a more personal attraction.

A sculpture presented by the Directors of the
San Carlo in 1921 with the inscription,
'A Margherita Sheridan Butterfly Insuperabile'.

CHAPTER VII

PADDY DARLING
1927-1931

Although Toscanini seemed disinclined to include her in his plans at La Scala, Margaret had no shortage of offers elsewhere. On her return from London in Autumn 1924, she went straight into rehearsal at the famous Teatro Comunale Bologna, as Maddalena in *Andrea Chénier*. With a distinguished cast which included Giacomo Lauri Volpi as Chénier, Carlo Galeffi and Francesco Merli, and with Sergio Failoni conducting, the opera opened on 26th November for seven performances. 'Miss Sheridan was a real revelation for the freshness and fullness of her voice, for her most refined projection, for her perfect accent and for her dignified interpretation and style. She is a singer of great class and with a great future.'[1] The *L'Avvenire d'Italia* correspondent was even more enthusiastic:

> 'The newly arrived La Sheridan immediately conquered the Comunale audience. The young Irish singer has a voice of most beautiful timbre in every register, fluid, wide and flexible in every tone, capable of intense vibration when necessary. Like Maddalena, La Sheridan showed herself to be mistress of the part which she interpreted with intelligence and finesse.'[2]

Her success in Bologna was widely reported, both in the Italian and English press. In the December issue of the operatic advertising review, *Rassegna Melodrammatica*, the front page, under the heading, 'Fra Le Dive – Margherita Sheridan',[3] was devoted to her career in Italy and her success at Bologna.

Barely pausing to catch her breath, Margaret hurried on to her next engagement at the Carlo Felice Theatre at Genova. Genova, birthplace of Christopher Columbus, city of mariners and traders, of commerce and shipping, in both language and outlook, was different to the more leisurely-paced south. Even native Italians considered Genova a city

Recita Fuori Abbonamento   Recita 8°

TEATRO COMUNALE - BOLOGNA

STAGIONE AUTUNNO 1924

Per iniziativa e sotto il patronato del "RESTO DEL CARLINO„

DOMENICA 7 DICEMBRE ALLE ORE 15 PRECISE

UNICA MATTINATA

A PREZZI POPOLARI

ANDREA CHÉNIER

Dramma di ambiente storico in 4 atti di LUIGI ILLICA musicato da Umberto Giordano

PERSONAGGI

Andrea Chénier	Sig. Francesco Merli	Il Romanziere, pensionato del Re (Pietro Fiéville)	Sig. Luigi Bolpagni
Carlo Gérard	Carlo Galeffi	L'Abate, poeta	" Piero Girardi
La Contessa di Coigny	Sig.a Ida Mannarini	Schmidt carceriere a S. Lazzaro	" Mario Bassi
Maddalena di Coigny	Margherita Sheridan	Il maestro di casa	" Gino Cavina
La Mulatta Bersi	Irma Ronchi	Dumas, presidente del Tribunale di	
Roucher	Sig. Luigi Nocenti	Salute Pubblica	" Mario Zana
Il Sanculotto Mathieu detto "Populus„	Natale Villa	Fouquier Tinville accusatore pubblico	" Luigi Bolpagni
Madelon	Sig.a Franca Franchi		
Un "Incredibile„	Sig. Carlo Bonfanti		

Dame, Signori, Abati, Lacchè, Staffieri, Conduttori di slitte, Zagheri volanti, Musici, Servi, Paggi, Valletti, Pastorelle, Straccioni, Borghesi, Sanculotti, Carmagnole, Guardie nazionali, Soldati della Repubblica, Gendarmi, Mercatine, Pescivendole, Calzettaje, Venditrici ambulanti, Meravigliose, Incredibili, Rappresentanti della Nazione, Jiudici, Giurati, Prigionieri, Condannati, Ragazzi strilloni

Un maestro di musica, Alberto Roger, Fléandro Fiorinelli, Orazio Coclite, Un bambino, Un cancelliere, Il vecchio Gérard, Robespierre, Couthon, Barras, Un fratello servente (garzone di caffè), ecc.

Maestro Concertatore e Direttore:

SERGIO FAILONI

Maestri sostituti: A. SABINO - G. COLUCCI - O. GIORDANI   Maestro del Coro: F. MILANI   Maestro Suggeritore: E. DELEIDI

Direttore della messa in scena: EZIO CELLINI

Coreografa: Giacinta Gallini - Direttore del Macchinario: Francesco Sartorio - Capi Macchinisti: Fratelli Bassi

Costumi della Sartoria Teatrale CHIAPPA - Attrezzi della Ditta E. RANCATI di SORMANI e TRAGELLA di Milano - Scene di ROVESCALLI - Calzoleria: E. NICOLELLI di Bologna - Parrucchiere: ROCCO SARLO. Istrumenti Musicali delle Ditte BALBANI di Milano - BONGIOVANNI - BORSARI di Bologna.

PREZZI

Poltrone (oltre l'ingresso)	L.	30	Palchi di 3° ordine (centrali)	L.	60
Poltroncine (oltre l'ingresso)	"	20	Palchi di 3° ordine (di fianco)	"	50
Posti distinti (oltre l'ingresso)	"	10	Palchi di 4° ordine (centrali)	"	50
Palchi di 1° e 2° ordine (centrali)	"	80	Palchi di 4° ordine (di fianco)	"	40
Palchi di 1° e 2° ordine (di fianco)	"	60	Palchi di loggione (centrali)	"	30
			Palchi di loggione (di fianco)	"	20

Maddalena p *Andrea Chénier* – Bologna, 7 December, 1924.

apart. 'In Genova', Gigli recalled of his first performance there, 'I began to feel that I was out in the world.'[4] On 28th December 1924, under the baton once more of Sergio Failoni, she faced an audience described as 'the coldest audience that exists'.[5] Margaret scored another notable success in Catalani's *La Wally*. 'Her most beautiful voice gave power and feeling to the words', *Il Lavora* reported. 'She is an artist, not only by virtue of her natural calling but also by (her) intellect; conscious of her interpretation she preserved the character amidst the many psychological variations in the drama. Her singing was full of passion with vibrant phrasing and a thrilling timbre in her magnificent high notes.'[6] From Genova, Margaret moved on to Modena where, on 18th February, she performed *Madama Butterfly* in a production, commemorative of Puccini's death, at the Teatro Comunale. Accompanied by her fellow artistes Tumminello, Menikoff and Corti, Margaret also sang the quartet from Act III of *Bohème* directly after her performance of *Butterfly*. News of her continued success in Italy appeared regularly in the British press where plans to revive the International Season of Opera at Covent Garden were in process. But Margaret's reputation at Covent Garden did not depend solely on the critics' reports. Through her friendship with Eustace Blois, the managing director of the newly-formed syndicate, her successes in Italy had been well noted there.

After the 1919 Covent Garden International Season of Opera, the following season, given under the auspices of Sir Thomas Beecham, had proved a financial disaster. But the English operatic company which he had formed during the war and which was to eventually become the British National Opera Company continued to give seasons of opera at Covent Garden between 1922 and 1924. The theatre was also leased to the Carl Rosa Opera Company, to film distributors and, horror of horrors, for Jazz concerts! In 1925, the London Opera Syndicate was formed and financed by the wealthy industrialist, Samuel Courtauld and his wife. A love of opera induced them to once again present an international operatic season at the Royal Opera House. Colonel Eustace William Blois was appointed managing director of the newly-formed Courtauld syndicate.

Eustace Blois was described as 'a unique blend of soldier, business man and artist'.[7] Born in 1877, he seemed destined for a military career and joined the Rifle Brigade, serving with the regiment for six years in Dublin. His passion for music caused him to leave the army to study at Leipzig, Milan and Florence, where he settled for some time to study under the conductor and composer, Leopoldo Mugnone. He

composed an opera which he later conducted with the Moody Manners
Opera Company in England. On the outbreak of the war, he rejoined
his old regiment and served on the Salonica front until invalided home.
He had been associated in a minor capacity with the 1919 operatic
season at Covent Garden. In the intervening years, he worked for
Samuel Courtauld in his many business interests in London. 'Tall,
broad-shouldered, distinguished looking, his grey-blue eyes would
often twinkle with humour. A sense of humour was one of his most
valuable as well as lovable traits.'[8] A brilliant linguist, an acknowledged
diplomat, his background in business, his discipline, a legacy from his
army days, combined with an interest and knowledge of music,
especially opera, made him the ideal choice for the difficult task of
organising an international season at extremely short notice. His work
at Covent Garden necessitated much travel to the continental opera
houses to assess and sign suitable operatic artistes. Often pressurised
by 'the tantrums of tenors and prima donnas who could swear and did
in several different languages . . . (Blois) . . . developed the guile of a
tolerant master, handling a school of temperamental and intolerant
pupils'.[9] His relationship with one of those students, Margaret Sheridan, was to develop into something more.

They met during her first season at Covent Garden. His association
with Ireland was perhaps an initial attraction. As a young boy, long
before his army career in Dublin, he had spent numerous summer
vacations in Margaret's home county of Mayo with his grandmother
who was one of the Knox family. It was under the pseudonym, 'David
Knox', that he had later composed his opera. During her occasional
visits to London, Margaret may have renewed contact with Blois.
Towards the end of 1924, in search of suitable artistes for Covent
Garden, he telegrammed Margaret: 'I hope to come on the first of
December, love, Blois'.[10] It was the first in a long series of telegrams
and letters, developing into a friendship that was to be protracted and
tortuous. Blois was already married and, throughout the course of his
relationship with Margaret, seemed unable or unwilling to break free.
At first Margaret seemed able to cope with the strain the relationship
posed, interspersed as it was with lengthy periods of absence while she
continued with her career in Italy and he remained in London. When
his travels abroad coincided with her singing schedule he came to Milan
and at Bellagio they spent many happy interludes. Margaret's love
for Blois was real. Indeed, there was almost a sense of desperation
about it, as if she were making one final attempt to capture an elusive
dream. Her need for love and affection was great, as her mentor,

Margaret at the height of her London fame. (Courtesy: EMI Archives).

Margaret's long-time friend, Colonel Eustace Blois, Managing Director of the Royal Opera House, Covent Garden. (Courtesy: The Royal Opera House).

T. P. O'Connor realised. 'It is natural that you should think of love,' he wrote her, 'that is human nature. It is in accord with all life. But don't let it get an obsession with you as I think it is getting to be. Let it come in its own time.'[11] Her Irish, Catholic, convent upbringing initially restrained her: 'You who know me better than others understood how much I suffered and am suffering at the thought that I could become the lover of a married man . . . Peggy Sheridan from Ireland!'[12] But T.P. knew her still better: 'I pray that love may come and in the right way, the wrong way will never suit you and it would be a tragedy.'[13]

Now in her mid-thirties, an exceptionally desirable woman, idolised in the public eye, she had experienced her share of admirers and potential lovers who had often made intense demands on her emotionally. The calm, steady and supportive character of Blois appealed to her deeply. He advised and helped in her financial and business affairs in which, as the years progressed, she had become no more proficient. But he also begged her not to accept the American offers which she had received. Blois' affection, even love, for his Peggie or 'Darling Paddy' as he called her, is apparent from his letters. But there was a limit to his commitment. The furtiveness and secrecy with which they had to pursue their relationship and the basic impediment of Blois' married status was at variance with her personality and background. Initially, she coped outwardly with the emotional strain and the more practical advantages of their association benefited them both. As the hasty preparations for the 1925 International Season continued, as he would often do in the future, Blois sought her views on the choice of suitable singers. 'What sort of a singer is Toti Dal Monte?' he wrote from London in January 1925. 'What is thought of her in Italy and what is your private opinion?'[14] Her opinion of Toti was high and she was to become the star of the new season at Covent Garden. Through her friendship with Blois over the years, Margaret was instrumental in bringing many of her Italian colleagues to the attention of the British opera public, including her friend, the conductor, Vincenzo Bellezza, as he later testified in 1958: 'It was through her that I was invited for the first time to London by the Directors of Covent Garden in 1926 and thus she helped to create for me that current of reciprocal understanding and sympathy with the London public which still exists to this day.'[15]

As the first of the operatic stars to arrive at Victoria Station in early June 1925 for the opening of the International Season at Covent Garden, Margaret was besieged by reporters. She was booked to sing in two operas, she informed them, *Madama Butterfly* and *Andrea*

Chénier. The composer of *Chénier*, Umberto Giordano, when asked to nominate the most suitable artiste for the role of Maddalena, had replied without hesitation, 'You must take La Sheridan, she has the true style.'[16] Aware of the importance of this new season to Blois, she warmly praised his efforts to revitalise Covent Garden. 'A few years ago the name Covent Garden failed to excite anything but remote memories of the great days before the war,' she stated. 'People used to shake their heads at the sad thought that London's Opera House no longer housed opera. That is changed now. Covent Garden,' she assured her listeners, 'is being talked about in Paris, Milan and Rome. I think that the day is not far distant when it will once more assert its position as the leading Opera House in Europe. To all Britishers that in itself must be a cause of gratification.'[17] Given the short time they had to organise the season, the Courtaulds and Eustace Blois had done an impressive job. Toti Dal Monte, Maria Jeritza, Benvenuto Franci, Giacomo Lauri Volpi, Ernesto Badini were among those signed for the Italian season.

The operatic season was an important feature in the social calendar and was accompanied by the mandatory parties and receptions. Prior to her opening performance, she attended a supper party with Blois at the Courtauld mansion in Grosvenor Square, where she was to become a frequent visitor. Under the warm summer night sky, the guests were entertained in the gardens 'which had been transformed into an Italian courtyard surrounded by a white pillared colonnade. In the centre, a mosaic-lined pond, lit by subtly arranged electric lights in the greenish blue water, over which a silvery fountain splashed. Beneath it swam goldfish.'[18]

On 16th June, the Italian section of the season opened with Maria Jeritza in *Tosca*. Margaret followed with *Madama Butterfly*, the role intended for her debut in 1919. With her friend and colleague, Ernesto Badini as Sharples, the Greek tenor, Ulysses Lappas as Pinkerton and Sergio Failoni conducting, the Irish soprano was reintroduced to the London audience. Wearing magnificent costumes that had belonged to Rosina Storchio, Margaret won a rapturous reception. As usual, the English newspapers, as they tend to do on occasions of an Irish success, hurriedly adopted her as one of their own and gloried in the success of a 'native'. 'Once again last night a huge audience filled Covent Garden,' they reported, 'when Miss Margaret Sheridan duly made what amounted to her debut here. It is not in itself amazing that we now have one of our own, a native (sic) who has earned a rich fame in a foreign land . . . one such singer who has arrived at Covent Garden

. . . not only by virtue of the fact of birthright but because of her art; that she has raised herself to the right level is a matter of justifiable pride. And that the right to so lofty a position is hers, is absolutely and entirely unquestionable.'[19] *The Times* critic noted, 'how experience has ripened her style. She sang the music finely and her whole treatment of the part grew in dramatic interest as the opera progressed'.[20] *The Daily Telegraph* noted 'her voice of loveliest most velvety character, beautifully used and used with all the ease of one born for the art . . . In addition a subtlety of brain behind the rest . . . a deep psychological study is hers that stands considerably apart from the famous Butterflys of a good many years, her representation is not a mere empty shell.'[21] The only dissenting criticism came from Francis Toye, writing in *The Express*, who suggested that her voice had been occasionally inflicted with a tremelo.

Telegrams and flowers from friends and well-wishers poured into her dressing room. Among the tributes, a magnificent harp of flowers from the Irish community in London, bedecked in the green, white and gold of the newly-created Irish Free State, made her feel proud. Her second performance of *Butterfly* on 22nd June, with the young Italian tenor, Franco Lo Guidice, with whom she had performed in 1922 in Naples, was received and reviewed with equal enthusiasm. On 3rd July she reappeared in *Andrea Chénier* as Maddalena with a similar cast as in Bologna. With Giacomo Lauri Volpi making his Covent Garden debut, their performance, as it did in Bologna, captivated the audience, especially in the dramatic final scene before the lovers disappear in the tumbrils to their death. 'This sent a very real thrill through the crowded auditorium . . . and received a thunderous response from the audience'.[22]

During her stay in London, her career received full coverage in the British newspapers. The personal details of her life, her orphan status and her convent upbringing were widely reported. 'For years she hesitated between the life of the nun and the life of a singer', one report proclaimed. 'Her face is beautiful with the beauty of an Irishwoman. Her eyes are quite wonderful, very blue, very frank and sometimes almost childish; and yet within their depths you catch gleams of shrewd and characteristic vigilance.'[23] Her return to Covent Garden had been a success. The critics, the public and the recording companies were impressed. Robin H. Legge, the music critic of *The Daily Telegraph*, in his assessment of the season, singled out her performance, particularly in *Andrea Chénier*, as one of the highlights. It was fitting that she should bring the season to a close on 11th July with the

final performance of *Chénier* on a note of 'utmost brilliance'.[24]
Rumours and newspaper reports abounded that she had signed a
contract with the Chicago Opera but in September, Margaret returned
to Italy.

Based again in Milan at the Hotel Parco on the Piazza Fiume, her
impressario, Ferone, arranged her next performance at the Teatro
Politeama Rossetti in Trieste. Recently united with Italy after six
hundred years dominance by Austria, the busy Adriatic seaport city
retained much of its Hapsburg elegance and atmosphere. For ten years
from 1906, Trieste had been home to Margaret's most famous compatriot, James Joyce (with whom she had shared the same singing teacher
in Dublin). On 15th and 17th November, with Lauri Volpi again as
Chénier and conducted by Angelo Ferrari, she sang Maddalena. On
29th November, to commemorate the first anniversary of the death of
Puccini, with Franco Tumminello as Pinkerton, she gave one performance of *Butterfly*. The Trieste papers highly praised 'her poetic
impersonation of Butterfly'[25] and the audience showered her with
flowers.

Christmas found her at the Hotel San Marco in Piacenza in preparation for the opening of the Carnival Season at the Teatro Municipale on
27th December. Her performance in *Manon Lescaut* with Angelo
Minghetti as Des Grieux and Giacomo Armani as conductor was a
triumph. *L'Obbonato*, the journal of theatre criticism, devoted a
special supplement to her appearances in Piacenza:

> 'All Piacenza, and one can rightly say "all", considering the huge
> crowd which literally filled our greatest temple of art, entered into
> and understood every nuance of her lyricism and was happy to pay
> tribute with spontaneous applause to this beautiful and sensitive
> artist, possessed of natural delicacy and authority. She indeed well
> knows how to impart the proper fascination and the colour of true
> humanity to the strange figure of Manon. Flirtatious, impudent,
> sentimental, gay, each facet was rendered with just balance and
> animation.'[26]

Reports of her success at Piacenza were carried in the English papers
and telegrams arrived from friends and admirers in London, including
the ever-faithful T.P. and one from Eustace Blois which read,
'Delighted with success. Ti adoro.'[27]

From Piacenza, she moved on to the Teatro Grande at Brescia where
she repeated her success as Manon with the celebrated tenor, Nino

Piccaluga. The conductor, Vincenzo Bellezza, remembered that, despite feeling unwell, she 'gave performances which were perfect examples of bel canto and expressive interpretation'.[28]

At the beginning of 1926, Margaret had an exchange of correspondence with her brother, Paddy, who, for the previous two years, had made unsuccessful attempts to contact her in Italy and in 'the old country'.[29] After demobilisation from the army and recuperation in a military hospital in Glasgow, he had returned to Quebec and, with his war service gratuity, had purchased a small home for his wife and two sons, John and David. With the assistance of the Department of Soldiers' Civil Re-establishment, a series of jobs were secured for him, but owing to his 'extremely nervous disposition and his irritability',[30] he had difficulty retaining them. By 1926, he was engaged in a clerical capacity in the Department of Customs, but concern about the illness of his eldest son, who had contracted tuberculosis, and about his financial situation, necessitated a further period in a military hospital in Quebec. From there, he eventually contacted his famous sister and sought her assistance.

Throughout her career, Margaret's connections with her family had remained tenuous. The only link she had retained with Paddy was a photo of him in uniform, dated 1915. Her sister Hester made many attempts to contact her, particularly during her sojourns in London. Hester's daughter, Moira, had never failed to send a card to 'Auntie Peggy' prior to her performances at Covent Garden. Hester's husband, Alfred Gaillton, who, after the war, became a surgeon with the P & O Line, wrote to her occasionally during his travels in the Far East and assured her that 'Hester would be delighted to have you stay with her . . . if you are ill or want a holiday, our house is ever and always open to you.'[31] With her eldest brother, Jack, there had been no apparent contact whatsoever. But Margaret was not inclined to resume relations with a family she hardly knew. All her brothers and sister seemed equally disinterested in one another. 'Do you ever hear from Hester or Jack?', Paddy enquired in his letter to her. 'You are the only one who has written to me at all. We are a queer lot.'[32] Margaret wrote to Paddy to see what she could do financially for him and received a reply seeking assistance towards the education of his children and asking her to think of him particularly on St. Patrick's Day which he would spend in hospital. 'I have only one ambition and that is to hear you sing before I die,'[33] he assured her. Although that desire was not to be fulfilled, his prospects improved. He moved with his family to Ottowa and advanced his position with the Customs Department there. Later, in 1928, Margaret's friend and fellow artist, Walter McNally, who met with Paddy in Canada, informed her of his success.

In 1927, Paddy sought her assistance in establishing what he considered to be their mutual claim to the fabled and then much publicised 'Blake Millions'. This was a legacy, then valued at an incredible 16 million pounds, to which the English Court of Chancery was publicly seeking lawful heirs. Paddy based their claim on 'a lengthy and impressive document' which, his lawyers advised Margaret, 'appears to be a copy of the genealogical tree of your family'.[34] Given her distinct disinterest in her family and in fortunes per se, there is no evidence among her papers that she assisted her brother in his intriguing quest. Despite Paddy's at times erratic behaviour, a result of his war service, it is a fascinating prospect that, through genealogical and legal material then in his possession, some connection, however tenuous, may have existed between his forbears and the Blake estate. (The descendants of Patrick Burke Sheridan are probably in Canada to this day and may still retain the details of the claim and the genealogical evidence on which it was based.)

In early 1926, Colonel Blois and his Courtauld backers made plans for a further International Season at Covent Garden. Blois cast his net far afield, drawing in Melba, Chaliapine, Lehmann, Badini, Jeritza, Melchior, Stabile and bringing back Bruno Walter as conductor, with a new conductor, Vincenzo Bellezza and Margaret Sheridan. Margaret had the honour on 24th May of opening the Italian section of the season. In her familiar role of Mimi in *La Bohème*, surrounded by her Italian friends and colleagues, Minghetti, Badini and Bellezza, she was warmly applauded. The unexpected appearance of the King and Queen in the royal box added to the excitement of the opening night. *Bohème* was the King's favourite opera. The media, however, as they had done with Melba and former interpreters of the fragile, consumptive heroine, began to note that Margaret's figure could not sustain the illusion of the fragile consumptive for much longer. Since her last appearance at Covent Garden, she was putting on weight and for the remainder of her operatic career had to struggle to keep it under control. This was the first season in which live recordings were made at the Royal Opera House and on 4th June, a recording of her performance in her second appearance in *Bohème* was broadcast.

Her performance in *Bohème* was followed on 25th May by the debut of the great Russian bass, Fyodor Chaliapine in *Mefistofele*. Margaret later became friendly with the dramatic singer and conversed with him in French, the Russian having little English. To his amusement, she mimicked his attempted English pronunciation. On many occasions, they attended concerts and theatre together, including a performance by the popular film-turned-operatic star, Grace Moore, and were both impressed. (Margaret often maintained that the film *One Night of Love*, which starred Grace Moore, mirrored her own life-story.) Another highlight of the 1926 season was Dame Nellie Melba's farewell concert. It was a memorable and nostalgic occasion. The King and Queen attended as the great Diva took a final curtain after a thirty-nine year association with the Royal Opera House.

Margaret gave three performances as Mimi and on 28th June she appeared as Lauretta in *Gianni Schicci* with the by now familiar cast of Badini, Minghetti, Malatesta Sampieri, conducted by Bellezza. In this one-act comic opera, the London audience, as *The Times* critic observed, 'were allowed to see Miss Sheridan in a non-tubercular role . . . singing with freshness and girlishness as Lauretta.'[35] During the course of the season, she suffered from a nose and throat infection, but this did little to spoil her enjoyment of a succession of dinners, soirées and supper parties. In London, there was little opportunity for Margaret and Blois to pursue what they referred to as 'nostra cosa'.[36] Their liaison was suspected and accepted within their operatic and social circles. Apart from occasional social appearances connected with their operatic backgrounds, the relationship was decorus, particularly during the course of Margaret's sojourns in London. 'We are much better off abroad than in London,'[37] Eustace Blois assured her when, on one occasion, she suggested coming to London out of opera season. The loneliness, deception and isolation that the relationship imposed upon her would eventually, as T.P. had feared, take its toll on her physical and mental well-being.

During the course of the 1926 Covent Garden season, she embarked on the first in a series of contracts with the recording company, HMV. The contract was signed on her behalf by Eustace Blois who had advised her on the financial details. Her first recordings with HMV, issued in 1927, included a twelve-inch, double-sided 'red label' record of the 'Ave Maria' from Verdi's *Othello* and the aria most popularly associated with her, 'Un Bel Di Vedremo' from *Butterfly* conducted by Eustace Blois. Later the same year, the first in a series of nine Irish melodies appeared on ten-inch, double-sided disc, including, 'I Know Where I'm Going', and 'Danny Boy'. During 1927 also, she made her recordings with Pertile, with the Scala orchestra conducted by Carlo Sabajno, and included the love duet from *Butterfly*. 'It seems impossible to imagine anything more heavenly than your duet with him

(Pertile) not excepting even a Stradivari cello and violin in the hands of virtuosi,'[38] one recording enthusiast wrote to her. These recordings were followed by 'Ancora un Passo' and 'E Questo' from *Butterfly*, 'Si Mi Chiamano Mimi' from *Bohème* and 'Elsa's Dream' from Wagner's *Lohengrin*.

Back in Italy in the Autumn, Margaret made a return visit to the San Carlo in Naples for the 1926/27 Carnival season. On 4th January 1927, she gave the first of nine performances of *Butterfly*. Again the Neapolitan audiences gave her a tumultuous reception. The critics however, while acclaiming her vocal ability, now questioned her continued suitability for the role of the diminutive and fragile Japanese heroine. During her season in Naples, a recurring bout of the nose and throat difficulties she had experienced in London necessitated medical attention and a respite from singing for the greater part of the year. It was at this time that her agent, Emilio Ferone, who had taken over the Lusardi agency, negotiated a new contract for her with La Scala to perform Dolly in the world premier of Ermanno Wolf-Ferrari's *Sly*. The cast included Pertile, Badini and Rossi-Morelli with Ettore Panizza as conductor. Due to open on 27th December, the production was postponed when Margaret fell ill. The new work was finally presented on 29th December with Mercedes Llopart replacing Margaret in the role of Dolly, much to the disappointment of Margaret's friends and colleagues who had looked forward with anticipation to her return to the stage of the Scala. 'I hope you have fully recovered by this time' her friend and admirer A. Beaumont, the Italian correspondent of *The Daily Telegraph*, wrote to her. 'I do not know if you are still in Milan or if you have gone to the Riviera or to a religious retreat to expiate your sins for not singing at the Scala! (wicked, is it not!) The next time I hope you will not make me come all the way from Rome and miss your beautiful voice that I longed to hear.'[39]

In early summer, she returned to London for a holiday. She did not participate in the 1927 Season but regularly attended the Royal Opera House as a spectator. She was spotted in the society boxes at the Covent Garden debut of the Irish-born tenor, John O'Sullivan, in *Gli Ugonotti*. A noted performer, both in Italy and in France, he was considered by Margaret to be a fine operatic tenor, a view endorsed by James Joyce who championed his cause at Covent Garden through his friendship with Lady Emerald Cunard.

The remainder of 1927 and the early part of 1928 were lean periods in Margaret's working life. Based at the Hotel Parco in Milan, she spent much of the Autumn with friends at Bellagio. Eustace Blois paid

TEATRO ALLA SCALA

(ENTE AUTONOMO)

Recita **20ᵃ** d' Abbonamento
(Serie **B**)

STAGIONE 1927-1928

Rec. **31ᵃ**
(15ᵃ del SECONDO Turno)

LUNEDI 26 DICEMBRE 1927 - alle ore 21 precise

PRIMA RAPPRESENTAZIONE
di

S L Y

Dramma lirico in 3 atti e 4 quadri di GIOVACCHINO FORZANO
Musica di ERMANNO WOLF FERRARI
(Proprietà Casa Musicale SONZOGNO)

NUOVISSIMA
PERSONAGGI

ATTO PRIMO

Sly	Sig. AURELIANO PERTILE
Dolly	Sig.a MARGHERITA SHERIDAN
Il Conte di Westmoreland	Sig. LUIGI ROSSI MORELLI
Gli amici del Conte	
John Plake, attore del teatro Blakfriars	ERNESTO BADINI
Snare, agente dello sceriffo	LUIGI MARCHI
L'Ostessa	Sig.a IDA MANNARINI
Il Giudice Campestre	Sig. PALMIRO DOMENICHETTI
Rosalina	Sig.a CESIRA FERRARI
Un Soldato	Sig. GIUSEPPE MENNI
Un Vetturale	GIOVANNI AZZIMONTI
Il Cuoco	AMLETO GALLI
Il Garzone	LUIGI NARDI

Paggi - Beoni - Avventori della Taverna - Servi del Conte

ATTO SECONDO

Sly	Sig. AURELIANO PERTILE
Il Conte	LUIGI ROSSI MORELLI
I Nobili della Brigata travestiti da:	
Un Moro	EMILIO VENTURINI
Un Cinese	NELLO PALAI
Un Pellerossa	ARISTIDE BARACCHI
Un Musico	GIUSEPPE NESSI
Un Vecchio Servo	ANTONIO LAFFI
Un Dottore	GIACOMO CARBONI
Un Gran Cerimoniere	GIOVANNI AZZIMONTI
Dolly	Sig.a MARGHERITA SHERIDAN
La Prima Ancella	MARIA NEVESO
La Seconda Ancella	GINA PEDRONI
La Terza Ancella	OLGA DE FRANCO
Un Paggetto	IRIS ADAMI CORRADETTI

Amici e Amiche del Conte - Uomini d'Arme - Servi - Gentiluomini

ATTO TERZO

Sly	Sig. AURELIANO PERTILE
Dolly	Sig.a MARGHERITA SHERIDAN
Il Primo Servo	Sig. LUIGI MARCHI
Il Secondo Servo	GIUSEPPE MENNI
Il Terzo Servo	AMLETO GALLI

Maestro Concertatore e Direttore
ETTORE PANIZZA

Maestro del Coro: **VITTORE VENEZIANI**

Direttore della messa in scena: **GIOVACCHINO FORZANO** - Direttore dell'allestimento scenico: **CARAMBA**

Maestro della Banda: **MARSILIO CECCARELLI**
Scene dipinte da **G. B. SANTONI** e **ALBERTO SCAJOLI**
Direttore del Macchinario: **GIOVANNI ANSALDO**
Costumi della Società Anonima CARAMBA - Attrezzi della Ditta E. RANCATI e C. di SORMANI TRAGELLA e C.

PREZZI

Biglietto d'ingresso alla Platea ed ai Palchi	L. **25,—**	Biglietto d'ingresso alla prima Galleria	L. **10,—**
Poltrone (oltre l'ingresso)	„ **100,—**	Posti numerati Prima Galleria (oltre l'ingresso)	„ **30,—**
Poltroncine (oltre l'ingresso)	„ **70,—**	Biglietto d' ingresso alla Seconda Galleria	„ **6 —**
Posti numerati di Platea (oltre l'ingresso)	„ **40,—**	Posti Numerati Seconda Galleria (oltre l'ingresso)	„ **25.—**

PALCHI

Prima fila . L. **400,—**　Seconda fila . L. **500,—**　Terza fila . L. **400,—**　Quarta fila . L. **300,—**

A tutti i prezzi suesposti sarà applicato l'aumento governativo del 12 %, come da R. Decreto del 23 gennaio 1921.
Le frazioni di centesimi devono essere arrotondate sino a 10 centesimi (R. Decreto 4 maggio 1920 N. 567).

IN PLATEA NON VI SONO POSTI IN PIEDI
È PRESCRITTO L'ABITO NERO PER LA PLATEA E PER I PALCHI

Durante l'esecuzione dello spettacolo è vietato di accedere alla Platea e alle Gallerie. È pure vietato di muoversi dal proprio posto prima della fine di ogni atto.
Gli indumenti e gli altri oggetti depositati alle guardarobe non possono essere ritirati che negli intervalli tra gli atti o alla fine dello spettacolo.
Ragioni d'ordine e d'arte hanno indotto la Direzione a vietare le repliche dei pezzi durante la rappresentazione. Il Pubblico è pregato di uniformarsi a tale disposizione.
Le biglietterie del Teatro e l'Ufficio Palchi si aprono alle ore 10 di ciascun giorno di rappresentazione per la vendita e per la prenotazione dei posti, dei palchi e per la vendita dei biglietti d'ingresso alla Platea e Palchi.
Per disposizione del Prefetto è assolutamente vietato agli spettatori di accedere a qualsiasi posto della Sala (Platea e Gallerie) con cappelli, soprabiti, pellicce, bastoni, ombrelli e simili.
Per disposizione del Regolamento sulla vigilanza dei Teatri il pubblico può lasciare la sala, alla fine dello spettacolo, da tutte indistintamente le porte d'uscita.

Il Teatro si apre alle ore 20,15 — Le Gallerie alle ore 20

LA DIREZIONE

Dolly – *Sly* – Teatro alla Scala. Poster for her final scheduled performance at La Scala which, due to illness, she did not fulfil. (Courtesy: Anne Chambers)

occasional visits to her during his travels in preparation for the new season at Covent Garden which, at the end of the previous one, had seemed unlikely to be held. The Courtaulds had withdrawn their financial support, initially intended merely 'in a visionary spirit to revive interest in opera'.[40] That, they had achieved. Amid rumours that the Opera House was to be demolished, Blois approached a wealthy City associate, the naturalized Hungarian banker, F. A. Szarvasy, who agreed to provide the financial backing necessary, with Blois to remain as managing director. As Blois became absorbed in preparation for the season, Margaret once more toyed with the idea of going to America or to the Colon Theatre in Buenos Aires. Work was scarce in Italy and the bills were mounting. 'If you love me don't go,' Blois telegraphed her. 'New situation here, also for you.'[41]

The 1928 Covent Garden prospectus announced by Blois in February, the production of some twenty operas, was ambitious. Margaret was scheduled to appear in three, *La Bohème*, *Othello* and in Puccini's last and unfinished work, *Turandot*. (Due to illness, she was subsequently replaced as Desdemona in *Othello* by the English soprano, Miriam Licette.) By now, with her solo and duet recordings with Pertile being promoted by HMV, there was much interest and anticipation surrounding her scheduled reappearance. 'Her voice, her appearance, her stage action, her command of the Italian language and her phrasing have been everywhere acclaimed',[42] *The Times* announced. And her performances still held social appeal. 'Lady Coventry is going up for *La Bohème* to hear Margherita Sheridan as Mimi,'[43] the social columnist of *The Field* revealed.

On 7th June, she opened once again in the first of five performances under the baton of Vincenzo Bellezza. Her favourite singing partner, Aureliano Pertile, played Rodolfo and the young Italian soprano, Margherita Carosio, whom she had heard singing at Brescia and had recommended to Covent Garden was Musetta. Inghillieri Baccaloni, the Italian bass, was making his début at the Royal Opera House. The King and Queen paid their first visit of the season to the opera house, accompanied by Princess Mary and the Duchess of York. Margaret's society friends thronged the boxes and John McCormack attended to hear for himself the Irish woman whose success in Italy had so outshone his own there. At the second interval, Margaret, Pertile, Bellezza and the other principals of the otherwise all-Italian cast, were summoned to the Royal Box to receive the personal congratulations of the King and the Royal party. King George V talked with the artistes who because of the language difficulty struggled to reply. Turning to Margaret, the King asked how she had obtained such fluency in Italian and such success at La Scala, being an English girl. 'And I told him,' Margaret recalled, 'it was probably because I was Irish.'[44] The following year, when she performed again at the Royal Opera House, the King remembered her and asked that she be presented to him. He greeted her with the words, 'Now I too have Irish blood in me,'[45] and explained to her that he had recently received a blood transfusion, the donor being a soldier in one of the Irish regiments of the British army.

Critical assessment of the performance was mixed. Bellezza was faulted for too spirited a tempo, while Pertile was accused of 'letting rip' too forcefully and of having a persistent vibrato. Most of the praise was reserved for Margaret's performance as Mimi. 'She is everything that is charming in singing, acting and looks,' *The Star* enthused, 'a rare combination and especially in the lovely aria in the third act was she inexpressively telling.'[46] The revered critic, Ernest Newman, more restrainedly commented that apart from 'the cool, clear singing of Miss Sheridan – as healthy-looking a Mimi as ever died of consumption,' there was little else to praise in the production.[47] The following performance on 7th June and again one on 29th June were broadcast live from the Opera House by the BBC.

Esconced at the Savoy, Margaret celebrated her first-night success. 'After theatre time, the Savoy grill room was like a theatre grill room, so many well known players were gathered there,' the press reported. 'Miss Margaret Sheridan had the place of honour at a large circular table . . . where she held a sort of a court.'[48] Surrounded by her fellow artists and adoring London friends, Margaret sparkled in the lime-light she adored. To the Press, she waxed lyrically but impracticably about her priorities and ambitions. 'I have no ambition to make money,' she declared, 'all I want is a cottage in the country. I have refused a number of offers to go to America because I like a quiet life.'[49] Even in retirement, it would have been improbable to see her exchanging the excitement of city life for the 'quiet life' of the country. But her real need for brief respites in the courtry, surrounded by nature, to which she had a deep and almost spiritual attachment, manifested itself in her many interludes at Bellagio and later on her return to Ireland, to the beauty of sea and mountain in Connemara. But the thought that, even in her retirement years, she could be at peace without the trappings of her profession and more importantly still, the company and admiration of people who understood her and her artistic achievements, was no more than a pipe-dream.

Selection of Posters and Programmes of her performances from the Sheridan Archives; and by permission from The Royal Opera House, Covent Garden, from Teatro Alla Scala; from Monte Carlo – Societe des Bains de Mer.

Mimi – *La Bohème* – Covent Garden, 27 May 1919. Her Covent Garden début.

SAVOY RESTAURANT FOR DINNER

Royal Opera Covent Garden
Proprietors . The Grand Opera Syndicate, Ltd.

[1919]

THIS EVENING'S PERFORMANCE

Tuesday, July 8th, at 7.45

FIRST PRODUCTION IN ENGLAND

MASCAGNI'S OPERA

IRIS
(In Italian)

Iris	MARGARET SHERIDAN
Il Cieco	GUSTAVE HUBERDEAU
Kyoto	ROBERT COUZINOU
Osaka	AGOSTINO CAPUZZO
Una Guecha	KATHLEEN DESTOURNEL
Un Merciaiuolo	ANGELO ALGOS
Un Cenciaiuolo	ANDRÉ GILLY
Conductor	LEOPOLDO MUGNONE

For future Announcements see inside

IMPERIAL RESTAURANT FOR LUNCHEON

Iris – *Iris* – Covent Garden, 8 July 1919.

TEATRO ALLA SCALA
(ENTE AUTONOMO)

Recita 57.ª d'abbonamento
STAGIONE 1922-1923
GIOVEDÌ 26 APRILE 1923 - alle ore 21 precise

PRIMA RAPPRESENTAZIONE

di

BELFAGOR

Commedia lirica in un prologo, due atti, un epilogo di CLAUDIO GUASTALLA
(dalla commedia di ERCOLE LUIGI MORSELLI)

Musica di OTTORINO RESPIGHI

NUOVISSIMA

(Proprietà G. RICORDI & C.)

PERSONAGGI

L'arcidiavolo BELFAGOR (al secolo: Signor Ipsilonne) ... Sig. MARIANO STABILE
Maestro MIROCLETO, organista emerito e speziale ... GAETANO AZZOLINI
La sua consorte ... Sig.ª ANNA GRAMEGNA
OLIMPIA ... MARGHERITA SHERIDAN
Le loro figliuole CANDIDA ... TEA VITULLI
FIDELIA ... CESIRA FERRARI
MADDALENA
Il marinaio BALDO ... Sig. FRANCESCO MERLI
L'arciprete DON BIAGIO ... GIOVANNI AZZIMONTI
La sua serva MICCA ... Sig.ª IDA MANNARINI
Un vecchio ... Sig. AMLETO GALLI
Due ragazzi { Un ragazzo ... GIUSEPPE NESSI
GIOVANNI AZZIMONTI

Gli invitati - I paesani - Il maggiordomo del Signor Ipsilonne - Servi - Contadini
In un piccolo paese del litorale toscano. Quando non tutti i diavoli portano corna.

Maestro Concertatore e Direttore:

ANTONIO GUARNIERI

Maestro del Coro: VITTORE VENEZIANI
Direttore Generale della messa in scena: GIOVACCHINO FORZANO
Direttore della messa in scena: CARAMBA
Scene da VITTORIO ROTA su bozzetti di CESARE FRATINO

PREZZI

Biglietto d'ingresso alla Prima Galleria (oltre l'ingresso)	L. 10.—
Posti Numerati Prima Galleria (oltre l'ingresso)	30.—
Biglietto d'ingresso alla Seconda Galleria	6.—
Posti Numerati Seconda Galleria (oltre l'ingresso)	18.—
Platea	L. 400.—
Palchi	L. 300.—

LA DIREZIONE

Candida – Belfagor – Teatro alla Scala, 26 April 1923.

TEATRO ALLA SCALA
(ENTE AUTONOMO)

Recita 41.ª d'abbonamento
STAGIONE DI CARNEVALE-QUARESIMA 1921-22
GIOVEDÌ 6 APRILE 1922 - alle ore 20.45 precise

PRIMA RAPPRESENTAZIONE

di

LA WALLY

di W. DE HILLERN - Riduzione Drammatica in 4 atti di LUIGI ILLICA

Musica di ALFREDO CATALANI

(Proprietà G. RICORDI & C.)

PERSONAGGI

Wally ... Sig.ª MARGHERITA SHERIDAN
Stromminger, suo Padre ... Sig. UMBERTO DE LELIO
Afra ... Sig.ª LUISA BERTANA
Walter, suonatore di città ... Sig.ª MAFALDA DE VOLTRI
Giuseppe Hagenbach di Sölden ... Sig. LUIGI MARINI
Vincenzo Gelner dell'Hochstoff ... GIUSEPPE NOTO
Il Pedone di Schnals ... ARISTIDE BARACCHI

Cori:
Alpigiani — Paesani — Borghesi — Vecchie — Contadini — Cacciatori — Giovinetti e fanciulle di Sölden e dell'Hochstoff

Danze di fanciulle e Cacciatori.

Maestro Concertatore e Direttore:

ETTORE PANIZZA

Maestro del Coro: VITTORE VENEZIANI
Direttore di Scena: EDOARDO MARCHIORO

PREZZI PER QUESTA SERA

Biglietto d'ingresso alla Platea e Palchi	L. 20.—
Poltrone (oltre l'ingresso)	L. 100.—
Poltroncine (oltre l'ingresso)	80.—
Posti Distinti e Numerati di Platea (oltre l'ingresso)	50.—
Poltroncine Centrali I.ª fila (oltre l'ingresso)	90.—
Palcoscenico Centrale III.ª fila (oltre l'ingresso)	L. 80.—
Biglietto d'ingresso alla Prima Galleria	10.—
Posti Numerati Prima Galleria (oltre l'ingresso)	45.—
Biglietto d'ingresso alla Seconda Galleria	6.—
Posti Numerati Seconda Galleria (oltre l'ingresso)	18.—

LA DIREZIONE

Wally – La Wally, Teatro alla Scala, 6 April 1922.

TEATRO ALLA SCALA
(ENTE AUTONOMO)

Recita 1ª

STAGIONE 1923-1924

GIOVEDI 15 NOVEMBRE 1923, alle ore 20.45 precise
PRIMA RAPPRESENTAZIONE

SALOME

Dramma musicale in un atto dal poema di OSCAR WILDE
Musica di RICCARDO STRAUSS
(Propr. A. FÜRSTNER)

PERSONAGGI

Erode, tetrarca di Galilea	Sig. ALFREDO TEDESCHI
Erodiade, di lui sposa	GIUSEPPE NESSI
Salome, di lei figlia	FRANCESCO DOMINICI
Jokanaan, profeta	GIOVANNI GENZARDI
Narraboth, giovane centurione	Sig. AMLETO GALLI
Il Paggio d'Erodiade	GIUSEPPE MENNI
Der Nazarener	Sig.a GINA PEDRONI

Cinque Giudei
Due Soldati
Popolano di Cappadocia
Uno schiavo

Ornate Terrazzi nel Palazzo di Erode

Direttore della messa in scena ERNESTO LERT
Scenario di GIOVANNI GRANDI

I COMPAGNACCI

Libretto in un atto di GIOVACCHINO FORZANO
Musica di PRIMO RICCITELLI
(Propr. Soc. An. del Teatro Lirico Italiano)

NUOVA PER MILANO

PERSONAGGI

Bernardo del Nero, reggitore dei maestri	Sig. FILIPPO ROMITO
Anna Maria, sua nipote	Sig.a MARGHERITA SHERIDAN
Neri Di Cecone delle Corniole	Sig. AMLETO GALLI
Baldo	CARMELO ALABISO
Olindella	Sig. IDA MANNARINI
Noro del Grazzo, scolaro	NICOLA BAVARO
Vincenzio, venditore di cera	GIUSEPPE QUINZI TAPPEROLI

Compagnacci - Bandilori - Fanciulli del frate - Popolo

Direttore della messa in scena GIOVACCHINO FORZANO
Scenario di ANTONIO ROVESCALLI

Maestro Concertatore e Direttore d'Orchestra
VITTORIO GUI
Maestro del Coro VITTORE VENEZIANI
Direttore dell'allestimento scenico CARAMBA

PREZZI

Biglietto d'ingresso alla Prima Galleria	L. 20.	Biglietto d'ingresso alla Prima Galleria	L. 10.
Poltrona (oltre l'ingresso)	100.	Posti Numerati Prima Galleria (oltre l'ingresso)	30.
Poltroncina (oltre l'ingresso)	80.	Biglietto d'ingresso alla Seconda Galleria	8.
Posti Numerati di Platea (oltre l'ingresso)	40.	Posti Numerati di Seconda Galleria (oltre l'ingresso)	18.

PALCHI

Prima fila L. 500. — Seconda fila L. 400. — Terza fila L. 400. — Quarta fila L. 300.

IN PLATEA NON VI SONO POSTI IN PIEDI

La Lotteria "Pro Scala" sarà irrevocabilmente estratta il 31 Dicembre 1923
LA DIREZIONE

Anna Maria – *I Compagnacci* – Teatro alla Scala – 15 November 1923.

TEATRO ALLA SCALA
(ENTE AUTONOMO)

Recita 135ª

STAGIONE 1923-1924

Serie F(a) d'abbonamento
(Serie 19)

MERCOLEDI 14 MAGGIO 1924 - alle ore 21 precise
PRIMA RAPPRESENTAZIONE

ANDREA CHÉNIER

di

Dramma di Ambiente Storico in 4 quadri di LUIGI ILLICA
Musica di UMBERTO GIORDANO
(Proprietà Casa Musicale SONZOGNO)

PERSONAGGI

Andrea Chénier	Sig. LUIGI MARINI
Carlo Gérard	BENVENUTO FRANCI
Maddalena di Coigny	Sig.a MARGHERITA SHERIDAN
La mulâtre Bersi	GINA PEDRONI
La contessa di Coigny	IDA MANNARINI
Madelon	FRANCA FRANCHI
Roucher	Sig. FERNANDO FERRARI
Il romanziero pensionato del Re (Pietro Fléville)	AMLETO GALLI
Fouquier Tinville, accusatore pubblico	GIUSEPPE MENNI
Il Sanculotto Mathieu detto . Populus	ARISTIDE BARACCHI
Un . Incredibile	ALFREDO TEDESCHI
L'Abate, poeta	GIUSEPPE NESSI
Schmidt, carceriere a S. Lazzaro	FABIO RONCHI
Il Maestro di casa	FILIPPO ROMITO
Dumas, presidente del tribunale di Salute Pubblica	Serv. - Paggi, Valletti, Pastorelle, Straccioni

Borghesi, Sanculotti, Carmagnole, Guardie Nazionali, Soldati della Nazione, Giudici, Gendarmi, Mercatine, Rescendole, Calzettaie, Venditrici ambulanti, Meravigliose
Incredibili, Rappresentanti della Nazione, Giudici, Gendarmi.
Un Maestro di Musica, Alberto Roger, Filandro Farinelli, Orazio Coclès, un bambino, un Cancelliere, il vecchio Gérard, Robespierre, Couthon, Barras

Un fanello servente, garzone di caffè, ecc.

Maestro Concertatore e Direttore
VITTORIO GUI

Maestro del Coro VITTORE VENEZIANI
Direttore della messa in scena GIOVACCHINO FORZANO - Direttore del machinario scenico CARAMBA
Scene dipinte di ANTONIO ROVESCALLI - G. B. SANTONI - Direttore del machinario GIOVANNI ANSALDI.
Attrezzi della Ditta RANCATI & C. di SORBARI TRAGELLA & C.

PREZZI

Biglietto d'ingresso alla Prima Galleria	L. 20.	Biglietto d'ingresso alla Prima Galleria	L. 10.
Poltrona (oltre l'ingresso)	100.	Posti Numerati Prima Galleria (oltre l'ingresso)	30.
Poltroncina (oltre l'ingresso)	80.	Biglietto d'ingresso alla Seconda Galleria	8.
Posti Numerati di Platea (oltre l'ingresso)	30.	Posti Numerati di Seconda Galleria (oltre l'ingresso)	18.

PALCHI

Prima fila L. 500. — Seconda fila L. 400. — Terza fila L. 400. — Quarta fila L. 300.

IN PLATEA NON VI SONO POSTI IN PIEDI

LA DIREZIONE

Maddalena – *Andrea Chénier* – Teatro alla Scala, 14 May 1924.

Cho Cho San – *Madama Butterfly* – Modena, 18 February 1925.

Cho Cho San – *Madama Butterfly* – Monte Carlo.
Programmes from 27th and 31st January 1924.

Lauretta – *Gianni Schicchi* – Covent Garden, 28 June 1926.

Liù – *Turandot* – Covent Garden, 5 July 1928.

Maddalena – *Andrea Chénier* – Covent Garden, 27 May 1930.

Desdemona – *Otello* – Covent Garden, 16 June 1930.

On 27th June, for the first time in her career, she played a secondary role as the tragic slave girl, Liù, in Puccini's *Turandot*. The great dramatic soprano, Eva Turner, was Turandot. It was not in Margaret's nature to play second fiddle to anyone. Ernest Newman, on being asked by his wife, Vera, if Turner and Sheridan were indeed to appear together in *Turandot*, succinctly summed up the situation. 'You can set your mind at rest about Turandot,' he advised her. 'It is Turner and the Liù is Sheridan, but I doubt whether Sheridan will be Liù.'[50] But she played Liù, the timid, child-like figure who represents the forces of good in the strange Chinese fable, in contrast to the icy cruelty of Princess Turandot. Margaret often remarked that Puccini had told her that he had her in mind when he created the music for the character of Liù. In 1928, the choice of voices to represent the two extremes was superb. The cold, crystal, dramatic voice of Eva Turner contrasted so effectively with Margaret's rich, warm timbre. The performance was warmly applauded. It was Turner who, as an English soprano, had also won acclaim in Italy and who, not unnaturally, was the toast of the season in her Covent Garden debut as *Turandot*, a part for which she was to attain international fame. During the course of her 1928 appearances at Covent Garden, Margaret was made a fellow of the Royal Academy of Music from which she had graduated in 1911. Throughout the season in London, however, she was afflicted yet again with throat infections which necessitated many visits by physicians to her rooms at the Savoy and at least one visit to a Harley Street specialist.

In September, she went to Paris to visit the De Sousas at the Ambassador Hotel. Prompted by T.P., De Sousa once more discussed the possibility of extending her career to America. The impresario, Morris Gest, had contacted her in London with an offer of a concert tour there. This time, with De Sousa's assistance, she went so far as to draft a letter outlining the conditions under which she was prepared to sing in the States. 'I am not sure,' she wrote, 'what fee to ask but basing myself on the fact that I receive one hundred guineas a performance at Covent Garden, I suggest that you guarantee me a fee of five hundred dollars per concert.'[51] This time the arrangements almost reached fruition and letters of introduction were procured to influential people in America, including one from the Roman Catholic Bishop of Killala in County Mayo to the Archbishop of New York, Cardinal Hayes; but once again, she backed away from the challenge and change, preferring to let the matter rest until the next time.

CLOSE UPS *by Fernando Autori.*

CHALIAPINE   SHERIDAN   PERTILE
INGHILLERI   PONSELLE   STABILE
BARBIROLLI   AUTORI   GOOSSENS

Margaret and company in caricature by her colleague and friend, Fernando Autori.
From *The Gramophone*, October 1929.

CHAPTER VIII
ADDIO FIORITO ASIL
The Final Curtain 1928-1934

On returning from Paris to Milan, Margaret moved into the Hotel Touring on the Piazza La Republica. Her agent secured her contracts for return Autumn engagements at the Comunale in Bologna and the Carlo Felice in Genova. She also received an invitation from the Irish baritone, Walter McNally, to perform with him again in Dublin in two concerts he was planning for the following August during the Dublin premier social event – Horse Show Week. 'Just the two of us,' he wrote her, 'and a good instrumentalist. As you know you would always get top billing and preference in every way.'[1] But like so many of her planned recitals in Ireland, it did not materialise.

In early November, she returned to Bologna, the scene of her triumph in 1924, in *Andrea Chénier*. Illness once more forced her to cancel the important engagement. On 30th December, however, she opened in *Manon Lescaut* at Genova with Nino Piccaluga once more as her tenor and under the musical direction of Giacomo Armani. She gave five performances at the Carlo Felice and again received favourable reviews from the critics and warm applause from the Genoese public. On 22nd January, she gave a special performance with Pertile as Des Grieux. Together with the conductor, Armani, they received several encores before they were allowed by a delighted audience to leave the stage.

In March, she renewed her contract with HMV and prepared to make additional recordings at La Scala. With Pertile and the Scala orchestra, conducted by Carlo Sabajno, she recorded duets from *Manon Lescaut* and *Andrea Chénier*. The recording sessions were temperamental affairs, since Margaret was restless and impatient with the technical dictates and requirements. Further solo recording sessions, scheduled for London during the Summer months, were postponed and temporarily abandoned as she became embroiled in disagreements with the proposed arrangements by Hubert Hughes of the Irish melodies she was contracted to sing. At one stage, in exasperation, Hughes wrote her, 'As this is the second thing you have turned down in a few weeks . . . I do not propose that there shall be a third.'[2] But, of course, there was. Margaret was usually forgiven for her at times vexing nature. But it was more than just temperamental quirks that caused her to object to various arrangements and scores, particularly of the Irish songs and melodies she loved and knew so well. Throughout her career, she had set herself high standards of interpretative as well as vocal perfection. Friends remember her almost obsessive determination as she repeated individual words and phrases, to achieve the correct inflection, the appropriate emphasis. And when she fell short of the high standards she set herself, she faced the inevitable with honesty and courage.

For the 1929 Covent Garden season, she was contracted to sing in *Turandot*, *Manon Lescaut* and *Bohème*. Blois had managed to present a mix of old and new faces to the London public. The main attraction of the season was the debut of the American soprano, Rosa Ponsella, 'acclaimed as being in the true line of great bel canto singers'.[3] Among the more familiar faces were Margaret's colleagues from La Scala – Pertile, Stabile, Inghilleri, Merli, Autori and her friend, the soprano, Carmen Melis. The return of Chaliapine and Eva Turner was also announced. The season opened on 27th May with *Don Giovanni*, with Stabile in the title role, Schumann as Zerlina and the debut of the English tenor, Heddle Nash, as Ottavio. Scheduled to appear as Liù in *Turandot* on 29th May, Margaret's performance was cancelled at the last minute and her place was taken by the American soprano, Ina Souez. The cancellation was said to have been caused by health problems but the gossips whispered that late-night partying was more likely the reason for Margaret's sudden indisposition. By 31st May, she was ready to go on with Eva Turner as Turandot, accompanied by Pertile, Autori, Merli, Cilla, Baracchi, Dua and Sampieri and with Bellezza conducting. The second act of the opera was relayed live on radio by the BBC.

On 18th June, she gave her first Covent Garden performance of *Manon*, with Pertile, Badini, Baccaloni and Bellezza. The performance was enthusiastically received by the audience and by the critics. '*Manon Lescaut* Revived. Margherita Sheridan in Title Role – A Notable Triumph',[4] proclaimed *The Daily Telegraph*. 'Most of the lyrical moments depend on the two lovers', *The Times* noted, 'and with Signor Pertile's powerful voice to impress all the climaxes from his first approach to Manon to his sobbing appeal to the ship's captain and with Margherita Sheridan bringing more subtle qualities to the several phases of Manon's character (a warmth and richness of tone used without effort) all the charm and pathos of the sentimental tragedy was secured.'[5] 'Such richly lyrical music calls for fine singing', *The Daily Chronicle* reported, 'and last night Margaret Sheridan as Manon and Signor Pertile as Des Grieux gave their duets in superb style, each artist in splendid voice and blending their singing most effectively.'[6] Margaret and Pertile received an ovation from the audience at the end of the third act and there was general agreement that one had seen a superb *Manon*.

A performance of *Bohème* on 24th June was to be her final appearance in the role most associated with her Covent Garden successes. Carmen Melis sang Musetta and Autori, Nash and Inghilleri complemented the cast who once more were conducted by Vincenzo Bellezza. The Irish opera buff, journalist and radio presenter, the late Tommy O'Brien, met his famous compatriot during the course of the 1929 season. He sought an interview with her and, after the obligatory bribe at the stage door, was admitted to the presence of La Sheridan after her performance in *La Bohème*. To impress her he had implied in his note of introduction that he was from *The Irish Times*. Seated at her dressing table, she was removing her make-up. 'I see you're from *The Irish Times*.' Her voice, he later said, was the most beautiful he had ever heard. Tommy admitted the truth. 'I thought not,' the diva replied, 'you're a bit young looking for *The Times*'. She chatted to him about her life in opera and Tommy recorded her words in his Pitman shorthand. As he was about to leave, she suddenly asked him, 'what did you think of tonight's performance'. 'Miss Sheridan,' Tommy replied, 'to tell you the truth, I often heard you sing better.' Then she told him she had been ill prior to the performance which could not be cancelled at such short notice. 'Well,' replied Tommy, 'I should tell you, Miss Sheridan, that I saw you and Pertile in *Manon Lescaut* last week and you were both marvellous. I saw the opera again a few nights ago with Merli and Pampanini and they were like puppets after you and Pertile.' As he left her dressing room, he heard her remark in a voice tinged with a west of Ireland brogue, 'There you are now . . . and all the talk about that Pampanini one!'[7] He waited to escort her down the stairs at Covent Garden and into the street, where a Rolls Royce waited to take her to Lady Courtaulds.

In July, she returned again to the HMV studios to record additional melodies, including 'Killarney', 'I Dreamt I Dwelt in Marble Halls' and 'Must I Go Bound'. On her return to Milan in October, arrangements for the first electrical recording of *Butterfly* were put in train by HMV. Margaret suggested numerous tenors to sing Pinkerton, including the young Alessandro Ziliani, whom she had heard in his debut at the Dal Verme. HMV decided however, on the Australian tenor, Lionelo Cecil, the Italian pseudonym of one Cecil Sherwood. Margaret, furious and disappointed with the company's choice, prior to the recording locked herself in her room for two days. Eventually, she relented and confided later to friends her dislike of the quality of the duets with Cecil. A comparison of her duets with Cecil and those she had made with Aureliano Pertile forces one to agree that the difference was palpable and to sympathise with her dilemma. The recording of *Butterfly* (thirty-two sides) continued until January. Among the artistes who performed this historical recording were Ida Mannarini (mezzo-soprano), Nello Palai (tenor), Antonio Gelli (bass) and Guglielmo Masini (bass). Members of the chorus and orchestra of La Scala were conducted by Carlo Sabajno.

On top of her artistic problems, her relationship with Blois was becoming strained. Her need for love, attention and companionship was not being realised by their infrequent and fleeting meetings. He was committed to a hectic work schedule. The fond farewells at Como station, which she had come to dread, were inevitably followed by periods of loneliness and sadness which, in turn, led to embittered reproaches and accusations. The practical and expedient manner in which he approached his business commitments and which he sought to apply to his relationship with Margaret, could find little reciprocation in her emotional, sensitive and honest nature. Regardless of his affection for her, Blois was intent on maintaining appearances. 'I hoped so much that we had opened a new book of our lives and I still hope and think so', he wrote her after a holiday at Bellagio. 'But I think, if this is the case, that the past must not be brought up and referred to in the way you have done in your last two letters. If our future is to be what we have planned it to be at Bellagio, it must not, Paddy darling, be subjected to the risk of embitterment . . . I denoted to you', he continued, 'that I could see things from your point of view but this did not mean that I agreed with your view in everything.'[8] At Bellagio, they agreed to arrange their business affairs so that they might be together more often and endeavour to help each others' careers. 'I told you that I loved you,' he assured her, 'as I always have and that there had never been anyone else for me and that there never would be and that therefore in spite of all our obstacles, I wanted as much of you and your life as was possible.'[9] Seemingly oblivious to the sensitive, emotional nature of the woman he professed to know and to love, he advocated the impossible. 'When we meet after being apart it should be as if the clock had stopped during the interval, not gone back.'[10] This self-centred approach to the relationship is evident in the many letters Blois wrote to her over the years of their friendship. They invariably commence with advice and instructions on her business and financial affairs while discussion of 'nostra cosa' is left to the end. His advice was practical, particularly on her dealings with HMV with whom she was in almost constant disagreement over payment of royalties and selection of recording material. In her dispute over the choice of tenor for the *Butterfly* recording, her instant reaction, much to Blois' horror, was to withdraw from the prestigious and profitable contract altogether. 'Of course you must do *Butterfly*,' he scolded her. 'It would be absurd for you to lose that fee because you are annoyed with the company.'[11] But since Margaret valued artistic excellence over financial gain, she considered her threatened action to be the honourable course.

Towards the end of September 1929, declining Blois' request to join her, Margaret departed with her friend, Carmen Melis, for a short stay at Bellagio. In November, her faithful friend and mentor, T. P. O'Connor, died in London. The old radical Parnellite had lived to see some semblance of independence and stabilization at last in Ireland, whose cause he had championed both in England and in America. Margaret had lost her most loyal and caring father-figure. While at times she had failed to act on his advice, she appreciated and cherished his concern for her wellbeing and benefited from their long, affectionate relationship. She spent Christmas 1929 in a manner to which she had by then become well accustomed, alone in her hotel in Milan. Work had become scarce and Blois advised a move to Germany where he had organised contracts and appointments for her. But once more, she refused to leave Italy. In the New Year however, her prospects improved and she was contracted to sing in the Teatro Regio, Turin. In *Andrea Chénier*, with Aureliano Pertile in the title role, they gave a spirited and dramatic rendition of the familiar work. And once again, she received the lion's share of the praise: 'From the large group of performers, Margherita Sheridan, who in a short time has won much fame in Italy, stood out,'[12] observed *La Stampa*. Following several performances of *Chénier* at the Regio, Margaret was awarded a singular honour. On 10 February, she was invited to sing in a gala performance of *Gianni Schicchi*, held in honour of the newly-married Crown Prince of Italy, Umberto and his Belgian Princess, Maria José. It was a unique tribute and honour for a foreigner. The wedding of the Crown Prince on 8th January had excited great interest throughout the country. For the Prince's first official visit to Turin since his marriage, the city was en fête. Margaret and her colleagues, Pertile and Badini gave 'an exceptional *Gianni Schicchi*'.[13] As the applause continued loud and long, few in the great theatre or among her friends and fellow artists realised that they had heard the voice of the great La Sheridan for the last time on stage in Italy.

Following a successful 1929 opera season at Covent Garden, rumours circulated of an amalgamation between the opera Syndicate, of which Eustace Blois was managing director, and Sir Thomas Beecham's Imperial League of Opera. But difficulties arose between Beecham and Blois about government subsidisation of the new venture and, more significantly, over who would wield the power. The personality clash between the two men was accentuated at a series of meetings to discuss amalgamation. 'Beecham was in his worst vein,' Blois wrote to Margaret after one such meeting in January 1930. 'He spoke as if he was addressing a meeting of his admirers for nearly half an hour without any interruption from me. A mixture of preposterous impossibilities, hot air and deliberate mis-statements . . . his idea of an amalgamation between the Covent Garden Syndicate and the League of Opera is that the latter should completely swallow the former and the united body should carry on the impossible policy of the League with him as head.'[14] Beecham's preference, the development of opera in English by British performers and his aversion to Italian artists in particular, was in conflict with the policy of Blois and the Syndicate. Blois sought a merger of both policies as a logical solution but feared that Beecham would attempt to monopolise the proposed union. 'I think I have done everything for a common cause,' he wrote to Margaret, 'but the interviews (with Beecham) seem to prove what I have always been afraid to be true, that the man is an impossible megalomaniac.'[15]

Regardless of the power struggle with Beecham, Blois prepared for the 1930 International Season and concentrated more than ever on the promotion of the Italian section. In this, he was actively encouraged by Margaret who had never ceased to promote Italian opera at Covent Garden, both through her influence with Blois and with the British press. During her career in Italy, she had been instrumental in the introduction to English audiences of many hitherto unknown Italian artistes, including, among others, Ernesto Badini, Aurora Rettore, Autori and Minghetti. After retirement, she continued her interest and support. 'You can rest assured,' a contact in *The Daily Telegraph* wrote to her, 'that we will do all we can . . . to keep up the prestige of your beloved Italians. The Italians need more organisation and a few more friends like yourself'.[16] Her efforts in promoting Italian interests at Covent Garden never received official recognition and she never looked for personal gratitude. Mussolini however, pleased with Blois' efforts in this regard, had him conferred with the honour of a 'Commendatore' of the Italian crown. (Commendatore della Corona d'Italia). 'I was rather inclined to make fun of it,' Blois informed Margaret, 'but Autori tells me that it is a great honour for a foreigner under the Mussolini regime. Anyhow it was very nice of the Italiani.'[17] The 1930 Covent Garden season showed an Italian bias; thirty out of the fifty evenings were devoted to non-German and mainly Italian works. The highlight of the season promised to be the Covent Garden debut of Beniamino Gigli who chose Margaret to partner him in his favourite role, *Andrea Chénier*.

In May, Margaret arrived in London. Staying at the Savoy, she prepared for her important reunion with Gigli, by then 'the greatest tenor in the world'.[18] With a familiar cast which included Inghilleri, Sampieri, Dua, Baracchi and with Vincenzo Bellezza conducting, Gigli, with Margaret as his Maddalena, made his first appearance on 27th May at the Royal Opera House. Many in the audience were Italian and applauded their countryman with shouts of 'Bis' after Gigli's every aria. But La Sheridan had her share of plaudits too. 'He had excellent support from Miss Margaret Sheridan,' *The Daily Mirror* reported, 'whose appealing singing as Maddalena earned her tremendous applause in Act 3.'[19]

Two nights later she stepped into the breach, literally at the last minute, when the American soprano, Edith Mason, became indisposed and *Madama Butterfly* seemed destined to be cancelled. 'There was never a sign of unpreparedness, of unreadiness and the voice rang out with even a greater significance than before,'[20] *The Daily Telegraph* concluded. But one critic struck a discordant note, a portent, perhaps, of the disaster that lay ahead. 'The gaps in her technique remain serious,' *The Evening News* reported. 'Miss Sheridan's voice, naturally a fine one, wants consolidation'.[21] On 10th June, in a repeat performance of *Butterfly*, which was being broadcast live from the Opera House, Margaret became ill and was forced to retire after the first act. The English soprano, Maggie Teyte, sang the remainder of the role, in English, the rest of the cast continuing in Italian.

But Margaret soon recovered and was called upon to replace Iva

Pacetti, who had received indifferent reviews, in the demanding role of Desdemona in Verdi's *Othello*. Othello was being sung by her recording colleague, Renato Zanelli, in his second season appearance at Covent Garden. And so, on 16th June (a date resonant with Irish literary echoes as Joyce's Bloomsday), surrounded by a cast of her friends – Autori, Stabile, Cilla, Dua, Sampieri, Beltacchi and Bellezza – La Sheridan, Irish prima donna and diva, took the operatic stage for the last time. Her final performance, as her first, had been twelve years earlier, was at short notice and without previous orchestral rehearsal. Nervous initially, she grew in confidence and the critics noted significantly that 'in the lovely 'Salce', the upper notes of her voice were as pure and as clear as her lower notes were rich and full.'[22]

So ended not only her career at Covent Garden but her entire operatic career. Her final performance gave no indication of the imminent collapse of voice and nerve. She was a popular performer at the Royal Opera House with her fellow artistes and management and also, if one is to judge from her substantial fan mail, the opera-going public. One English fan wrote to her to tell her 'how much your smiles are appreciated by members of the gallery queue at Covent Garden, especially by people such as myself who queue for up to eight or nine hours at a time.'[23] The tenor, Luigi Marini, who had sung with Margaret at La Scala, was well-known for being tightfisted with money. During the course of an International Season at the Royal Opera House, he went shopping for neck-ties in a store adjacent to Covent Garden. He complained at the cost and asked for a reduction in the price on the basis 'that he was a dear and close friend of Margherita Sheridan'.[24] He departed from the store with the price of the neck-ties substantially reduced and an added bonus of four complimentary handkerchiefs! Margaret often returned to Covent Garden during her retirement. She was an especially invited guest for some of the International Seasons when, with usual Sheridan aplomb, she would stride down the central aisle just as the curtain was about to be raised, or sit in a box and receive the homage of friends, admirers and colleagues.

During the summer, she stayed on in London at the home of her friend, Ginnie Courtauld in Grosvenor Square. She recorded with HMV two additional Irish melodies, 'Killarney' and 'An Irish Love Song', at the small Queen's Hall with a string quartet conducted by Lawrence Collingwood. Another protracted dispute with HMV arose over the two songs which Margaret maintained were part of her previous contract (for which she claimed she had not received payment) and not, as HMV considered, as two out of the eight songs of her new contract with the Company. 'All this sort of thing is very upsetting to an artist who is very willing to do her duty and only asks fair play,'[25] she complained to Fred Gaisberg. On her return to Italy in the Autumn, HMV tried to persuade her to record additional duets from *Bohème* with Pertile. Carlo Sabajno was asked to intervene. 'We know that Miss Sheridan is not one of the easiest artistes, but we are sure that with your usual tact you will be able to get some good work accomplished with her.'[26] An additional eight operatic extracts, including 'Ei m'ama' (*Faust*), 'O mio babbino caro' (*Gianni Schicchi*), 'C'e Rudolfo' (*Bohème*, with the baritone, Franci), and 'Spunta l'aurora pallida' (*Mefistofele*) were suggested by HMV. Margaret requested that they should be recorded in London at the same time as she was to record the outstanding Irish melodies of her contract. This did not suit HMV who, in any event, were more anxious to complete the operatic numbers and to leave the recording of the Irish melodies until a later date. Throughout 1930 and 1931, the Company arranged recording dates in Milan which had to be cancelled when Margaret disagreed with the company's choice of material or for health reasons was unable to attend. In late 1931, the company suggested that if she agreed to record a complete *Othello* (Desdemona) they would release her from the contract to sing eight songs for which she had been paid in advance and concede her a five per cent royalty on the *Othello*. But by this time she had more critical problems to worry her than unfulfilled recording contracts. Eventually, HMV, in exasperation, advised their Milan office in March 1933, that even though 'Miss Sheridan owes us 8 songs on her contract we have not the slightest desire to hold her to this debt and are rather inclined to relieve her of the obligation.'[27] It was many years before Margaret recorded again with HMV, and it would be an engagement as tempestuous as her previous ones with the company.

After her 1930 appearances at Covent Garden, the New York concert manager, Richard Copley, attempted to sign her for concert recitals in America and Canada, but mainly because of the continuing U.S. depression, the idea was abandoned. Her operatic prospects in Italy for the coming season did not appear promising. Her agent, Emilio Ferone, could only offer her recitals of *Butterfly*, more to boost their sagging morale than for any appreciable commercial gain. Ferone and the other independent theatrical agencies in Italy were hard pressed by government attempts to replace them with state controlled agencies, and their former influence was severely curtailed. Nevertheless, refusing offers of concert recitals in England, Margaret returned to Italy in September and was joined by Blois at Bellagio. The Covent Garden Syndicate had taken over the management of the British National Opera Company's provincial tours, previously managed by Sir Thomas Beecham. Contrary to his promises to reduce his work so that he might spend more time with Margaret, Blois' schedule had vastly increased and forced him to cut short his stay at Bellagio. 'I miss you terribly darling,' he wrote her, 'all our jokes and talk. Bellagio seems like a dream.'[28] Yet when she suggested that she might do her recording with HMV in November in London rather than in Milan, his opinion 'that we are much better off abroad than in London'[29] prevailed and he suggested she might join him instead in Berlin. Because of the dearth of work in Italy, he urged her to see Anita Colombo who had succeeded Angelo Scandiani as the administrative director at La Scala, and investigate the possibility of returning to prominence at La Scala, especially in view of Toscanini's recent departure from the theatre. But though ever willing to do favours for others, she was loathe to ask them for herself. 'I quite understand your feeling that you don't like to appear to be seeking favours when you go to see people,'[30] Blois assured her, but nevertheless urged her to seek the advice of the new Scala administrator. She received an unexpected and welcome invitation to sing the unfamiliar role of Eva in Wagner's *Die Meistersinger* at the San Carlo however, and by mid-October had commenced her study for the part. But her nose and throat problems recurred. An operation on her sinuses had been suggested more than a year previously but she had continued to postpone her decision. If she wished to continue her singing career, the medical advice was that an operation was now imperative. In early 1931, she entered hospital in Milan. 'All is well,' she assured Fred Gaisberg in April. 'But it (the operation) has held me up and given me a great deal more suffering than I bargained for.'[31] But this was merely the beginning of her medical troubles. A throat infection ensued and by the end of the year, it was apparent that the operation had been unsuccessful and had to be repeated in 1932. In between, gynaecological problems beset her, also necessitating surgery. All this greatly affected her nerves, already overwrought by the suspension of her career and particularly by the emotional strain of her inconclusive relationship with Eustace Blois. Now totally immersed in his struggle with Beecham for control at Covent Garden, Blois had even less time to devote to Margaret in Milan. She had to cope with her medical and accompanying financial problems without his support. And when for the time being, her medical anxieties were allayed, the emotional strain became even more acute. No longer able to cope with Blois' apparent ability to dedicate himself equally to business and to her, Margaret decided to terminate their friendship. For her, the need for love, to be loved, involved sacrifice. 'For a feeling, an ideal, I'm ready to give my life, you wouldn't allow it to distract your thoughts from your next season,'[32] she wrote to him. She no longer believed his avowals of love. 'Facts not words count,' she admonished him. 'You tell me I am very Irish, yes it's true and you are very English . . . 'There's a time for everything' you think and maybe you are right – You are not like me, as T.P. told me . . . I messed up everybody and everything just to dedicate myself to you and this against my judgement, my principles, religion, life, everything.'[33] And it was to her deep spiritual faith that she now turned for direction in this painful decision. During a brief holiday in London, and without consciously deciding to go there, she found herself in St. Patrick's Church in Soho and made there, as she later confided to a friend, 'the most important decision of my life'.[34] 'It was very touching, the end of that affair,' her friend later recalled. 'She struggled very much against it before ending it.'[35] She needed Blois more than he needed her; her expectations of the relationship were highly idealised. She was prepared, as were her heroines on stage, to sacrifice everything, even her art, for love. It was a difficult, painful decision but she approached it with bravery and determination. 'I have suffered these past days because of how much I love you,' she told him, 'but I controlled myself and I wore again my armour, it covers a wound, I know, and it will save me from a deeper one. Be affectionate, it is enough, I don't believe anymore in your love and it's better for all of us.'[36] Blois' love for her, while reserved, less emotional and at times selfish, was nonetheless sincere as her many friends in London, who kept her informed of his respiratory illness during 1933, realised. But they also realised the strains the relationship imposed on her. 'Right or wrong,' a journalist friend wrote to her, 'you were the only woman he loved, tho' he ruined your career and perhaps your happiness.'[37]

Eustace Blois died in 1933. As Margaret struggled to recover her confidence from both the physical debility of her operations and the emotional trauma of her break-up with Blois, followed by his subsequent death, her friends encouraged her with references to him. 'You mustn't be depressed or unhappy', one advised her, 'because I feel you have so much to do on this earth before you join him. I'm sure he wants us to help and encourage you.'[38] She had still many admirers, many potential lovers, especially in Italy, who continued to write extravagantly to her. She listened and even lingered occasionally, needing the companionship, the security, as she once more faced life on her own. But these friendships were no more than empty shells, the pearl had long since drifted away on the ebbing tide. 'You have really revealed yourself' one admirer wrote to her, 'one foot in heaven the other burning in hell'.[39]

In September 1932, she signed a contract to sing *Butterfly* at the Carlo Felice in Genova. But her continuing medical and emotional problems had forced her to cancel. Through the good offices of Mother Clement, she was invited to the Eucharistic Congress in Dublin. But after her second operation, which was presumed a success, she retreated, like a wounded bird, to Bellagio to recuperate and did not accept the invitation. But Bellagio merely re-opened the emotional wounds. She fled from the memories the idyllic quiet Lake Como evoked. From Milan she sent optimistic letters to her recording company, to her agent, to her colleagues, that soon, very soon, La Sheridan would make her operatic comeback. Privately to her close friends, she wrote of her fear, her despair, that she would never sing again. Loyally her friends rallied. Letters from her former patron, Lady Howard de Walden; her close friend and benefactor Mrs. Stephen Courtauld; Lady Hambledon; Olga Lynn; her operatic and political friends in Italy, brought words of love and encouragement and wishes for her recovery and return to where she belonged, in opera. As if addressing a child, they scolded and cajoled her in letters and personal visits. 'I wish I was with you to hold your hand,' one well-wisher wrote, 'but in spirit you will have me with you all the time, so be a good girl.'[40] 'Don't underrate yourself and your gifts. They *are* there,' assured another, 'and you must remember you have something to give to the world, so give it . . . you have been blessed with a voice not just for yourself but for others.'[41] 'Corraggio little one,' Ginnie Courtauld directed her, 'the silver lining must be very near and then you'll have a long period of prosperity (if the Irish in you can hold on to it!!).'[42] Friends in the London office of the Irish Free State, including the High Commissioner, Dulanty, wrote encouragingly, as did her sister Hester, then involved in divorce proceedings against her husband, Alfred Gaillton. 'Why on earth did you not wire for me,' she admonished her. 'You should realise by now that blood is thicker than water and that however indifferent you are to me I am always loving you and as proud of you as if I were also your mother.'[43]

Three years had passed since her last stage appearance. Fearfully and in private, she had tried to test and recapture the bell-like quality of the high Bs and Cs, but to her horror, discovered that she now had cracked on notes that once came effortlessly. Hers had been a 'natural' voice or, as Puccini had told her, 'she sang instinctively'. Her training with Maestro Martino, and especially the development of her vocal technique, was essential if she was to extend the range and life of her voice. But it had been interupted by Emma Carelli's offer of early stardom in 1918. Margaret now reaped the bitter harvest of a late beginning combined with inadequate preparation. Technique, according to one of the century's greatest prima donnas, Maria Callas, was what a singer relied upon from as early as twenty-three years of age. Margaret's technique had not been properly developed and she had no safety net to rely on when the natural elements of her voice wore away. Like most singers, she had never tried to conserve her voice in order to prolong her career. 'I gave capital on my voice when others gave only the interest,'[44] she later told a friend in Dublin. Ebe Stignani, the great and enduring mezzo, would communicate in a whisper after a performance and then only to excuse herself for not speaking at all. Gigli refused all financial inducements to sing Radames in *Aida* because he considered that his voice was not then ready. But a late start, made La Sheridan intent on recovering lost time. With objectivity, she acknowledged her deficiency:

> 'Having myself made a successful career with a completely natural voice, which from my earliest years functioned to perfection from the mechanical point of view and which no master 'trained' in the usually accepted meaning of the term, I was, however, to realize after some years the absolute necessity for the singer to have a *complete* knowledge of vocal technique without which no true control can ever be exercised over the voice.'[45]

Her financial situation was rapidly deteriorating. As living expenses mounted, aggravated by heavy medical outlay, she was forced to borrow from her 'nest egg' as she referred to her securities account in London. She was welcomed back to 'her haven', the Courtauld mansion on Grosvenor Square, by Ginnie Courtauld. In London, friends such as Olga Lynn, attempted to rally her flagging spirits and urged her to sing again. 'We really must get at it,' Olga advised, 'otherwise you will not be ready for Thomas Beecham in the Autumn.'[46] But dispirited, irritable and emotionally drained, Margaret made excuses. Friends in Italy persuaded her to attend a voice clinic near Vienna where many colleagues, including Lotte Lehman, had attended in a bid to restore tired and bruised vocal chords. But it was expensive and

Margaret's financial resources were slim. Once again, she was dependent on the generosity of her friends in London. Lady Howard de Walden, Mr. and Mrs. Courtauld and others, provided the means to seek treatment. She left for Austria in January 1935, stopping at Monte Carlo to attend a gala performance of *Rigoletto* in February.

The disciplined regime of the clinic did not suit her and while new friendships emerged during her year-long stay, there was little in the way of vocal restoration. Her colleagues at La Scala, Maria Caniglia, Pertile, Stabile, urged her to return. 'Everyone here wants you back, how we long for you,'[47] they wrote. She went to Milan briefly. At La Scala, the conductors, Victor de Sabata and Gino Marinuzzi, maintained the high standards established by Toscanini. From the centre stage limelight to the anonymity of an audience seat was difficult. She left Milan, sadly ending a brilliant career and leaving a country to which she had been ever faithful, and which had cherished and adopted her.

Her success in Italy was indeed quite remarkable, given her relatively short operatic career and the difficulties singing in Italy posed for a foreigner. Competition in the mercurial operatic world, during Margaret's tenure there, was particularly fierce. Nevertheless, she was accepted and became enormously popular with Italian audiences for her vocal ability, her personality and her unique stage presence. Once when asked to recall her most thrilling first-night performance in Italy her answer was, as ever, candid:

'The career of any successful prima donna in grand opera in Italy is just a continuation of dangerously thrilling first nights. Because, although the Italians adore their artists, they expect them to give of their very best and renew their success in every different place and in each new role. A great success in Rome does not necessarily mean one in Milan and vice versa.'[48]

She often said that on the Italian stage 'she felt humble in the realization that in the chorus of the great opera houses, such as La Scala for example, were many sopranos with as good a voice as her own but who lacked the ability to project themselves.'[49] Projection she considered a vital element of one's performance in Italy. She was adamant that the impression made in the first seconds of an entrance set the tone of the entire performance. The many spontaneous outbursts of applause she received on her appearance on stage during her career in Italy are ample testimony to her rapport with Italian audiences. And her vocal performance matched her stage presence. 'Her splendid operatic voice was of the highest quality,' Mimi Zuccari (private secretary to her fellow artiste at La Scala, Claudia Muzio) remembered, 'and of warm, pure timbre, she possessed perfect equality in all registers and a forced note was never heard – her voice often seemed like a stringed instrument for its vibration and beautiful legato.'[50] She was well liked by her Italian colleagues. Many of these ended their days at the 'Casa Verdi' (Casa di Reposa) near Milan, an artists' retirement home established in 1902 by the great composer. There they spoke of La Sheridan with affection and remembered her as a 'real signora'; 'true artist'; 'a lovely lady having no malice or envy of others'.[51] Her colleague the tenor Nino Piccaluga remembered her 'ever smiling, an artist, a lady and a great human being'.[52] Gigli on his return to the Albert Hall, London in 1947 recalled her 'as one of the greatest sopranos of all time'.[53] The son of her fellow artist and friend, Dottore Arnaldo Pertile, recalled, 'I remember how my father spoke of her as being a fine artiste and a fascinating colleague. On the occasion of my father's centenary in 1985, the celeb-rated artists who assembled on that occasion reiterated the great admiration my father had for this illustrious colleague and the affection and respect in which they held each other'.[54]

Margaret belonged in the first division of Italian opera and the venues in which she sang reflected her premier ranking. Of the numer-ous opera theatres throughout Italy, about a dozen were in the top category. She began her career at the top, in the Costanzi in Rome, and finished at the top, at the Regio in Turin. For her, there was to be no ignominious slide down to the lower divisions. 'If one cannot go higher, do not go lower' would seem to have been her maxim.

The Irish soprano, Veronica Dunne, who in more recent years has had first-hand knowledge of the obstacles facing foreign artistes in Italy, appreciated the significance of Margaret's achievement:

'For an Irish soprano to command operatic limelight during a polit-ically sensitive time in virtually every prestigious opera house in Italy was an incredible achievement. Even in later years for a foreigner, even one as famous as Callas, to break the closed-shop environment of Italian opera was a daunting undertaking. But sheer will-power, vocal excellence, personality and presence, helped undoubtedly by her ability and desire to integrate totally into the social environment of her adopted and beloved Italy, ensured Peggie's success where so many had failed before and since. Had she access to modern recording technology, media coverage, the hype of television and publicity, I feel that her impact on the wider world of opera would have been immense.'[55]

Dottore A. G. Viani recalled that she

'possessed in her voice a pure soprano top register and yet her middle register and chest register had almost the quality of a mezzo, full of intense romance'.[56]

When asked in an interview as to her favourite opera, Margaret's reply was not surprising. Like the composer, in love with the characters of his own creation, she identified with the traits and personalities of his creations:

'When I sing, I am Mimi who makes artificial flowers and longs for the kiss of Spring . . . I cling to every shattered hope of Butterfly as she sees the cherry blossom year after year. I am Iris, transfixed with horror before the wasted dead ocean of molten brass wherein the monster writhes, the mighty monster, Pleasure. I am Tosca who upbraids Heaven for having forsaken her in her hour of need. I am like the Aeolian harp, which when played upon by the sighing music of the breeze responds to its touch and becomes the lyrical expression of the wind's will.'[57]

For years her many outstanding interpretations remained a verdant memory in Italy as her colleague, Maria Caniglia, related to her:

'New Butterflys come and go here but people say we heard La Sheridan.'[58]

She returned to London in 1934 once more determined to embark on a course of study in a further bid to restore her vocal technique. She enlisted the assistance of E. Herbert Caesari, an ardent advocate of natural training methods. Professor of Music, author of *The Alchemy of Voice* and of the treatise *The Science and Sensations of Vocal Tone*, Caesari had, in 1959, dedicated the third edition of this work 'to the memory of Margaret Sheridan'. Margaret began her initial therapy with Caesari in early 1935. Valiantly he tried to boost her confidence, to dispel her by then morbid fear of the high B flats, B naturals and Cs, the 'BBC complex' as he jokingly referred to them. He urged calmness, no temperamental outbursts but a cool and calculated approach to gradually building a solid foundation of lower notes on which to eventually recapture the elusive higher notes. Caesari became extremely fond of his temperamental pupil and forgave her outbursts and walk-outs from his studio. 'I am determined to put you on the boards again,'[59] he told her. His judgement on the state of her voice and her progress with him is interesting but must be interpreted with care as he was a passionate critic of the methods of voice renewal in vogue elsewhere and may have exaggerated the success of the methods he himself had devised.

'In 1939, when she was fifty' [he wrote] 'her voice was as sound as a bell. There was not the slightest symptom or sign of wear or age in it. The quality was truly exquisite and more than ever evident as a result of her technical studies. If only certain inhibitions could have been uprooted and mental readjustments crystallised there was nothing whatever to prevent her returning to her well-loved opera stage. The desire was now there, but not the full will. At times, where singing was concerned, she could be revealed as fearful, hesitant, self-doubting, everything the exact opposite of herself. This (he recorded] is a statement of fact . . . What a voice was hers. There was an intangible but highly seductive timbre in her voice, a power of attraction that brooked no denial, endearing one and all. It was matched by a first class singing brain . . . ever ready to grasp the essentials, the inner meaning of the musical-vocal phrase, as conceived by the composer. A rare gift indeed! . . . A forceful personality shone through those laughing blue Irish eyes of hers. A sparkling wit and a ready repartee that could out-smart even a Q.C.'[60]

And that complex nature outsmarted, unfortunately, Caesari's best efforts to restore her confidence in herself and in her vocal ability. Despite the desire and, it seemed evident, the ability to make the comeback sought by herself, her friends and the Italian theatres that innundated her, even as late as 1956, with offers and contracts, the will to do so failed to materialise. World War II intervened and the dream of a return to operatic glory receded further and further.

The agent, Harold Holt, encouraged her to think in terms of the concert platform once more. Many concert promoters sought her as a recitalist. She shuddered at the very thought. Opera was her natural medium. By contrast, however financially rewarding, concert platforms were stark and confined. Ginnie Courtauld suggested the growing musical film market, reminding her of Grace Moore's great success in *One Night of Love*. But, for Margaret, there was simply no substitute for the operatic stage.

She again became irritable and restless, testing the patience of her loyal London friends. 'Peggy, I hate your guts,'[61] wrote one exasperated friend irritated by her persistent chatter during a performance at Covent Garden. She drifted aimlessly from one social function to another, from the office of the Irish High Commissioner where she made her first acquaintance with the Irish Taoiseach (Prime Minister), Eamon De Valera, with George Bernard Shaw and G. K. Chesterton, to a garden party at Buckingham Palace. Finally, the long-resisted lure of Ireland, prevailed.

CHAPTER IX

UNA DONNA SOLETTA
Retirement 1934-1950

The summer of 1937 saw her first visit home since 1922 and there had been many changes. The new Irish Free State had survived the disruption of the Civil War that had been in course during her previous visit. A constitutional democracy had been firmly established in the newly independent nation during her years away. There were two dominant political parties: Fianna Fail, led by Eamon De Valera, and Fine Gael, led by W. T Cosgrave. A new constitution had just been adopted and Éire – in the English language, Ireland – had become the official name of the State. A national currency a broadcasting station, an airline service and the many other trappings of an independent state had been established. The Tricolour, the nation's green, white and orange flag flew high over every public building.

Making a brief stop-over in Dublin Margaret visited Eccles Street. She presented Mother Clement with a complete set of the *Butterfly* recording. Her inscription revealed her indebtedness to her first teacher: 'To my very best and most careful teacher in memory of my very young and happy days in the Dominican Convent, Eccles Street. Gratefully and lovingly, Margaret Sheridan'.[1] Then alone she set off to the west of Ireland, to the wild, beautiful spaces of Renvyle in Connemara where she hoped to find a little peace and rest 'in my own country'.[2] Signing herself 'Margherita Burke Sheridan',[3] on 16th August, she registered at Renvyle House, the hotel home of the celebrated poet, surgeon and wit, Oliver St. John Gogarty. Once a strong-hold of the O'Flaherty chieftains, former overlords of the remote 'kingdom' of Connemara, the house had been acquired by Gogarty from the Blake family in 1917 as a holiday home. Renvyle House was burned by the Republican side during the Civil War in retribution for Gogarty's acceptance of a seat in the Senate of the Irish Free State. Compensated by the Government, Gogarty determined that 'as I could no longer afford to keep a country house, I conceived the idea of making the country keep me',[4] and in 1930 opened it as a hotel. Renvyle House Hotel attracted literary, artistic, political and aristocratic patrons. An Italian historian and philosopher, Professor Mario Rossi, author of *Storia Inghilterra*, recorded his impressions of the unique atmosphere of the hotel. 'Renvyle House is the kingdom of Gogarty, the most westerly hotel in Europe, beaten by all the Atlantic winds, crowded with guests, a peculiar combination of the great Atlantic Hotel and the hospitable home. It is not easy to say who is there as the guest of the hotel. You fail to understand how so many people have arrived there across 18 miles of impossible road. Nevertheless you find there a sort of mundane tone which couples insensibly with the wildest nature.'[5]

Almost unknown, certainly not readily recognised, in her own country, Margaret went by train to Galway and by bus along the winding, narrow roads through the rocks, bogs, mountains and moorlands of O'Flaherty and Joyce country. On the bus journey, she talked with her fellow travellers, the ordinary Connemara men and women who wondered at the rather exotic, golden-haired lady with a 'foreign' way of speaking, dressed in soft pastel colours, a large hat shading the lovely, if plump, face. With typical western forthrightness (which she herself understood and practised), one gaunt Connemara man, on hearing who she was, as the bus trundled towards Renvyle, exclaimed to her, ''Tis a wonder you never got married Miss Sheridan. You must have had great chances in your day'.[6] Had one of her more sophisticated circle of friends even alluded to her unmarried state, it would have produced a temperamental outburst, but in Connemara, among her own, it was easier to forgive and even to smile.

'I'm in love with the West,'[7] she wrote to her former teacher, Vincent O'Brien. When she returned to live permanently in Ireland at the outbreak of the Second World War, Renvyle became her Irish 'Bellagio' where, amidst the beauty of mountain, sea and lake, she could rest and be at peace if not with everyone else, then at least with herself. She remained friends with the Gogartys and especially with Maude (Neenie) who, during their residency in London, invited Margaret to musical soirées at her Chelsea home. Gogarty was in medical practice at Mansfield Street and his devoted wife was tireless in her efforts to bring him new clients: 'If you know of any one who wants a good throat, nose or ear surgeon do send them to Oliver,'[8] she wrote to Margaret. Gogarty departed for America in 1939, leaving Maude in Connemara to look after the guests. Gogarty's amorous exploits were known to most but not to his wife. A stickler for good taste and the custom of yesteryear, Maude insisted on dressing in resplendent style each evening for dinner in Renvyle. Descending the staircase in regal fashion one evening to her waiting guests below, she plaintively asked Margaret, 'How do you think Oliver will find me when he comes home?' Margaret was overheard to remark wickedly, 'Well, my dear, I should think it all depends on who he is seeing in New York.'⁹

She later met the eminent barrister, Sean McBride and his family who had a summer cottage in Renvyle and dined at Renvyle House each evening. Still engaged in organising and defending the Irish Republican Army, McBride, with his Irish and international background, his charm and intelligence, struck a chord with her. They enjoyed long discussions and Margaret continued her friendship with the family in Dublin, writing a letter of congratulations on the success-ful outcome of one of McBride's many court-room triumphs. However, in later years as her friendship with the then Taoiseach, Mr. De Valera, developed, her relationship with McBride (then at political loggerheads with De Valera over the Republican prisoners and intern-ment issues) became quite strained.

In an interview given to *The Connaught Telegraph* during her holiday at Renvyle in August 1939, she expressed an interest in visiting 'Castlebar where I was born. I would like to see the Mall again'.¹⁰ A 'monster carnival', a highly popular method of raising funds for parish social and sporting activities at the time, was being organised in the town for September. The Committee, thought, not unnaturally, that, as part of the carnival, an appearance by the town's most illustrious daughter at a grand 'Celebrity Concert' in the local cinema would be a major attraction. But somewhere along the line, communications as to why precisely she was invited to Castlebar became unclear. Margaret was under the impression that she was to receive the homage of the citizens of her native town. Members of the organising Committee were under the impression that she had come to sing and posted bills around the town to that effect.

The concert was a sell-out. Luring the prima donna back to the limelight – what Dublin, Covent Garden or La Scala could not achieve – seemed to be the good fortune of Castlebar, even though the stage was that of the local cinema. With a great ship's trunk firmly strapped on the roof of the car, the famous diva and her trousseau were driven through the streets of the town she had left as a young child in 1901. Installed in the house of a relation, the Committee allowed their illus-trious guest some hours to recuperate after the exhausting journey

*The Lord Chamberlain is
commanded by Their Majesties to invite*

Miss Margaret Sheridan

*to an Afternoon Party in the Garden of Buckingham Palace,
on Tuesday 22nd June 1937 from 4 to 6.30 p.m.
(Weather permitting)*

Morning Dress

Invitation to Buckingham Palace, 1937.

Miss Margaret Sheridan

eire

The High Commissioner for Ireland

At Home

Piccadilly House,

St. Patrick's Day, 17th March, 1939.

R.S.V.P.
The Private Secretary,
   High Commissioner's Office,
     33-37, Regent Street, S.W.1.

Please bring this card.
3 p.m. to 5.30 p.m.

Invitation to the High Commissioner's Office, 1939.

Renvyle House, Connemara. (Courtesy: Hugh Coyle)

from Renvyle. Two members then presented themselves to welcome her home and to find out what she wished to sing that evening. It all went charmingly well until the question of singing was broached. According to one of the Committee, 'she threw her ample frame into a chaise longue in the room, burst into hysterics, kicking her legs in the air and shouting that she would not sing in public'.[11] On the pretext of 'a sudden indisposition' of the star, the news was communicated to the disappointed audience waiting in the cinema. As she refused to appear on stage, the address of the welcome ceremony, prepared by the town council, had also to be abandoned. The County Manager later wrote to her to apologise for any misunderstanding and in return received a copy of a painting of her (by the Dublin-domiciled Italian artist, Gaetanno de Gennaro) with the inscription, 'Misunderstanding once cleared am looking forward to happy reunion with my own people – "When it's moonlight in Mayo"'[12] (quoting the title of a popular song about the county). Sadly, that reunion with her native town never took place.

On her return to London after her holiday at Renvyle, war clouds once more darkened Europe. Friends in London and in Ireland advised her to return home permanently. 'You have the humour of coming – soon I hope,' the Director of Irish broadcasting, Dr. T. J. Kiernan, husband of her friend, the Irish ballad singer Delia Murphy, wrote to her. 'London will be a dangerous place soon and Dublin will be safer – a cot in Connemara safest of all'.[13] His reference to a cottage in Connemara originated in Margaret's own expressed desire, after her summer vacation there, to retire in splendid solitude to the west of Ireland. Those who knew her better realised that the likelihood of permanent residence in the remoteness of Connemara was no more than a romantic whim. In 1939, she left London and returned to live permanently in Dublin. After a brief stay with her Cooley relations in Mount Merrion, she moved to the more familiar surroundings of one of Dublin's premier hotels, the Gresham. While her financial resources were slender, her personality and status demanded and received, for a while at least, one of the superior suites at the hotel at reduced rates. After the fame and adulation she had enjoyed in Italy and in London, her homecoming was in many ways a disappointment. Outside a small circle of artistic friends in the Ireland of the 1940s – drab, narrow-minded, censorious, and in tortuous search for its own identity – few knew or cared about the past operatic triumphs of an ageing, tempera-mental eccentric. 'She walks along the street smiling to everybody, bowing to most in case she should know them'.[14] In Dublin, people 'paid her scant attention except to be mildly witty at her expense, but in London,' a friend recalled, 'she is feted and adored, while in Italy, they kissed the hem of her dress'.[15] The best one could say about her life in Dublin was that it was safer than wartime Milan or London. 'An alien among her own, outrageous and witty, a complete revelation,'[16] an acquaintance described her during these years in Dublin. 'Of medium height, a natural blonde, she had a most gloriously fair complexion,'[17] another recalled. Her large-bosomed (my 'balcone' as she called it) figure emerged daily down the steps of the Gresham. As the trams trundled to and from the Pillar, she sallied flamboyantly forth, wearing high Italian platform-soled shoes, dressed in pastel blue, with flowing chiffon scarves and draperies and a large brimmed hat with veil. Her cupid-bow lips were accentuated with a dash of lipstick. Inviting the curious stares of passers-by or greeting friends and admirers with animation she journeyed down O'Connell Street, via Westmoreland and Grafton Streets to St. Stephen's Green where, among the flower beds and ponds, 'she provided a burst of exotic glamour'.[18]

One friend and admirer was the actor, Micheál MacLiammóir. Their meetings in the street were straight from the stage. Playing to the gallery of passers-by and in a mixture of Italian and English, Margaret and Micheál loudly proclaimed their mutual joy at meeting: 'Caro Michele,' Margaret would cry, arms out-stretched. 'Ah! Margherita bellissima,'[19] Micheál would respond, embracing her Continental style with kisses on both cheeks. Micheál's great friend and colleague, Hilton Edwards, however, had little time or tolerance for Margaret's insistence 'on acting when the curtain has come down',[20] as he rather sourly put it.

The actor, Cyril Cusack, recalls with affection his numerous encounters with the Diva on walks on Grafton Street. 'I cannot remember exactly where or when I first met her except that she always seemed to be a familiar to me from the very beginning. She had an international flavour about her. There was nothing insular about her, on the contrary, she made you feel that in her presence you were in the world, in her world, that you were not confined. Although I knew little about her career, one didn't need to be informed of the details of her achievements, one instinctively knew that there was a great career behind her. When she moved on after our brief meetings, I always felt that I was floating', he remembered. He never heard her sing but bought a copy of one of her recordings. 'There was a superstition in our profession that certain songs bring bad luck, for example, Balfe's "Lily of

Lily and John McCormack. (Courtesy: Liam Breen).

Prima Donnas – Past and Present: with Elena Danielli in Dublin.

Louis Elliman of The Gaiety Theatre, Dublin, Margaret Burke Sheridan, Princess Maria d'Ardia Caracciola, unidentified priest, Prince Ferdinando d'Ardia Caracciola. (Courtesy: Niccolo d'Ardia Caracciola).

Margaret with Veronica Dunne.

Margaret and Beniamino Gigli, Dublin, 1954.

Killarney", "When Other Lips" and "I Dreamt I Dwelt in Marble Halls"', he recalled. 'I had inherited this superstition from my mother who passionately believed it. However, I got a record of Margaret Burke Sheridan singing "I Dreamt I Dwelt in Marble Halls" and all I can say is that it broke the spell forever.'[21]

Slowly but surely, as she had done in Italy and in London, she attracted a coterie of friends and admirers, usually from theatrical, musical, literary or political backgrounds. Her extrovert behaviour and her fading but yet exotic glamour fascinated and bound them to her. If you had something to contribute to the conversation, time and patience to listen to her reminiscences, you were allowed to bask in the glow she radiated. R. W. Lightbody (Bobbie), then a young, successful Belfast businessman fell under the spell of 'The Enchantress" after an accidental meeting in the Gresham. Almost thirty years her junior, he found her company both scintillating and vibrant. 'You never thought of her age,' he remembered and when the subject was tentatively approached, she laughingly remarked, 'I've told so many lies about my age I simply cannot remember.' 'She made other company seem dull by comparison,' he recalled, 'and she had the unique ability to make you feel that you were sparkling in your own conversation when you were with her.'[22] Her gaiety, her sense of mischief and fun are his abiding memories of her. He recalls the imaginary servants who tended 'Madame Sheridan' when she later moved to an apartment at number 6, Fitzwilliam Street. Alternatively, 'Fifi the French Maid' or 'Mary, the Housekeeper from Galway', was liable to answer his telephone call to Madame Sheridan and in response to his enquiry as to her whereabouts would reply with perfect French affectation or a western brogue that Madame was either in or out according to her prevailing mood. He took her driving or walking at weekends in the Dublin environs. One Sunday evening, as they drove through the Phoenix Park, she decided, despite his protests, to walk the remainder of the way back to the Gresham Hotel. As she sauntered along with a carefree air she was accosted by a man who surreptitiously asked her fee. Returning to Bobbie as he sat in the car, she gaily related the encounter, adding, 'one time I would have been insulted, now I am flattered'.[23] Her financial resources at this time, he recalled, were meagre, her clothes, although of couture quality, were of the fashions of yesteryear. On his offer of assistance to take off her coat, she once jokingly replied, 'Any assistance and the sleeves might well fall out.'[24] Any attempt to advise her on her business affairs, he remembered, 'met with a blank wall. The vital pause before singing a phrase in an opera score was a more important consideration than trifling business concerns.'[25]

The present President of the United Arts Club, Gwladys McCabe, was introduced to the prima donna and remained a friend until her death in 1958. She wrote her impressions of Margaret during her retirement years in Dublin. 'She is so entertaining, so pathetic in a way, so pleased at praise but always doubting its sincerity and so deflated by anyone's unkindness . . . I don't know her age . . . it's unimportant. She looks exactly what she is, a prima donna. Small tiny hands which she uses beautifully, small feet and built up shoes . . . that make her walk like a little mermaid: blonde hair worn with a sweep on her forehead, tied back and falling in almost a curl on her nape.'[26] Her rather theatrical use of cosmetics, unnecessary for such an unblemished, fair complexion, made 'the shape of her mouth hard to determine as she overpaints it rather grotesquely. Eyebrows likewise sketched far too high, all right for her own mirror face but as she has such an expressive one to show the world they take on a slightly ridiculous look when the outlines of where they should be are underneath. A small, well-shaped, rather provocative nose and the bluest of blue eyes, still soft and innocent looking; there is no hardness in the face. She must have been incredibly lovely at the height of her fame.'[27]

In the lounge of the Gresham Hotel, she held her audience spellbound as she told and retold the exciting moments of her glamorous life and the famous people who had crossed her path – Toscanini, Respighi, Puccini, Marconi, Lauri Volpi, Gigli . . . the names, the incidents, the memories were deftly shuffled in a mixture of English, Italian, German and French. 'Never did expert card-men, nearing the end of a railway-journey, flash out their kings, queens and aces with such dexterity as La Sheridan flashes out the celebrities,'[28] one reporter wrote. If she accepted your invitation to lunch or dinner, one's expenditure was well rewarded by a performance as theatrical and emotional as one could see on the stage of La Scala. Before the ceremonial opening of the coat and the lowering of the fur, she would not begin to talk. As the waiters hovered she changed and rechanged her mind as to choice of food, position of or at the table. When the logistics were reorganised to her satisfaction – usually with Margaret occupying a strategic corner where she could see and be seen – a tantalising performance ensued. She never referred to her past unless directly asked or if it happened to enter by chance into the conversation; she never praised her own performances; but one could count on a conversation glittering with references to the stars of the music world, interspaced with witty, anecdotal reminiscences, sprinkled with bon mots in a weave of English, Italian and French. 'To get La Sheridan to talk reasonably according to plan,' one reviewer wrote, 'is about as simple as trapping sunbeams in a wickerbasket. With her, conversation is all tangent and sky-rockets – a sort of celestial *camogie* with La Sheridan as full-back, centre-forward and goal-keeper simultaneously.'[29]

But underneath the worldly sophistication and flamboyance flourished a residual layer of 'Maggie from Mayo'. Used to send up or amuse, it was still an integral part of the beautifully modulated timbre of her speaking voice. Despite the continental mannerisms and outlook, she was attuned to the more parochial elements of Irish society as if she had never left it. During the weekend of an all-Ireland Hurling Final, a robust bunch of Cork supporters came into the Gresham dining room. One burly fellow, on sitting down to the table, emitted a loud sneeze. There was a brief embarrassed hush, where-upon, from a corner seat across the room, came the voice of Margaret, aimed at the Corkonian table, 'Germs and *foreign* germs at that'.[30] accompanied by a dainty wave of her hand to acknowledge the laughs of the Cork supporters and everyone else in the dining room. Or the day when, in the lounge, when she discovered that a young First Communicant in white was named Margaret, the prima donna bent over her and told her that she was a little saint and asked her to say a prayer for her. Later, during lunch, Margaret paused in mid-sentence to remark, seeing the young child leaving the hotel, 'There goes little Margaret. If that child doesn't keep her promise to pray for me today, I'll wring her neck'.[31]

Dr. Michael Browne, then Bishop of Galway, a somewhat pompous and arrogant man, with a distinct penchant for high living, met her in the Gresham. A fluent Italian speaker, his Lordship sought her company on his occasional visits to Dublin and entertained her to dinner. Never one to tolerate pomposity, Margaret insisted on calling him by his christian name, Michael John. She often accused him of being arrogant and too fond of worldly luxuries. 'If Christ were here,' she told him one evening at dinner, 'he'd have to move to another table.'[32] The Bishop also possessed finely shaped hands which, like Margaret, he tended to use for emphasis in conversation. Margaret tolerated the competitive weavings until, exasperated, said, 'all right, Michael John, we've all seen them, now put them away under the table!'[33]

She also numbered among her friends Dr. Pádraig Browne (de Brún), the brilliant academic, wit and President of University College

Galway. He seldom saw eye-to-eye with his namesake (but no relation) the Bishop. Both men made little secret of their mutual animosity. Margaret danced merrily between the company of the two, encouraging both in their criticism of each other.

The worldly and extrovert prima donna had warmed to the outwardly austere figure of the Taoiseach, Mr. De Valera. 'I made him laugh so much that he rocked on his long legs,'[34] she later recalled. Initially, she was in awe of De Valera whose exploits during Ireland's struggle for independence had been widely reported in Italian newspapers. 'Mr. De Valera's tremendous personality always makes me ill at ease,' she confessed. 'In his company my eyelashes fall off, my lipstick fades. I say "no" for "yes and "thanks" for "please"'.[35] De Valera at first knew little of the background and achievements of the only Irish person whose name was more familiar than his own in Italy. She related how, at a dinner party in Dublin where De Valera was also a guest, she was silent and overawed. 'A London doctor in the party,' she related, 'gallantly came to my rescue. To make conversation with me he recalled the wonderful gala night in Covent Garden when the audience included four kings. He recalled how I was summoned to the Royal Box and how the King paid me great compliments, talked to me about Ireland and Italy and my command of Italian. And,' she continued, 'the Taoiseach's brow wrinkled. He looked at us interrogatively. 'Which Miss Sheridan?' he asked, 'and which King?' 'This Margaret Burke Sheridan from Mayo,' the doctor replied, pointing to me and King George V.'[36] She visited De Valera occasionally in his office in the Dáil and regaled his secretary, Miss Kathleen O'Connell with the choicest of her most outrageous stories and anecdotes, often bringing a blush to the cheeks of the less worldly secretary. Through De Valera, she received many invitations to social functions and events. In 1947, Vincenzo Bellezza, on a visit to Dublin, recalled how he was presented by Margaret to Mr. De Valera and invited later by the Taoiseach to a private tea-party.

During this time, her gynaecological problems surfaced once more and necessitated major surgery. She was operated on in Holles Street Hospital by the Taoiseach's son, Professor De Valera and after some weeks convalescence in the Linden Nursing Home in Blackrock, she rented a flat at Number 6, Fitzwilliam Street, abandoning her Gresham suite. Her insistence there of practising her singing and accompanying herself on a piano, provided for her by the Gresham management, had brought a torrent of complaints from guests who did not necessarily appreciate having their rest disturbed, albeit by such a famous and still lovely voice. Moreover, her financial affairs had further deteriorated. Royalties from her records were practically non-existent due to fall-off in demand in the war and the imposition of a luxury tax. HMV received recriminatory letters from her, accusing the company of not promoting her records and not making them available, especially in Ireland. 'I have come back', she wrote, 'and this plan to try to kill Margaret Sheridan is bad business now and may be even more so when we return to normal, peaceful, musical life.'[37] Turning her ire on the HMV office in Dublin, she wrote to Head Office in London. 'Your representatives in Dublin *still* ignore the fact that Miss Sheridan is a red label Artiste of HMV.'[38] When the recording company deleted her *Chénier* duets with Pertile from their catalogue it brought a stinging Margaret-style rebuke. 'Just because I stopped singing for a few years now I may start singing again even if only for spite,'[39] she threatened. Publicly, she let it be known that she had not retired but was merely resting. Plans for her operatic come-back, concert tours of Ireland and America, of 'singing to the troops'[40] were discussed at length but when it came to implementation, plans were inevitably postponed yet again. Her records, especially her *Butterfly*, were regularly played on British and Continental radio stations and she accused HMV of deliberately boycotting her records in Ireland. By 1943, only three of her titles were still retained on the HMV catalogue. This hurt her pride as well as affecting her income. For the thousands of her compatriots who may have doubted that she had a major operatic career, her records were the only proof of her greatness.

She next turned her attention to Radio Eireann. She heard, she often informed her friend and Minister for Posts and Telegraphs, P. J. Little, that not only were RE (the Irish national radio station) not playing her records, but that they had been smashed by vindictive people there. The sound librarian, Mrs. Kathleen Joy (nee Evans) was sent to assure her that this was certainly not the case. P. J. Little, an opera lover and one of Margaret's circle of loyal friends, tried his very best to increase the air play of her records (many of which were, for technical and quality reasons, below par for transmission by the 1940s) and spent his own money in having a new set recorded. Margaret insisted on being kept fully informed of his progress and when the poor man failed in one of his endeavours on her behalf, the withering remark from Margaret was, 'P.J., you're what the Americans call "futile",'[41] (pronounced fewtle). Kathleen Joy remained on friendly terms with the prima donna for many years and treasures the memory of her brief association. Impervious to the restrictions and responsibilities pertaining to a semi-state occupation, Margaret would summon the librarian to join her 'immediately'[42] for afternoon tea at the Gresham or the Shelbourne hotels. To Kathleen Joy's excuse that she could not possibly leave her post in the middle of a working day, the reply, from one for whom such restrictions had never applied, was, 'Don't be absurd. Of *course* you can.'[43]

To many in Ireland at the time, Margaret's refusal to sing opera or concert work in her own country meant either of two things: that she had lost her voice completely or that it was beneath her to sing in Ireland. It was even rumoured that she was not Margaret Sheridan but a housekeeper or dresser who impersonated her. Such unkind criticisms cut her deeply. 'But of course I sing,' she wrote in a newspaper article. 'I am always singing. Ask the nurses at the National Maternity Hospital when the wind blows from my Fitzwilliam Street flat in that direction. But', she added, quoting her friend, the writer, Kate O'Brien, 'how can I sing "without my cloak"!'[44] Her 'cloak' was the unique atmosphere, the rich setting, the high standards of artistry and production of international grand opera to which she had ever been accustomed. Ireland simply did not have the facilities nor the standards. And, of course, she demanded equally high standards of herself, standards of which she was no longer capable. She declined, as diplomatically as possible, to give her second best to 'her own people' and resolved to remain silent.

In 1944, she did, however, sing in Dublin, not quite in public, but for HMV. Margaret delayed the ordeal as long as she could. 'She's desperately afraid to sing now,' Gwladys McCabe noted at the time, 'and keeps the gramophone companies waiting for her. It costs £200 each time for an orchestra – so now, she says, she is down to a piano!'[45] The recording eventually took place in the Aula Maxima of 86 St. Stephen's Green. An orchestra, conducted by Terry O'Connor, was assembled especially for the occasion. Amid tension and tantrums, Margaret was cajoled into the hall. Disregarding the technical recording requirements, she insisted on facing the orchestra which had to be formed in a horseshoe format around her as if she were singing in opera. Nobody was to be allowed enter. Even De Valera, who had come to listen, had to suffer the indignity, it was rumoured, of listening through a keyhole. The songs recorded include Moore's 'When He Who Adores Thee', 'O Breathe Not His Name', 'Galway Bay' and 'L'Altra Notte' (from *Mefistofele*). While her breathing was somewhat more laboured and her voice had reverted back, not merely to its original mezzo pitch, but to a rich contralto, she sang with the old expressiveness of her youth. Like Maria Callas, two decades later, she had acquired another voice but one which her pride and memories of her glories as a soprano would not allow her to utilise. Despite repeated offers of concert tours of the country, she resolutely refused.

In 1946, a grieving Margaret attended the funeral of her friend and teacher, Mother Clement, who died at Eccles Street. Throughout her life the relationship of affection and respect between pupil and teacher was preserved by Margaret's brief and sporadic bulletins from Italy and the more lengthy letters of encouragement and advice from Mother Clement in Dublin.

Drifting from one social function to the next, entertaining friends in the foyers of the Shelbourne or the Gresham, her life in Dublin continued aimlessly. During the war years, she was a much sought-after guest at German, Italian and British Embassy and consulate functions. She was a frequent visitor to the United Arts Club in Fitzwilliam Street where she contributed to the cut and thrust conversation and gossip of the Dublin literary and artistic set. At Jammets and the Unicorn, two famed Dublin restaurants, she presided with aplomb over the dinner table. In 1941, she was made co-patron, with her fellow-artist (but, as she declared, 'not my friend',[46]) John McCormack, of the newly-founded Dublin Grand Opera Society. At the Society's seasons of opera to which both famous patrons were invited they assiduously avoided one another. They received admirers and friends in their separate boxes, rarely acknowledging each other's presence, but nevertheless surreptitiously observing who paid court at the rival box. The President of the Irish Tourist Board, Christopher F. Reddin, was among the many who admired both artists. Having paid his respects at the Count's box, unobserved as he imagined, he made his way along the back of the circle and entered La Sheridan's. 'Christopher,' she greeted him, 'are you on the side of the Montagues or Capulets tonight?'[47] The basis for her antipathy to McCormack is difficult to ascertain. McCormack's success, financially and otherwise, as a concert recitalist, particularly in the United States, and the warm regard he undoubtedly commanded in his own country as well as abroad, may have rankled with her. And yet, in opera, McCormack had never reached the heights in Italy which she had achieved. His career in opera in Italy had been, in effect, unsuccessful. McCormack's preferred medium was as definitely the concert platform as Margaret's was the operatic stage. His instincts were not of the theatre. She was of true theatrical mould. 'I never felt at ease in opera',[48] he confessed and it showed. On stage, he lacked credibility. 'By comparison, on the concert platform, by himself, as himself, McCormack exhibited a rare authenticity.'[49] Like Caruso, Margaret could declare, 'I am for opera – in costume, I am in character and comfortable.'[50] Margaret blamed McCormack, perhaps incorrectly, for blackening her name at HMV and at the Metropolitan in New York and in Chicago by saying that she was too temperamental to be employed. In view of Margaret's indecision on the offers received from the United States, neither the Metropolitan nor the Chicago Opera required McCormack to tell them something that was already apparent. However, the 'quarrel' seemed resolved during a performance at the Gaiety when Margaret agreed to visit the tenor in his box and on her return declared to her friends; 'When I saw the condition of the poor man, the spleen left me'.[51] When he died in 1945, her barely disguised slight that 'he had been a very fine lieder singer'[52] was revealing.

Louis Elliman, managing director of the Gaiety Theatre, usually reserved a box for Margaret, especially during opera seasons, the singer declaring that 'she did not mind where she sat in the theatre provided there was no-one in front of her'!'[53] As the lights dimmed, she would take her seat, and regally acknowledge the applause which regularly greeted her appearance. She was often irritatingly childish and wont to chatter and become a source of distraction, particularly if displeased by a performance. During the war years, when foreign companies were unable to travel to Ireland, opera was maintained at a high standard by local artists. During one such opera, a local soprano gave a memorable performance, receiving a standing ovation from the audience. In her box, Margaret rose also to acclaim the performance and momentarily the spotlight operator moved the light from the soprano on stage to the famous prima donna. The audience in turn applauded Margaret as she paid her tribute. At the curtain, Margaret went back-stage to convey her congratulations in person to the soprano only to be verbally attacked and accused of stealing her applause by the indignant singer. The incident serves to illustrate the parochial attitude frequently encountered by Margaret in Ireland. That an artist of her calibre would attend the performance of an almost-amateur production and generously laud the performance of an unknown artist was a tribute that was unfortunately lost on the singer, who misinterpreted a generous tribute, seeing only that her moment of glory had been stolen by 'another'. But as ever, Margaret had the last word: as she turned in disdain from the outburst, she cuttingly remarked, 'My dear, you're just a Woolworths' soprano'.[54]

On another occasion Margaret was called upon for an impromptu judgement from her box on the all-Irish production of *Madama Butterfly*. With disarming generosity, she expressed 'praise and appreciation of the achievements of my own fellow-countrymen and women . . . (who) . . . thrown on their own resources presented opera after opera in a manner which, believe me, compares favourably with any of the larger and richer companies in these islands'.[55] During the DGOS international season at the Gaiety in 1956, Margaret made a rare stage appearance. The final opera of the season was Verdi's *La Traviata*, which Margaret had seen performed on countless occasions by eminent artists in the most prestigious opera houses in Europe. Making her Dublin debut in the role of Violetta, a part which she would sing a record 648 times, was the Romanian soprano, Virginia Zeani. Highly impressed by the young artiste's performance, Margaret presented her with a much-treasured possession, the fan she herself had received from the great Melba many years previously at Covent Garden. 'I never saw anybody that I wanted to give the fan to before,' she explained, 'but this girl has so many qualities – temperament, voice, acting ability. I defy anybody to give the desperation of the *demi-mondaine* as perfectly as Zeani gave it in the second part of the first act. I've heard all the others, but she got it in every note. I have already written to the Metropolitan Opera House in New York commending Zeani to them. I think that she's as good as there is in opera today.'[56] Margaret's praise and recommendation of Zeani was fully vindicated by the soprano's subsequent brilliant career at the Metropoplitan. Now married to the celebrated bass, Nicolo Rossi-Lemeni, and Professor of Music at Indiana University, Zeani remembers meeting La Sheridan with great affection. 'Even before I had the pleasure of meeting her in person, I had often heard my teacher, the great Italian tenor, Aureliano Pertile, speaking of her beautiful voice, her stage presence and her musical personality.'[57] Regarding the fan, Madame Zeani recalled, 'I was particularly impressed by this fantastic present that she gave me with such generosity and even more impressed with her vibrant and elegant personality.'[58]

During her years in Dublin, Margaret always made time for any student who showed talent. She regularly attended the annual Feis Ceoil in Dublin, the launching pad of her own career, and was often called upon to present the awards to the successful competitors. One recipient, Phyllis Sullivan (nee Boland), recalled the interest and assistance given to her by the prima donna. In her apartment in Fitzwilliam Street, she coached her. 'Although temperamental,' she recalled, 'she never got annoyed when I made a mistake but would say "stop" and then she herself would sing it the right way.'[59] Her protegée concluded that Margaret's voice was still strong although she never sang the 'high notes'. 'It was very dramatic when she sang,' she remembered, 'her face would light up as though she "lived" every note and phrase.'[60] And in reply to her pupil's question as to why she did not sing in public, the Diva confided, 'My voice is finished. It's all right singing for you, darling, but I would break on my top notes and', she added, 'I am nervous.'[61]

A beautiful perpetual trophy, known as the 'Margaret Burke Sheridan Cup' presented in her memory by her friend, Prince Ferdinando d'Ardia Caracciolo, to the Feis Ceoil authorities, is now awarded annually to the most promising female vocalist in the competition.

The Irish soprano, Veronica Dunne, recalled and acknowledged Margaret's interest and help in the initial stages of her career and her dismay at Veronica's decision to put marriage and family before opera. 'She was as tremendous help to me in *La Bohème*', she recalled. 'She went through the entire opera with me, every movement, every subtlety. She showed me how to cry and how to express many of the more psychological aspects inherent in the character of Mimi. For instance, in the second act, when everyone is fussing over payment of the bill, to steal across to where Musetta's fur cape is lying, to take it up and to rub it against my face, then hesitantly to try it on, as a woman would something, especially fur, that she could not afford.'[62] For Veronica's Covent Garden debut in 1952, Margaret flew to London to see her protegée perform on the stage and in the part that she herself had rendered there so often in the past. It was Margaret's first plane journey and on entering the cabin, she looked intently at the faces of her fellow passengers and was heard to remark, 'Not a single face I would care to die with'.[63]

She had told her friends in Italy that she had returned to Ireland to establish a school of singing as colleagues like Pertile and Melis had done in Italy. But in this respect also she was to be disappointed. It was her one major regret that her undoubted talent in this regard was never capitalised upon by the music authorities. But Ireland was not Italy. Operatic training was very much a minority need and had low priority in the overall educational programme. 'She loved to teach,' her friend, May Piggott, wrote, 'because she learned so much from the difficulties of others. Her great ambition was to teach young Irish singers, not the elements of voice production, but the finishing touches that give poise and confidence. She asked me to get people interested in establishing her here . . . and was so hurt when no-one wanted to take advantage of all that she had to give.'[64] Her operatic colleagues in Italy urged her to return there. As late as 1946, Umberto Giordano wrote to invite 'La Bella Margherita'[65] to return to Milan to sing Maddalena once again in the fiftieth anniversary performance of *Andrea Chénier* at La Scala which Giordano, then seventy-nine years of age, was to and did conduct. Margaret declined and her friend, Maria Caniglia, sang in her place. She rarely alluded to the invitations that continued to come her way from Italy, but silently, perhaps sadly, added them to her ever increasing collection of operatic memorabilia.

When the war was over she made several return visits to London. In 1949, she went at the invitation of Lady Hambledon, to renew acquaintance with the conductor, Victor de Sabata, and, on the invitation of the Royal Opera House, to receive members of the La Scala Company. In June, she made some test recordings for Decca with piano accompaniment by Hubert Greenslade. The material recorded included 'L'Ultima Canzone' (Tosti), 'Rich and Rare' and 'Has Sorrow Thy Young Days Shaded'. The tests were, by her express orders, to be vetted by a 'committee' of her friends (in her absence) so that they might truthfully attest if they were of a standard she would approve. When they wrote to her that the collective opinion was in the negative, her reply was, 'thanks for the mercy killing'.[66] Apart from her visits to London and time spent with her friends Ferdinando and Maria d'Ardia Caracciolo on their estate, the Island in County Waterford, life seemed destined to continue along the aimless, empty path she had chosen, when incredibly America beckoned once again.

Margaret and the Taoiseach, Eamonn De Valera.

Margaret and the Irish tenor, Hubert Valentine, New York, 1952. (Courtesy: Hubert Valentine).

Tarrytown Castle, New York. Margaret's 'home' in America.

Mrs. Ruth Haughton Axe, Margaret and Mr. Frederick Rogers at the Metropolitan Opera House, New York. (Courtesy: *Capuchin Annual*).

CHAPTER X

VISSI d'ARTE
I Lived For Art 1950-1958

In 1950, Margaret was invited to New York by the director of the American National Arts Foundation, Carlton Smith. A philanthropic organisation, the Foundation was established to stimulate creation, interpretation and appreciation of the arts and to foster interchange of art and artists between nations. Members of the Advisory Committee included the Earl of Harewood, Sir Laurence Olivier, Katherine Cornell and, in the operatic field, the conductor, Bruno Walter, the general manager of the Metropolitan Opera, Rudolf Bing, and Ralph Vaughan Williams. This Committee advised the Foundation on the selection and training of promising young singers. In the spring, somewhat apprehensively, Margaret finally set out for the country whose allure she had resisted on so many occasions. Taking the tender from Cobh, County Cork, she sailed to New York on the *Queen Mary*.

Initially overcome by the sheer size, vitality and hospitality of the vast city, with typical astute assessment she soon found New York's measure. 'A scintillating, exacting and fascinating city,' she noted. 'It is a challenge from the first moment. New York can annihilate a person as easily as she can create a celebrity out of a nobody.'[1] She found it difficult at first to adapt to the lifestyle, and especially 'to the incessant noise which almost did for me'[2] but she soon found her feet and began to enjoy the experience and even to regret the missed opportunities of her career. 'I never went to the United States in all my career because I preferred to remain at La Scala. When I saw the United States and met the Americans I was very sorry for myself but too late . . . or was it?'[3] she wrote. As it transpired, it was not quite too late. Together with her former colleague at La Scala, Ezio Pinza, who had moved from opera to the Broadway stage where he was appearing in *South Pacific*, she was invited to become a member of the Advisory Committee of the Arts Foundation. Her function was one which she had hoped to have in

Ireland – to impart her knowledge and experience in the roles for which she had become famous to selected young artists.

News of her appointment was carried by American and Irish papers. Cardinal Spellman of New York wrote his congratulations; her records were featured on a coast-to-coast network radio programme entitled 'Voices that Live Forever' and messages of welcome and invitations poured into her rooms at the Barclay Hotel. As had happened in London and in Italy, her American friends whom (the Broadway producer and author Guthrie McClintic testified) 'she kept in a constant state of merriment, surprise, sometimes amounting to near-shock and, in some, utter enchantment'[4] fell under the spell of La Sheridan. She had previously met McClintic and his wife, the actress, Katherine Cornell, at a party in the Merrion Square apartment of the Irish novelist, Kate O'Brien, in Dublin. Late as ever, Margaret floated into the party and spoke with McClintic, who became fascinated with her. He confided to her that he was to have been introduced to some old broken-down prima donna whom Kate had invited but who thankfully had not turned up. Margaret drew him on even further, until Kate O'Brien came across and said to McClintic, 'I see you've met our famous prima donna'.[5] McClintic, naturally embarrassed, vowed that if ever Margaret came to the States, he would throw the best party ever in her honour. And at that party, Margaret met the millionaire couple, Emerson and Ruth Axe, who were to become her next and final patrons. Enjoying enormous wealth, even by American standards, they owned the Axe-Houghton Management Organisation, a mutual fund investment company. An economist, financial analyst, astute businessman, wine connoisseur and chess exponent, Emerson Axe's reserve and short temper were destined to be purposely fused and ignited by Margaret's temperamental behaviour and devastating jibes. Ruth Axe, with placid acceptance, endured the oftentimes erratic behaviour of her new friend. An intelligent woman and wealthy in her own right, she owned much property on Fifth Avenue where she had her office, was a member of the prestigious Fifth Avenue Cosmopolitan Club and a director of the Carlisle Hotel, the much-favoured haunt of the future president, John F. Kennedy. The Axes were agnostics, but Ruth, as her friendship with Margaret grew over the years, was impressed by the underlying spirituality she observed within Margaret's complex personality. Patrons of the arts and particularly of opera, the Axes were smitten by the extrovert prima donna and readily offered her hospitality during her American visits. Their home was an imposing castle near Tarrytown overlooking Sleepy Hollow on the

Hudson. Built in 1900 by General Howard Carroll, the son of a Civil War general, Tarrytown Castle resembles Lismore Castle in County Waterford. Special masons and carpenters were brought from Germany to quarry the stone and to fashion the hewn oak girders, beams and joists and the furniture. The dining hall accommodated one hundred guests beneath its beautiful rose window. The spacious grounds, enclosed by stone-cut walls, contained an arboretum of evergreens and rare varieties of deciduous trees and flowers. This extraordinary mansion was to become Margaret's American 'home' during her annual visits to America from 1951 to 1957.

Her friendship with the Axes deepened over the years and the couple, especially Ruth, went to quite extraordinary lengths to ensure that her every whim, and she had many, was satisfied. When she complained about the decor of the wing of the castle that had been especially designated for her use, her apartments were immediately redecorated to her choice. When she got bored with Tarrytown, they placed a Fifth Avenue apartment at her disposal, complete with a private maid. When she criticised the way the castle was administered, the servants, her apartments, or whatever happened to irritate her at the time, or disdainfully referred to Emerson, whom she seemed to delight in taunting, as 'patrone di casa', Ruth just shrugged and waited for the storm to pass, as it invariably did. But, as usual, her benefactors were well rewarded. 'Wherever Margherita was, there was theatre and excitement,' Emerson Axe remembered. 'She drew adventure to her. She was in fact a being of an older race, a sorceress with a personal magnetism and power beyond that of normal human beings today.'[7] And while she may have considered Tarrytown and its owners somewhat nouveau and lacking the authenticity and tradition of her Italian, British and Irish aristocratic connections, she did, however, meet many interesting people there. On one occasion, much to her delight, she was introduced to Penelope Witherington Hyde, the great-great-grand-daughter of the Irish patriot, Theobald Wolfe Tone. Margaret readily acknowledged the debt she owed the Axes. 'In New York,' she wrote, 'I made some very dear friends whose kindness and hospitality I can never forget and whose appreciation took me out of the dustbin and put me back on a pedestal.'[8]

The Axes introduced her to the wealthy and famous and, above all, to appreciative people. Her photo appeared in society magazines and newspapers; parties were given in her honour; she was regularly photographed with artists performing at the Metropolitan. In the Axe box at the opera, she once more renewed her contact with opera of the

Margaret with the soprano, Dorothy
Kirsten, at the Metropolitan, New York.
(Photo: *Opera News*).

Margaret congratulates Hilda Gueden, soprano at the
Metropolitan, New York. (Courtesy: *Capuchin Annual*).

With Mr. and Mrs. Barton G. Tremaine on a New York opening night.

At the fifty-third banquet of the American–Irish Historical Society in the Hotel Baltimore, New York.

Virginia Zeani, to whom Margaret presented her Melba fan in Dublin in 1954, with the fan inset. (Courtesy: Virginia Zeani).

highest quality. In October 1956, she attended the long-awaited and exciting debut of Maria Callas and she too was impressed by the sheer dramatic talent and vocal ability of the diva. As T. P. O'Connor had foretold, many of her compatriots welcomed her presence among them and well might she have wondered how different her life could have been had she accepted the offers to perform in the Metropolitan and in Chicago. She attended Irish literary evenings at Oriel House on Park Avenue, the home of the Irish-born scholar, Dr. Maurice Leahy, Professor at Columbia University, and attended many functions at the American Irish Historical Society. The Irish tenor, Hubert Valentine, then performing in opera and in concert in New York, remembered her 'as a really wonderful witty lady'.[9] He had originally met her at the HMV studios in Dublin on her return from Italy. She attended two of his concerts in Carnegie Hall and he met her socially subsequently. 'Hello Hubert. This is Maggie from Mayo',[10] was invariably how she would greet him on the phone. Now a broadcaster and presenter of a classical musical programme on radio in America, Hubert Valentine still plays her recordings 'for that special timbre and vocal quality I do not think we will ever have another to surpass her,' he wrote. 'There could only be ever one Sheridan.'[11]

She tired frequently of the hectic social pace and luxurious living and pined for home to which she returned for six months each year. Her friend, Father Leo Clifford, O.F.M., recalled how, on occasions when she needed to be alone and to rest, she would stay for short periods in a convent on Long Island. He had initially met the prima donna at a luncheon she gave in honour of the Italian priest composer, Monsignor Licinio Refice, then in Dublin to conduct his opera *Santa Cecilia* and whom Margaret had known in Italy. Like so many of his countrymen and women, Father Leo had then but a vague knowledge of her career. 'I saw the tremendous respect and veneration in which he (Monsignor Refice) held her as a person, as an artist; to him she was La Sheridan, the toast of musical Italy. She was the singer, he recalled, for whom his friend Pope Pius XI, sent so often when he was Archbishop of Milan. He told the Monsignor that when he heard her sing, 'the clouds were rifted and heaven came very near'.[12] Later, when he became Pope, he wanted to make her a Contessa. She declined. When he later asked her why she had refused the honour, Margaret told him that she had informed His Holiness, in her usual forthright manner, "I wouldn't know how to behave. I would let you down."[13]

Shortly after their first meeting in Dublin on a grey morning in November in 1954, Father Leo found himself standing alongside

Margaret in Cobh as they waited for the tender to take them out to the
S.S. America. 'It was a long, arduous journey,' he recalled. 'We parted
at the pier in New York and I thought I had seen Margaret for the last
time. How wrong I was. She came to visit me again and again and
became my closest friend in the New World.'[14] In no sense her spiritual
advisor, nonetheless he was struck by her deep-set, almost child-like
spirituality:

> 'She played at being very impious' [he recalled] 'but that was only a
> veneer. She had tremendous character and a great integrity and
> passion for the truth. Even the truth about herself as she had to face
> up to the unpalatable reality that she had lost her voice, her career
> and had little means. But she still maintained a sense of wonder, a
> sense of beauty, a sense of humour and an inner strength and
> belief.'[15]

She engaged him in long discourses on aspects of religion and life, on
death and things of the spirit. The applause, acclaim, the trappings of
her success, seemed to her by then, both artificial and empty. Perhaps
quoting from her own experience of life, she told him 'that for the
artist, in the world of profane pursuits, there had to be emptiness,
freedom, and detachment before there can be any dedication.'[16] He
remembered her in Tarrytown castle at times lonely and anxiously
awaiting the date of her departure to Ireland. 'She was restless in the
castle, restless in her apartment on Fifth Avenue, restless in the
convent where she occasionally went to relax and be at peace. She
talked about "my own country", of being among "her own people"
and fretfully awaited the date of her return to Ireland when her term at
the Foundation was completed.'[17] Among her personal papers, scrib-
bled in her hand at this time, are numerous biblical extracts, prayers
copied from religious articles, phrases and quotations which clearly
had a particular spiritual meaning for her. 'For I Jehovah thy God will
hold thy right hand saying unto thee, fear not I will help thee',[18] read
one such extracted piece.

   She was not possessive about her good fortune in America but was
generously prepared to share it with others less fortunate, often
spectacularly. On one of her return visits to Ireland, she encountered
Gabriel Walsh, later stage and film actor and scriptwriter of such box-
office hits as 'Quackser Fortune Has a Cousin in the Bronx' and 'Night
Flowers'. He was then a fifteen year-old commis waiter at the
Shelbourne Hotel. Seventh of fourteen children, he had left school at

A late photograph of Margaret in Dublin, c. 1956.

twelve years of age. In his first week at the Shelbourne, a breakfast tray arrived on the fifth floor via the dumb-waiter and young Walsh was told by another waiter, 'This is for you know who',[19] pointing to a door in the corridor. Not knowing the identity of the mystery occupant whom the rest of the staff regarded with some trepidation, the young waiter bravely knocked on the door and on receiving no reply, entered the room which appeared to be empty. But as he advanced, he heard movement from under the bed. 'In my innocence,' he later recalled, 'I got down on the floor, pushing the tray along the carpet towards the person whom I realised was a woman . . . a very beautiful woman. She looked at me through the folds of the overhanging bedclothes and burst out laughing.'[20] She rose from where she had been searching for a mislaid lipstick. Embarrassed, the young waiter fled from the room. Margaret left instructions that for the duration of her stay at the hotel, young Walsh was to serve her meals. That she was Margaret Sheridan, a prima donna, meant little to the young Dubliner. She spoke kindly to him and asked him about his background and his circumstances. He told her of his ambition, impossible as it then appeared, of one day going to America. Later, the Axes came to stay at the Shelbourne and Margaret arranged with the management that the young waiter was to serve them exclusively. Unknown to him, Margaret urged them to 'adopt' her protégé and bring him to America. With the agreement of his mother, the young waiter returned with the Axes, worked at Tarrytown castle and later was educated by them and eventually came to prominence on stage and screen. 'I was but a young lad running about with a tray in my hand . . . She made the effort to take the tray from me'[21] he later recorded in tribute to his famous benefactress.

Her work at the Foundation was interspersed with annual return visits to Ireland where her exploits and adventures in faraway America were reported to the surviving members of her coterie. Holding court in the lounge of the Shelbourne, she continued to entertain and amuse. All eyes and ears strained to look and listen in as the still bell-like musical voice rang through the air. Mischievously, she often deliberately misled the eavesdroppers – as when, relating to her friends (all the while conscious that her words were being listened to by a wider audience) of how she 'was so delighted to leave America and get back to my real homeland (pause) . . . *England.* "That shook them"',[22] she laughingly whispered to her friends. In 1954, she was on hand to welcome Gigli to Dublin when he performed at a concert at the Theatre Royal. With Ferdinando and Maria d'Ardia Caracciolo, she entertained him to lunch and re-lived their days of glory in *Andrea Chénier* in Rimini and London.

Behind the gaiety and the smile remained loneliness. To the outside world, it rarely manifested itself; within her it gnawed deep. Sometimes the mask dropped and the pain surfaced. Asked by a friend if she ever felt lonely, Margaret's honest reply revealed all. 'I've almost died of it',[23] she said. A fellow passenger recalled at Kingsbridge railway station how she observed the Diva's luggage being taken from the Cobh train after her return from a trip to America and piled high on the platform while Margaret searched for a taxi. 'My overwhelming thought was how strange and how sad that such a well-known and important lady should have arrived back in Dublin after a trans-atlantic voyage and have nobody to meet her. I wondered about her going into her house or flat and finding it empty and cold.'[24] Kathleen Joy Evans recalled the many midnight phone calls she received from Margaret, often lasting into the early hours of the morning as she sought someone to talk to. While the calls were often inconvenient and communicatively one-sided, there was always the compensation of Margaret's witticisms and irreverent comments. During one such late-night discourse, Margaret interrupted herself. 'Hold on', she told her friend. 'I've lost my beads in the bed.' There was a pause while she rummaged for the mislaid rosary beads and then with a chuckle, she said, 'One can lose so many things in a bed you know'.[25]

Without the assistance of Ruth Axe and a few close friends, her financial position at this time would have been untenable. Royalties from her records were negligible. But Ruth Axe was generous to her and ensured in the difficult final years that she lacked for no material comfort. The American's fortune was estimated to have been £500 million. She had no family and her intention was to leave a sizeable bequest to Margaret. In the event, Margaret predeceased her potential benefactor. What she might have done with such wealth is anybody's guess. Money never loomed large in her life and doubtless it would have been disposed of impulsively.

In 1951, Radio Eireann persuaded her to record her life-story which was appropriately entitled 'Vissi d'Arte'. Throughout the protracted recording, as ever fretful and temperamental, she was coaxed by her former school-friend, May Piggott, and by the charm and tact of a patient presenter, Norris Davidson, who, as a young man, had seen Margaret perform in Milan in her days of glory. During the production, her final singing performance was recorded. It was 'Galway Bay' – her recording of which, May Piggott recalled, 'was dramatic, operatic and much too low but so sincere that we decided to record it with no-one but the producer and myself in the studio.'[26] The recording was not broadcast. Norris Davidson endured the many tantrums of the Diva throughout the recording sessions. He understood, however, that, 'this arrogance, this superbia was with her all her life. She gloried in it; it was part of her period and of her brilliant career.'[27] As he recognised, Margaret was a product of her ancestral background, of the aristoratic society that befriended her in Ireland, England and in Italy and she was unquestionably in the tradition of the prima donna assoluta. There could be nothing ordinary or mundane about Margaret Sheridan and the normal conventions of society did not apply to her. She was 'beautiful, autocratic, witty, intelligent, with the most beautiful hands I have ever seen,'[28] according to the Irish actor, Joe Lynch, who looked forward to meeting her in the corridors of Radio Eireann during the recording of her life-story. He often carried her heavy box of records up the four flights of stairs to the studios. 'Thank you darling, you are the only Continental in the entire building,'[29] was her inimitable response to his gesture. He had never heard her sing and one day, as he struggled up the stairs with her records, told her so; whereupon she stopped abruptly in the corridor and sang 'Caro Nome', much to his delight and that of the occupants of the offices along the corridor who came to their doors to listen.

Margaret's last visit to the United States was from October 1956 to April 1957. During her stay there, she complained of feeling unwell, but nevertheless struggled to fulfill her professional and social commitments. Towards the New Year, it became apparent that she was indeed quite ill. Ruth Axe persuaded her to seek medical assistance. It was diagnosed that she had developed cancer of the breast. She entered a clinic in New York where she underwent treatment in an attempt to arrest the malignant growth. The treatment was painful. 'I've gone through hell, hell, hell,'[30] she confided to Father Leo. Pressed by her friends to remain in New York and continue the treatment, her longing for home proved too strong. 'I am on my way home,' she wrote to a friend in Dublin from the *S.S. America*. 'I have not been so well.'[31] Ruth Axe booked her into the Shelbourne Hotel. It became apparent, however, shortly after her return to Dublin, that she had developed secondary cancer of the spine.

Some months before her death, she entered the Pembroke Nursing Home attached to Saint Vincent's Hospital. In her hospital room, she played out the remaining months of her remarkable life with dignity and not a little courage. Ruth Axe arranged that she should have the best suite in the exclusive section of the nursing home. The suite had once been occupied by the Irish patriot, Arthur Griffith, who had died there in 1922. Margaret irreverently professed experiencing 'a great sense of history "every time she went to the loo!"'[32]

Her physician, Dr. Roderick Mansfield, remembered with affection his fascinating patient. 'From the first moment of our meeting we established a rapport that happily continued throughout the duration of her final illness. It was a wonderful experience to have known her. After meeting her she somehow became part of your life and made you part of hers. She was extremely perceptive and sensitive to people, to atmosphere. She could instantly sense insincerity, flattery (smarm as she called it) or if somebody tried to be patronising towards her, and she had little tolerance in this regard. While outwardly she appeared worldly and sophisticated, inwardly there was a simplicity, an almost virginal innocence and an impish sense of fun.'[33] He recalled that hypnosis was tried in an attempt to alleviate the pain (she had refused morphine, preferring to endure the pain so that she might retain complete mental awareness until the last). As the hypnotist went through the various stages, telling her that she was feeling drowsy, that her eyelids were closing, that one arm was feeling light as air, etc., the phone suddenly rang beside her bed. With eyes closed in an apparent totally relaxed state, she lifted one arm, brought the phone slowly to her ear and in a low voice, told the caller, 'I'm being hypnotised, call back later,' and to the hypnotist said, 'please continue'.[34]

She knew she was dying, and confided with her friends as Micheál Mac Liammóir reported: 'She gave us the news carelessly, gaily, with a certain delicate irony in her own characteristic blend of Italian and English words all mixed together, "Caro mio, non veramente, sono finita. I'm not joking, you know".'[35] Temperamental still in her illness, she nevertheless faced the end with gay, even impudent, courage, her spirit undimmed. Events from her eventful and colourful past she related now, often prefaced with humorous reminders to herself of the inevitability of her illness. 'I'll remember that story till the day I die . . . and that won't be long'[36] she would say. Although never religious in a narrow, pious way, she had a deep faith in God and in the hereafter. Clutching her mother's prayerbook from her far-off childhood days in Castlebar, she, at times almost cheerfully, endured the pain and discomfort. A picture of Christ hung at the bottom of her bed and her opinion was that, 'He was not only a supreme Artist but a great Sport as well'.[37] Her friends, including Father Leo Clifford and Ruth Axe, who arrived from America to be near her, Prince and Princess d'Ardia Caracciolo, Colonel John Fagan, Gwladys McCabe, the Taoiseach

Mr. De Valera and James Dillon, visited her regularly and watched the sands of time run their course on a spirit which seemed too vital to be thought mortal.

Light-heartedly, she made her final arrangements for her funeral, her grave ('I'll be tippy toes with Dev's secretary, Kathleen O'Connell',[38] she told Cyril Cusack), and her personal estate. She appointed Major John Fagan, Princess Mary d'Ardia Caracciolo and Ruth Axe as executors. She instructed John Fagan in detail regarding the disposal of her small estate, with bequests to friends and acquaintances and mementos to the porter and elevator operator in the Shelbourne Hotel. She ordered that her mother's prayerbook and a rosary beads given her by Mother Clement were to be placed in her coffin.

For months she lingered, waiting as ever to go on; knowing that her next entrance would be as she had predicted, 'an entry when you deliver all your operatic visiting cards at once'.[39]

On 16th April 1958 – the eve of the opening of the Dublin Grand Opera Society's presentation of *Manon Lescaut* by the visiting Italian Opera Company, Margaret, with perfect timing, chose to make her final exit. From the stage of the Gaiety Theatre, silence for a little while replaced the music of Puccini as members of the cast, Italian and Irish, paid tribute to the memory of one of the greatest Manons of all time. His excellency, Sean T. O'Kelly, President of Ireland and long-time friend, paid a personal tribute. 'When I first met the girl from Mayo who was to become and for many years to remain, one of Italy's most admired, most beloved prima donnas', he recalled, she was young and full of gaiety and charm, sparkling, radiant, devoted to her art. That was many years ago. To very few women', he added, 'or men, was it given to grow old with such grace and dignity. Something of the warmth and colour of life went with her when she died.'[40] The Italian Ambassador to Ireland, his Excellency Signore Aldo Mazio, on behalf of his 'Government, country and countrymen', spoke words in tribute that would have gladdened her heart. 'She was a great friend of my country,' he said. 'Italy admired and loved her. She was more than a prima donna. She was literally the first great lady of the opera houses of Rome, Milan and Naples. Toscanini and Puccini will ever be linked with her name. My countrymen cherish the memory of the years she spent with us. She made us the gift not only of her golden voice but of her generous, warm Irish heart.'[41] Her friend and executrix, Mary (Boodie) d'Ardia Caracciolo, an Irishwoman married to an Italian, aptly described La Sheridan. 'The sunshine of Italy was in her eyes;

Ebe Stignani, who sang at Margaret's
funeral requiem.

Major John Fagan, her executor.
(Courtesy: *Capuchin Annual*).

Her grave at Glasnevin Cemetery.
Inscription: FRONT; Margaret Burke-Sheridan.
Castlebar October 15, 1889. Dublin April 16, 1958.
BACK; Margherita Sheridan. Prima Donna.
La Scala, Milan. Covent Garden, London.
(Photo: S. Cashman)

the age-old sorrows of Ireland were in her voice, rich with the deep beauty of her native land.'[42]

In Italy, news of her death was received with sorrow by those who remembered her as a friend and an artist. At La Scala, a spokesman declared that her death 'had spread a veil of sorrow'[43] over the centenary celebrations of Puccini's birth, then in progress there. The composer's daughter-in-law gave testimony to anyone who may have doubted or who never knew in what high regard she had been held by the famous composer.

Led by the Taoiseach, Mr. De Valera, government ministers, singers, musicians, representatives of every branch of the theatrical profession, members of the visiting Italian opera company, friends and acquaintances, her remains were removed to University Chapel on St. Stephen's Green. Her requiem mass was appropriately sung by the great Italian mezzo-soprano, Ebe Stignani and by the American soprano, Gloria Davy. A handful of faithful friends followed her cortege to Glasnevin cemetery.

And it is there she lies, surrounded by many whose lives had been touched and brightened by the unforgettable and lovable La Sheridan. Alongside is the grave of her good friend and executor, John Fagan, across from her the graves of De Valera and Dr. Pádraig de Brún, and at her feet, her friend, Kathleen O'Connell, who died before her in 1956. Her tomb, which Ruth Axe arranged to be executed and placed in perpetual care, is inscribed with the simple epitaph she would have most appreciated, 'Margherita Sheridan, Prima Donna'.

'She has passed on', Micheál Mac Liammóir recorded in tribute,

'as I believe and as she believed herself to another cycle of labours, of adventures in a sphere of fathomless mystery and we who are left behind for a little may well feel reassured that she will acquit herself with beauty and with honour. Her faith in God was great. God will be good to her. Arrivaderci, Carissima Margherita.'[44]

Commemorative stamp issue by An Post, the Irish Post Office,
27th July 1989. By kind permission.

IN MEMORIAM

Puccini's favourite Butterfly —
thrice silent nor the fluttering fan
on stage in your Opera House, Milan
when you of the soaring feather-voice
caught in the throat that MacSwiney
   should die
stopped for country you could not work
the scene. And now, dear Margaret Burke-
Sheridan, how could we not rejoice
gladdened in memory — Butterfly feet
a twinkle down Dublin's Grafton Street.

— Cyril Cusack

Mícheál Mac Liammóir (left)
with Hilton Edwards.
(Courtesy: The Gate Theatre)

APPENDIX 1

Margaret Sheridan: Performed Operatic Repertoire

Opera	Composer	Date of First Performance	Theatre
La Bohème (Mimi)	Puccini	3 February 1918	Costanzi, Roma
Iris (Iris)	Mascagni	8 July 1919	Covent Garden, London
Madama Butterfly (Cho Cho San)	Puccini	30 December 1919	Dal Verme, Milano
Mefistofele (Marguerite)	Boito	26 December 1920	Dal Verme, Milano
La Wally (Wally)	Catalani	7 January 1922	San Carlo, Napoli
Belfagor (Candida)	Respighi	26 April 1923	La Scala, Milano
Andrea Chénier (Maddalena)	Giordano	August 1923	Vittorio Emanuele, Rimini
Manon Lescaut (Manon)	Puccini	September 1923	Vittorio Emanuele, Rimini
I Compagnacci (Anna Maria)	Riccitelli	15 November 1923	La Scala, Milano
Gianni Schicchi (Lauretta)	Puccini	28 June 1926	Covent Garden, London
Turandot (Liù)	Puccini	27 June 1928	Covent Garden, London
Othello (Desdemona)	Verdi	16 June 1930	Covent Garden, London

APPENDIX 2

Performances

1918
Costanzi, Roma - *La Bohème* - Puccini 3rd February - 13 performances
M. Sheridan / N. Marmora (Mimi); S. Paoli; C. Hackett / U. Macnez L. Bergamini; A. Romboli / B. Franci; / L. Peroni; A. Muzio; C. Melocchi / G. Cirino; C. Di Cola. Orchestra Conductor: T. De Angelis

1919
Covent Garden, London - *La Bohème* - Puccini - 27th May - 4 performances
M. Sheridan (Mimi); O. Lynn; T. Burke; A. Maguenat; E. Cotreuil; P. Malatesta; U. Scaravelli. Orchestra Conductor: P. Pitt.

Covent Garden, London – *Iris* – Mascagni – 8th July – 3 performances (British première)
M. Sheridan (Iris); G. Huberdeau; R. Couzinou; A. Capuzzo; K. Destournel; A. Algos; A. Gilly. Orchestra Conductor: L. Mugnone

Dal Verme, Milano – *Madama Butterfly* – Puccini – 30th December – 8 performances
M. Sheridan / L. Villani (Cho Cho San); N. Garrone; T. Schinetti; R. Endrigo; E. De Marco; A. Delgado; P. Friggi; A. Beneditti. Orchestra Conductor: A. Ferrari

1920
Dal Verme, Milano – *La Bohème* – Puccini – 22nd February – 10 performances
M. Sheridan (Mimi); R. Bardelli / A. Rettore; R. Endrigo; C. Del Corso; F. Autori; D. Cremonesi; A. Benedetti / D. Carmenali. Orchestra Conductor: A. Ferrari / G. Tronchi

Dal Verme, Milano – *Mefistofele* – Boiti – 26th December
M. Sheridan (Marguerite); N. De Angelis; A. Giorgini. Orchestra Conductor: A. Ferrari

1921
San Carlo, Napoli – *Madama Butterfly* – Puccini – 26th February – 14 performances
M. Sheridan / T. Mura (Cho Cho San); G. Di Bernardo / F. Villa; F. Tafuro; L. Paci / M. Gubbiani / Tisci-Rubini; Papaccio. Orchestra Conductor: V. Bellezza / A. Canepa

1922
San Carlo, Napoli – *La Wally* – Catalani – 7th January – 6 performances
M. Sheridan / H. Spani (Wally); L. Paikin; F. Lo Giudice; G. Baratto; C. Percy / M. Dupui. Orchestra Conductor: E. Mascheroni

La Scala, Milano – *La Wally* – Catalani – 6th April – 7 performances
M. Sheridan (Wally); M. De Voltri; L. Bertana; U. Di Lelio; L. Marini / N. Piccaluga; G. Noto; A. Baracchi. Orchestra Conductor: E. Panizza

Theatre Royal, Dublin – Concert Recital – 30th November – 2 performances
M. Sheridan; W. McNally; Barzotti; C. Diaz. Accompanists: Dr. V. O'Brien, L. Malajoli

1923
La Scala, Milano – *Belfagor* – Respighi – 26th April – 4 performances (World Première)
M. Sheridan (Candida); F. Merli; M. Stabile; G. Azzimonti; G. Azzolini; C. Ferrari; A. Gramegna; T. Vitulli; I. Mannarini; A. Galli; G. Nessi. Orchestra Conductor: A. Guarnieri

Teatro Vittorio Emanuele, Rimini – *Manon Lescaut* – Puccini – August
M. Sheridan (Manon)

Teatro Vittorio Emanuele, Rimini – *Andrea Chénier* – Giordano – 26th August
M. Sheridan (Maddalena); B. Gigli (Chènier); B. Franci. Orchestra Conductor: A. Guarnieri

Teatro Comunale di Cento – *Manon Lescaut* – Puccini – 15th September – 9 performances
M. Sheridan (Manon); E. Bergamaschi; E. Badini; G. Pedroni; G. Quinzi-Tapergi; L. Cilla; M. Sampieri; G. Marchesini; M. Zana. Orchestra Conductor: G. Bavagnoli

La Scala, Milano – *I Compagnacci* – Riccitelli – 15th November – 6 performances
M. Sheridan (Anna Maria); E. Badini; C. Alabiso; N. Bavaro; G. Nessi; G. Quinzi-Tapergi; A. Tedeschi. Orchestra Conductor: V. Gui

1924

Monte Carlo, Monaco – *Madama Butterfly* – Puccini – 27th January – 2 performances
M. Sheridan (Cho Cho San); Bilhon; Smirnoff; Castellaneto; A. Gilardi; Sorret; Garzo. Orchestra Conductor: V. De Sabata

Teatro Ponchelli, Cremona – *Manon Lescaut* – Puccini – 9th February – 6 performances
M. Sheridan (Manon); P. Menescaldi; G. Spadarotti / M. Gubbioli; A. Gilardi; O. Carozzi; G. Novelli; V. Ferraro. Orchestra Conductor: F. Ghione

La Scala, Milano – *Andrea Chénier* – Giordano – 14th May – 3 performances
M. Sheridan (Maddalena); L. Marini; B. Franci; F. Franchi; F. Autori; A. Baracchi; G. Pedroni; A. Tedeschi; I. Mannarini; G. Nessi; G. Menni; A. Galli; F. Ronchi. Orchestra Conductor: V. Gui

Teatro Comunale, Bologna – *Andrea Chénier* – Giordano – 26th November – 7 performances
M. Sheridan (Maddalena); G. Lauri Volpi; F. Merli; C. Galeffi; L. Nocenti; I. Ronchi; I. Mannarini; F. Franchi; N. Villa; P. Girardi; C. Bonfanti. Orchestra Conductor: S. Failoni

Carlo Felice, Genova – *La Wally* – Catalani – 28th December
M. Sheridan (Wally); E. Marchini; G. Ciampaglia; S. Caceffo / A. Gingolani; E. Grandini; L. Fabbronni. Orchestra Conductor: S. Failoni

1925

Teatro Comunale, Modena – *Madama Butterfly* – Puccini – 18th February
M. Sheridan (Cho Cho San); F. Tumminello; N. Menikoff
and
The quartette from Act III of *La Bohème*

M. Sheridan; E. Corti; F. Tumminello; N. Menikoff. Orchestra Conductor: I. Nini-Bellucci

Covent Garden, London – *Madama Butterfly* – Puccini – 17th June – 2 performances
M. Sheridan (Cho Cho San); E. Bennie / M. Blyth; J. Bourguignon; E. Badini; U. Lappas / F. Lo Giudice; L. Cilla / O. Dua; P. Jones; M. Sampieri; D. Noble; W. Roger; E. Wynn; C. Crang. Orchestra Conductor: S. Failoni

Covent Garden, London – *Andrea Chénier* – Giordano – 2nd July – 3 performances
M. Sheridan (Maddalena); G. Lauri Volpi; B. Franci; J. Bourguignon; G. Caro; E. Cotreuil; D. Noble; M. Sampieri; P. Malatesta; L. Cilla; O. Dua; F. Hitchin. Orchestra Conductor: L. Mugnone

Politeama Rossetti, Trieste – *Andrea Chénier* – Giordano – 15th November – 5 performances
M. Sheridan (Maddalena); G. Lauri Volpi; V. Guicciardi; F. Franchi; P. Votto; R. Autori; S. Beccucci; A. Brambilla; M. Basili; C. Bernini; V. Vittori; B. Silvani; G. Salani; B. Prodam. Orchestra Conductor: A. Ferrari

Politeama Rossetti, Trieste – *Madama Butterfly* – Puccini – 29th November – 1 performance
M. Sheridan (Cho Cho San); F. Tumminello; G. Vanelli; F. Franchi; Bertini. Orchestra Conductor: A. Ferrari

Teatro Municipale di Piacenza – *Manon Lescaut* – Puccini – 27th December – 3 performances
M. Sheridan (Manon); C. Togliani; A. Minghetti; A. Ailfieri; A. Bregola; P. Sbrana; G. Moresco; A. Caravello. Orchestra Conductor: G. Armani

1926

Teatro Grande di Brescia – *Manon Lescaut* – Puccini – 26th January – 10 performances
M. Sheridan (Manon); N. Piccaluga; C. Togliani; A. Ailfieri; A. Bregola; G. Moresco; A. Caravello; P. Sbrana. Orchestra Conductor: V. Bellezza

Covent Garden, London – *La Bohème* – Puccini – 24th May – 3 performances
M. Sheridan (Mimi); R. Torri / A. Rettore; A. Minghetti; G. Noto / J. Brownlee; E. Badini; E. Cotreuil; P. Malatesta; N. Schocknov. Orchestra Conductor: V. Bellezza

Covent Garden, London – *Gianni Schicchi* – Puccini – 28th June – 1 performance
M. Sheridan (Lauretta); E. Badini; J. Bourguignon; C. Willis; A. Rettore; E. McDermid; A. Minghetti; L. Cilla; F. Collier; E. Cotreuil; D. Noble; P. Malatesta; M. Sampieri; F. Le Pla; N. Roe. Orchestra Conductor: V. Bellezza

1927

San Carlo, Napoli – *Madama Butterfly* – Puccini – 4th January – 9 performances
M. Sheridan / B. Wallrott (Cho Cho San); D. Borgioli / N. Ederle; E. Ghirardini; A. Apolloni; S. Jamadori; O. Arduino. Orchestra Conductor: E. Vitale / T. De Angelis

1928

Covent Garden, London – *La Bohème* – Puccini – 7th June – 5 performances
M. Sheridan (Mimi); M. Carosio; A. Pertile; S. Inghilleri; S. Baccaloni; A. Baracchi; P. Harris; L. Manfrini. Orchestra Conductor: V. Bellezza

Covent Garden, London – *Turandot* – Puccini – 27th June – 4 performances
M. Sheridan (Liù); E. Turner (Turandot); S. Baccaloni; A. Baracchi; A. Lindi; N. Palai; G. Nessi; M. Sampieri; O. Dua. Orchestra Conductor: V. Bellezza

Carlo Felice, Genova – *Manon Lescaut* – Puccini – 30th December – 5 performances
M. Sheridan / A. Oltrabella (Manon); G. Amato; N. Piccaluga; A. Rubino; F. Belli. Orchestra Conductor: G. Armani

1929

Covent Garden, London – *Turandot* – Puccini – 6th June – 1 performance
M. Sheridan (Liù); E. Turner (Turandot); F. Autori; A. Baracchi; L. Cilla; F. Merli; G. Nessi; M. Sampieri; O. Dua. Orchestra Conductor: V. Bellezza

Covent Garden, London – *Manon Lescaut* – Puccini – 18th June – 1 performance
M. Sheridan (Manon); A. Pertile; E. Badini; S. Baccaloni; L. Cilla; N. Kovaceva; A. Barrett; G. Nessi; M. Sampieri. Orchestra Conductor: V. Bellezza

Covent Garden, London – *La Bohème* – Puccini – 24th June – 1 performance
M. Sheridan (Mimi); C. Melis; H. Nash; G. Inghilleri; F. Autori; A. Baracchi; S. Baccaloni; P. Harris. Orchestra Conductor: V. Bellezza

1930

Il Teatro Regio, Torino – *Andrea Chénier* – Giordano – 26th January – 9 performances
M. Sheridan / E. Maroli / M. L. Fanelli (Maddalena); A. Pertile / L. Marini; A. Granforte; Pantalloni; M. Neveso; E. Carabelli; Coletti; L. Cilla; S. Serra; P. Ferretti; B. Carmassi. Orchestra Conductor: F. Capuana

Il Teatro Regio Torino – *Gianni Schicchi* – Puccini – 10th February – 5 performances
M. Sheridan / A. Gargiula (Lauretta); E. Badini; A. Pertile / C. Solari; E. Carabelli; L. Cilla; A. Muzio; V. Bettoni; M. Serra; A. Righi-Tarugi; P. Ferretti; P. Giuliani; E. Gorone; G. De Rosa; M. Neveso; N. Caduana. Orchestra Conductor: F. Capuana

Covent Garden, London – *Andrea Chénier* – Giordano – 27th May – 2 performances
M. Sheridan (Maddalena); B. Gigli; G. Inghilleri; N. Kovaceva; G. Palmer; G. Tomei; D. Noble; M. Sampieri; A. Baracchi; L. Cilla; O. Dua. Orchestra Conductor: V. Bellezza

Covent Garden, London – *Madama Butterfly* – Puccini – 30th May – 1 performance
M. Sheridan (Cho Cho San); T. Beltacchi; A. Minghetti; C. Groome; D. Noble; O. Dua; A. Baracchi; G. Tomei; M. Sampieri; C. Crang; J. Mitchell; H. Wilton. Orchestra Conductor: J. Barbirolli

Covent Garden, London – *Othello* – Verdi – 16th June – 1 performance
M. Sheridan (Desdemona); T. Beltacchi; R. Zanelli; M. Stabile; L. Cilla; F. Autori; O. Dua; M. Sampieri; A. Baracchi. Orchestra Conductor: V. Bellezza

Other Venues –
Information unobtainable / unavailable
Cascina

APPENDIX 3

Margaret Sheridan — A Discography
BY ALAN KELLY

(All recordings were made for The Gramophone Company (HMV) except for the test sessions with Decca)

(1) *22nd November, 1915, Hayes* with piano.
HO 2125ab Test Mattinata (Leoncavallo)
HO 1269ac Test *Madama Butterfly*: Un bel di (Puccini)

(2) *4th June, 1926, Covent Garden Opera House, London.*
Recorded during a public performance with Angelo Minghetti (tenor), Giuseppe Noto (baritone), Aurora Rettore (soprano), Edouard Cotreuil (bass), Ernesto Badini (baritone) Pompilio Malatesta (bass), Chorus and Orchestra of the Royal Opera conducted by Vincenzo Bellezza.

(Performers are indicated by their initials; eg AM, GN, etc).

La Bohème (Puccini)
CR397—1: Non sono in vena, Act 1 MS AM; 1A: *do*; 1B: *do*.
CR398—1: O soave fanciulla, Act 1 MS AM; 1A: *do*; 1B: *do*.
CR399—1: Dal mio cervel, Act 2 AM GN EB; 1A: *do* 2-054159; 1B: *do*.
CR400—1: Gioventù mia, Finale Act 2 MS AM AR GN EC EB PM; 1A: *do* 2-054503 (RLS742); 1B: *do*.
CR401—1: Duo Mimi-Marcello, Act 3 MS GN; 1A: *do*; 1B: *do*.
CR402—1: Quartetto & Finale, Act 3 MS AM AR GN; 1A: *do*; 1B: *do*.
CR403—1: Io pur vidi, Act 4 2-054160 AM GN EB; 1A: *do*; 1B: *do*.
CR404—1: Gavotta, menuetto, Act 4 MS AM AR GN; 1A: *do*; 1B: *do*.
CR405—1: Dormè Ripose, Finale Act 4 2-054504 (RLS742) MS AM AR GN EC EB; 1A: *do*; 1B: *do*.

(3) *8th October, 1926, "C" Studio, small Queen's Hall, London* with piano accompaniments by Miss Goodman.

Bb9290-1 *Madama Butterfly*: Un bel di (Puccini)
Bb9291-1 Danny Boy (Weatherly)

(4) *13th October, 1926 "C" Studio, small Queen's Hall, London* with piano accompaniments by Madame Adami.
Bb9291—2: Danny Boy (Weatherley); 3: *do*.
Bb9304—1: Madama Butterfly: Un bel di (Puccini); 2: *do*.
Cc9305—1: *Otello:* Ave Maria (Verdi).

(5) *1st November, 1926, "C" Studio, small Queen's hall, London* with orchestra conducted by Eustace Blois (6 1st violins, 4 2nd violins, 2 violas, 2 cellos, double bass, tuba, 3 flutes, 2 oboes, cor anglais, 2 clarinets, harp, bass clarinet, 3 bassoons, 4 horns, 3 trumpets, 2 trombones, tympani.
Cc9380—1: *Otello:* Ave Maria (Verdi); 1A: *do*; 2: *do* 2-053274 DB981 IRX19 Victor 7102; 2A: *do*.
Cc9381—1: *Madama Butterfly*: Un bel di (Puccini); 1A: *do*; 2: *do*; 2A: *do*.
Cc9382—1: *Lohengrin*: Sola nei miei prim'anni (Wagner); 1A: *do*.

(6) *4th November, 1926 "C" Studio, small Queen's Hall, London* with piano accompaniments by Madame Adami.
Bb9291—4: Danny Boy (Weatherley); 4A: *do*; 5: *do*; 5A *do*.
Bb9403—1A: I know where I'm going (arr Hughes); 2: *do*; 2A: *do* 3-3115 DA832 IR307; 3: *do* 3A: *do*;

(7) *22nd November, 1926 "C" Studio, small Queen's Hall, London* with piano accompaniments by Madame Adami.
Bb9291—6: Danny Boy (Weatherley); 6A: *do*; 7: *do* 3-3120 DA832 IR307; 7A: *do*; 8: *do*; 8A: *do*.

(8) *24th November, 1926 "C" Studio, small Queen's Hall, London* with orchestra as above.
Cc9381—3: *Madama Butterfly*: Un bel di (Puccini); 3A: *do*; 4: *do*; 4A: *do*; 5: *do*; 5A: *do* 2-053275 DB981 IRX19 Victor 7102 (HLM7076).
Cc9382—2: *Lohengrin*: Sola nei miei prim'anni (Wagner); 2A: *do*; 3: *do* 2-053276 DB988 IRX20; 3A: *do*.
Cc9483—1: *Bohème*: Si, mi chiamano Mimi (Puccini), 2-053277 DB988 IRX20 (HLM7076); 1A: *do*; 2: *do*; 2A: *do*; 3 *do*.

(9) *7th July, 1927, "D" Studio, small Queen's Hall, London* (relayed from Kingsway Hall, London) with orchestra and chorus conducted by Eugene Goossens (1st violin - Marjorie Hayward, 2nd violin, harp, oboe, mustel organ, celeste, tuba)
CR1437—1: *Madama Butterfly*: Ancora un passo (Puccini), with chorus; 2: *do* 2-053298 DB1084 Victor 7064.
CR1438—1: *Madama Butterfly*: E questo, Act 2; 2: *do*; 3: *do* 2-053299 DB1084 Victor 7064 (HLM7076).
CR1439—1: *Madama Butterfly*: Death of Butterfly, with Browning Mummery; 2: *do* 2-054180 (E2901731, side 10 in EX29 0169 3).

(10) *14th July, 1927, "D" Studio, small Queen's Hall, London* (relayed from Kingsway hall, London) with orchestra as above.
BR1451—1: Believe me if all those endearing young charms (Moore arr G W Byng), violin by Marjorie Hayward; 2: *do* 3-3185 DA906 IR308; 3: *do*.
BR1452—1: Come back to Erin (Claribel arr G W Byng), violin by Marjorie Hayward; 2: *do* 3-3186 DA906 IR308; 3: *do*.

(11) *9th November, 1927, Conservatorio, Milan* with members of the Orchestra of La Scala conducted by Carlo Sabajno (12 1st violins, 10 2nd violins, 8 violas, 6 cellos, 6 double bass, piccolo, 2 flutes, 2 oboes, 2 clarinets, 2 cor anglais, 2 bassoons, 4 horns, 2 trumpets, 3 trombones, tuba, tympani, harp, drums, bass clarinet).

Duets with Aureliano Pertile
CD4916—1: *Madama Butterfly*: Bimba dagli occhi miei (Puccini); 2: *do*; 2-054185 DB1119 IRX21 Victor 6382 (HLM7076).
CD4917—1: *Madama Butterfly*: Io t'ho germita; 2: *do*; 2-054186 DB1119 IRX21 Victor 6382 (HLM7076).

(12) *12th November, 1927, Conservatorio, Milan* with orchestra as above.
Duet with Aureliano Pertile
CD4917-3: *Madama Butterfly*: Io t'ho germita (Puccini)

(13) *23rd July, 1928, 'C' Studio, small Queen's Hall, London* with piano accompaniments by Gerald Moore.
Bb14212—1: The lover's curse (arr. Hughes); 2: *do*; 3-3314 DA985.
Bb14213—1:Down by the Sally Gardens (arr. Hughes), 3-3315 DA987; 2: *do*; 3: *do*.
Bb14214—1: The Gartan Mother's lullaby (arr. Hughes); 2: *do* 3-3317 DA987.
Bb14215—1: The meeting of the waters (Moore); 2: *do* 3-3316 DA985

(14) *24th April, 1929, Milan* with members of the Orchestra of La Scala conducted by Carlo Sabajno

Duets with Aureliano Pertile
CM834—1: *Manon Lescaut*: Tu tu amore (Puccini), 2-054282 DB1281 Victor 7157 (HLM7076); 1A: *do*; 2: *do*; 2A: *do*.
CM835—1: *Manon Lescaut*: O tentatrice, 2-054283 DB1281 Victor 7157 (HLM7076); 1A: *do*; 2: *do*; 2A *do*.

(15) *29th April, 1929, Milan* with orchestra as above.

Duets with Aureliano Pertile
CM844—1: *Andrea Chénier*: Vicino a te (Giordano); 1A: *do*; 2: *do*; 2A: *do*; 3: *do* 2-054287 DB1289 Victor 7178 (HLM7076); 3A: *do*.
CM845—1: *Andrea Chénier*: La nostra morte, 2-054288 DB1289 Victor 7178 (HLM7076); 1A: *do*; 2: *do*; 2A: *do*.

(16) *15th July, 1929, 'C' Studio, small Queen's Hall, London* with string quintet conducted by Lawrance Collingwood (1st violin, 2nd violin, viola, cello, piano).
Bb17191—1: Killarney (trad) 2: *do*; 2A: *do*.
Bb17192—1: *Bohemian Girl*: I dreamt I dwelt (Balfe); 1A: *do*; 2: *do* 30-1022 DA1078 IR392; 2A: *do*.
Bb17193—1: An Irish love song Op 22 (Margaret Lang); 1A: *do*.
Bb17194—1: Barney O'Hea (Samuel Lover); 2: *do*; 2A: *do*.
Bb17195—1: The Kerry Dance (Molloy);

1A: *do*; 2: *do* 30-881 DA1078; 2A: *do*.
Bb17196—1: Must I go bound (arr H.
Hughes); 2: *do*; 2A: *do*.

(17) *13th December, 1929, Milan* with
members of the Orchestra of La Scala
conducted by Carlo Sabajno (12 1st violins,
10 2nd violins, 8 violas, 7 cellos, 6 double
bass, piccolo, 2 flutes, 2 clarinets, 2 oboes,
cor anglais, bassoon, contra bassoon, 4
horns, 3 trumpets, 3 tenor & 3 bass
trombones, tuba, tympani, drum, celeste,
harp).

Duets with Renato Zanelli
CM1333—1: *Otello*: Già nella notte densa
(Verdi); 2: *do* 32-1129 DB1395 Victor 7367 '
(HLM7076).
CM1334—1: *Otello*: Ed io vedea; 2: *do*
32-1130 DB1395 Victor 7367 (HLM7076).

(18) *8th July, 1930, 'C' Studio, small
Queen's Hall, London* with string quintet
conducted by Lawrance Collingwood (1st
violin, 2nd violin, viola, cello, piano).
Bb17191—3: Killarney (trad), 30-4167
DA1136; 4: *do*; 5: *do*.
Bb19890—1: An Irish love song Op 22
(Margaret Lang), 30-4168 DA1136 IR392;
2:*do*.

(19) 1944, *Aula Maxima, University
College, Dublin* with the Dublin String
Orchestra conducted by Terry O'Connor.
2ELI—1: - -; 2: - -.
2EL2—1: - - *Mefistofele*: L'altra notte
(Boito); 2: 2- 3-44 *do* IRX35.
2EL3—1: 14- 4-44 When he who adores
thee (Moore arr John F. Larchet), IRX35
(from Test 6949-1); 2: - -.
OEL332—1: - - O breathe not his name
(Moore arr J. F. Larchet); 2: - 3-44 *do*
IR316.
OEL333—1: *Gianni Schicchi*:
O mio babbino caro (Puccini); - 2: *do*.
OEL338—1: - - Galway Bay (Colehan arr
J. F. Larchet); 2: - - *do*.

(20) *18th June, 1949, Decca Studios,
London – 10" test recordings* with piano
accompaniments by Hubert Greenslade.
DDR13752—1: Oh! Breathe not his name
(Moore arr. J. F. Larchet); - 2: - -.
DDR13753—1: When he who adores thee
(Moore arr. J. F. Larchet); - 2: - -.

(21) *28th June, 1949, Decca Studios,
London – 10" test recordings for Decca* with

piano accompaniments by Hubert
Greenslade.
DR13779—1: Rich and rare.
DR13780—1: Has sorrow thy young days
shaded (Moore).

(22) *1949, London – 12" test recordings for
Decca* with orchestra.
Test 6: Danny Boy (Weatherley).
Test 7: L'ultima canzone (Tosti).

(23) *Radio Eireann Studio, GPO Building,
Dublin* ('recorded some time in the early
1950s').
Tape-recorded interview entitled 'Vissi
d'arte' later re-edited into a one hour radio
programme 'The Silenced Voice', broadcast
9th December, 1961. (Musical illustrations
from commercial recordings).

Untraced: Others in the OEL matrix series
(matrix numbers required):

DA 1078 *Bohemian Girl*: I dreamt I dwelt /
Kerry Dance
DA 1136 Killarney / Mavourneen.

[*Bohemian Girl* & Mavourneen were
re-issued as IR 392]

IRX 35 'L'Altra Notte' / 'When He Who
Adores Thee'.

(24) *23rd September, 1957, Radio Eireann
Studio, GPO Building, Dublin* (Private
Recording) Margaret Burke Sheridan —
Marchese P. Maracreda.

(25) *23rd October, 1929 to 3rd January,
1930, Milan.*
Madama Butterfly – complete recording on
32 sides with Lionello Cecil (tenor), Ida
Mannarini (mezzo-soprano), Elena Lomi
(mezzo-soprano), Vittorio Weinberg
(baritone), Nello Palai (tenor), Guglielmo
Masini (bass), Antonio Gelli (bass),
members of the Chorus and Orchestra of
La Scala, Milan, conducted by Carlo
Sabajno, Chorus Master Vittore Veneziani.
   (Orchestra: 10 1st violins, 8 2nd violins,
6 violas, 6 cellos, 6 double bass, piccolo, 2
flutes, 2 clarinets, 2 oboes, cor anglais,
bassoon, contra-bassoon, 4 horns, 2
trumpets, 3 tenor & 3 bass trombones,
tuba, tympani, drum, celeste, harp – but
may have varied slightly from session to
session).

Issue Numbers:
England:
C1950-C1965
C7391-C7406 (automatic couplings)
C7076-C7091 (automatic couplings)
Germany:
EH563-EH578
Italy:
S10190-S10205

[Face numbers in all cases run serially from 102-696 (side 1) to 102-727 (side 32)].

Victor:
9851-9866 (Manual album M97).
9867-9882 (Auto-Manual album AM97).

Contents of the set:
Side   1: E soffitto e areti IM LC NP
Side   2: Qui verran LC VW NP
Side   3: Ed è bella la sposa LC VW NP
Side   4: Ecco, son giunte MS NP
Side   5: Gran ventura MS LC VW NP
Side   6: Che burletta MS LC VW NP
Side   7: Lo Zio Bonzo MS LC VW NP AG
Side   8: Cio-Cio-San MS LC IM NP GM
Side   9: Viene la sera MS LC IM
Side 10: Bimba dagli occhi MS LC
Side 11: Vogliatemi bene MS LC
Side 12: Io t'ho germita MS LC
Side 13: E Izaghi e Izanami MS IM
Side 14: Perchè con tante cure MS IM
Side 15: Un bel di vedremo MS
Side 16: C'è entrate MS VW NP
Side 17: Ah, si – Goro MS VW NP AG
Side 18: Vi lascio il cuor MS VW AG
Side 19: Due cose potrei far MS VW
Side 20: Che tua madre MS VW
Side 21: Vespa! Respo! MS IM NP
Side 22: Scuoti quella fronda MS IM
Side 23: Gettiamo a mani pieni MS IM
Side 24: Nello Shosi MS
Side 25: Intermezzo, pt 1 Orch
Side 26: Intermezzo, pt 2 Orch
Side 27: Già il sole MS IM EL LC VW
Side 28: Io so che alle sue pene IM LC VW
Side 29: Addio fiorito asil MS IM EL LC VW
Side 30: Tu Suzuki MS IM VW
Side 31: A lui debbo obbedir MS IM EL VW
Side 32: Tu tu piccolo Iddio MS LC

Recording details:

CM1169-1	24-10-29	
-2	24-10-29	
-1T1	28- 5-30	Side 1
CM1170-1	24-10-29	Side 2
-2	24-10-29	
CM1176-1	25-10-29	
-2	25-10-29	Side 3
CM1263-1	26-11-29	
-2	26-11-29	
-3	1-4-30	
-4	1-4-30	
-4T1	- - 30	Side 4
CM1252-1	22-11-29	Side 5
-2	22-11-29	
CM1218-1	9-11-29	Side 6
-2	9-11-29	
CM1251-1	22-11-29	
-2	22-11-29	Side 7
CM1193-1	30-10-29	
-2	30-10-29	
-3	30-10-29	Side 8
CM1197-1	31-10-29	
-2	31-10-29	
-3	24- 3-30	Side 9
-4	24- 3-30	
CM1192-1	30-10-29	
-2	30-10-29	Side 10
CM1200-1	4-11-29	Side 11
-2	4-11-29	
CM1198-1	4-11-29	
-2	4-11-29	
-3	27- 3-30	
-4	27- 3-30	Side 12
CM1181-1	28-10-29	
-2	28-10-29	
-3	4-12-29	Side 13
-4	4-12-29	
CM1182-1	28-10-29	
-2	28-10-29	Side 14
-3	6- 5-30	
-4	6- 5-30	
CM1220-1	11-11-29	
-2	11-11-29	Side 15
CM1285-1	2-12-29	
-2	2-12-29	Side 16
CM1286-1	2-12-29	
-2	2-12-29	Side 17
CM1225-1	13-11-29	Side 18
-2	13-11-29	
CM1183-1	28-10-29	
-2	28-10-29	
-3	29-11-29	
-4	29-11-29	Side 19
CM1165-1	23-10-29	
-2	23-10-29	
-3	7- 1-30	Side 20
-4	7- 1-30	
CM1370-1	2- 1-30	
-2	2- 1-30	Side 21
CM1301-1	4-12-29	
-2	4-12-29	Side 22
CM1302-1	4-12-29	
-2	4-12-29	
-2T1	4- 6-30	Side 23

CM1262-1	26-11-29	Side 24		CM1371-1	2- 1-30	
-2	26-11-29			-2	2- 1-30	Side 30
CM1187-1	30-10-29			-3	2- 1-30	
-2	30-10-29	Side 25		CM1228-1	14-11-29	
CM1196-1	31-10-29			-2	14-11-29	Side 31
-2	31-10-29	Side 26		CM1164-1	23-10-29	
-3	31-10-29			-2	23-10-29	
CM1208-1	6-11-29	Side 27		-3	6- 1-30	
-2	6-11-29			-4	6- 1-30	Side 32
CM1177-1	25-10-29					
-2	25-10-29					
-3	21- 3-30					
-4	21- 3-30	Side 28				
CM1233-1	18-11-29					
-2	19-11-29					
-3	19-11-29	Side 29				

[Note: Victór renumbered the sides in sequence, allocating the matrix numbers from CVS67303-1 (side 1) to CVS67334-4 (side 32). The original take numbers were retained but without the 'T' suffix in the case of the three transfers.]

Notes on the Recording Sessions

1   These are the only acoustic recordings made by Sheridan.

2   Sheridan does not take part on CR399 and CR403; all the recordings made at this performance have been listed.

Take numbers (-1 / -2) are used to indicate different performances of the same work; the suffix letters (A/B) indicate different waxes cut from the same performance, on different machines and with different electrical characteristics.

9   EX 29 0169 3 is *The Record of Singing*, Volume 3.

11   Victor gave new matrix numbers, CVE45759-2 and CVE45760-2 respectively, to the issued takes from this session.

13   Bill Moran reports that his copy of DA987 is marked Bb14214-1. The matrix card, however, indicates that Bb14214-2 was used for making pressings. Whether the stamper for DA987 was wrongly marked or whether take one was used instead of (or as well as) take 2 remains to be determined conclusively.

16   The song on Bb17193 (Session 18) is listed as, and appears on the labels as, 'An Irish folk song' (Arthur Foote). Sheridan, however, sings the Lang song, which is quite different.

19   It has proved impossible to obtain details of Sheridan's last session for HMV. It seems that no Irish recording sheets were sent to Hayes, so that the matrix cards (which exist for masters used commercially) carry dates which may or may not be recording dates. A fire at the Irish branch then destroyed the original lists.
        It is also obvious that the person who numbered the matrixes did not fully understand the system in use and, never having met 12" matrixes before, believed that 2EL was a different series from OEL and numbered the Sheridans accordingly. This makes it seem likely that Sheridan also recorded some title on 2EL1.
        Listing the published recordings in the OEL matrix series reveals only one significant gap – which happens to run from 334 to 337, and no one knows what it contained!
        Sheridan was nervous about making these records and had them reviewed (in her absence) by a committee of friends whose opinion was that they did not 'represent her at her best'.

Under the terms of her contract they were therefore not published during her lifetime. (Information by courtesy of Norris Davidson). Presumably someone remembers what the records were and it is even possible that someone has copies of the test pressings but no further information has been forthcoming.

It has been reported that a copy of IRX35 was pressed using 2EL2-1 and not 2EL2-2 as shown by the matrix card. See note of Session 13.

20, 21, 22   The details given are all that is known of these sessions, but the test pressings have survived. (Information on 20 and 21: letter from Mr. Malcolm Walker. All recordings unpublished).

Acknowledgements

Grateful thanks are once again due to collectors who supplied information not available on file. Mrs. Ruth Edge, Chief Archivist at the EMI— Music Archive has again provided the essential help necessary to obtain anything approaching completeness and Bill Moran has supplied comprehensive details of Victor issues, while Geoffrey Child has provided the information on the series of tests made for Decca. Thanks are also due to Noel Shiels, Sound Archives Librarian of Radio Telefís Éireann and, particularly, to Norris Davidson, formerly Head of the Scriptwriters Department of Radio Éireann and Producer of the radio broadcast, for first hand information regarding the elusive last HMV records. Additional information supplied by Derek Walshe and Anne Chambers.

MARGARET SHERIDAN on LP

(Based on an article by Aldo Schiappapietra, Cesar A. Dillon & Neville Sumper
in *The Record Collector*, with additional information from
Derek Walshe and Anne Chambers)

PREISER LV 201 (M. Sheridan) —   Cc 9382 Lohengrin
                                  Cc 9380 Otello
                                  CM 844/5 Andrea Chénier
                                  Cc 9483 La Bohème
                                  CR 1437 Madama Butterfly
                                  CM 1197; 1192; 1200; 1198 Madama Butterfly (cp. rec.)
                                  Cc 9381 Madama Butterfly
                                  CR 1438 Madama Butterfly
                                  CM 1164 Madama Butterfly
PREISER LV 148 (R. Zanelli) —   CM 1333/4 Otello
PREISER LV 245 (A. Pertile Vol. 2) —   CD 4916/7 Madama Butterfly
PREISER LV 279 (A. Pertile Vol. 3) —   CM 844/5 Andrea Chénier
                                  CM 834/5 Manon Lescaut

CLUB 99: OP 1001: **MADAMA BUTTERFLY** Complete recording (sides A, B, C, D, E part)
plus sides E part / F —   Cc 9380 Otello
                           Cc 9381 Madama Butterfly
                           CR 1437 Madama Butterfly
                           CR 1438 Madama Butterfly
                           CD 4916/7 Madama Butterfly
                           CM 834/5 Manon Lescaut
                           CM 844/5 Andrea Chénier
                           CM 1333/4 Otello

TIMA 65/6 (Grandi Cantanti del Teatro Regio di Torino):
CM 844/5 Andrea Chénier

ETERNA 736 (Famous love duets in opera)
CM 845 Andrea Chénier (2nd part of duet)

RUBINI RS 320 (Covent Garden The story of five seasons 1899/1919):
Cc 9483 Bohème
Cc 9381 Madama Butterfly
HMV-HLM 7076 —   Cc 9380 Otello
Cc 9483 La Bohème
CR 1438 Madama Butterfly
CD 4916/7 Madama Butterfly
CM 834/5 Manon Lescaut
CM 844/5 Andrea Chénier
CM 1333/4 Otello

HMV — EX 2901693 (Record of singing Vol. 3) —
CR 1439 Madama Butterfly

VOCE DEL PADRONE: QALP 10414 (A. Pertile) —
CM 844/5 Andrea Chénier

VOCE DEL PADRONE: QBLP 5063 (10-inch) (A. Pertile) —
CM 834/5 Manon Lescaut & A. Chénier CM 844/5

SUPRAPHON 0120789 (A. Pertile) CM 844/5 Andrea Chénier

VOCAL RECORD COLLECTOR SOCIETY
VCRS 1977 — Test 6 (Decca) Danny Boy
VCRS 1981 — OEL 338 Galway Bay

AMERICAN LP ISSUE BY E. J. SMITH
CELEBRITY RECORDS (CRC101)
Side 1

Andrea Chénier:	Vicino a te	(Duet Pertile)
Madama Butterfly:	Love Duet	(Duet Pertile)
Manon Lescaut:	Love Duet	(Duet Pertile)
Otello:	Love Duet	(Duet Zanelli)

Side 2

Mefistofele:	L'Altra Notte
Otello:	Ave Maria
La Bohème:	Mi chiamano Mimi
Lohengrin:	Elsa's Dream
Bohemian Girl:	I dreamt I dwelt in Marble Halls

Danny Boy
Galway Bay

EMI Centenary Recording of her Operatic Arias and Irish Songs
Margaret Sheridan – Centenary. MBS1; TCMBS1 (October 1989, EMI, Ireland)

APPENDIX 4

THE FAMILY CONNECTIONS OF MARGARET BURKE SHERIDAN

Sources:
Cal. Grants of probate and letters of adm., PRO Dublin;
Landed Estates Court, PRO; Griffith Valuations;
Ms. 4855-6; PRO Marriage Licence Bonds 1769-1845,
Tuam, PRO; Census of Population (1901); Mary and
Dorothy Cooley, Newport, Co. Mayo;
Niamh Winklemann, Dublin; Registry of Births,
Marriages and Deaths, Dublin and Castlebar;
Parish Registers, Church of Holy Rosary,
Castlebar.

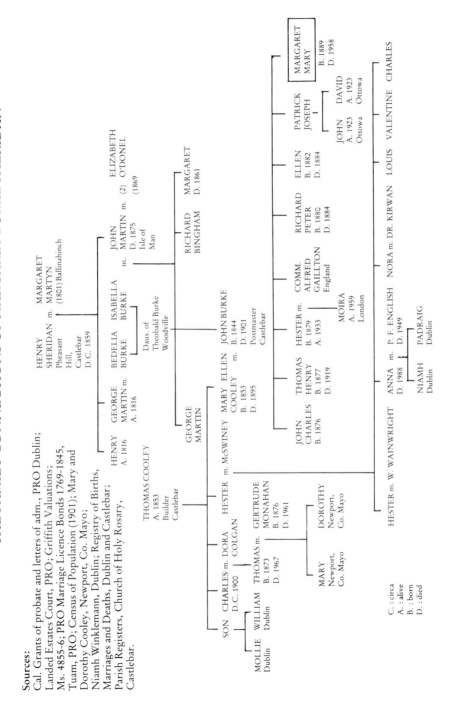

C. : circa
A. : alive
B. : born
D. : died

APPENDIX 5

References

Chapter 1

1 *Galway Vindicator*, October 9, 1871.
2 Last will and testament of John Burke Sheridan (PRO).
3 *Connaught Telegraph, July 15, 1899.*
4 *ibid*, October 1, 1898.
5 *ibid.*
6 *ibid*, June 4, 1898.
7 *ibid*, August 6, 1898.
8 *ibid*, March 30, 1901.
9 *Capuchin Annual*, Vol. 95, 1959, p. 173.
10 Miss Annie Walshe.
11 *Evening Press*, April 17, 1958.
12 *Capuchin Annual*, 1959, p. 169.
13 *Connaught Telegraph*, April 27, 1895.
14 *ibid*, January 12, 1901.
15 Last will and testament of John Burke Sheridan.
16 *ibid.*
17 *ibid.*
18 *ibid.*
19 *Connaught Telegraph*, February 16, 1901.
20 *Capuchin Annual*, p. 167.
21 *The Lanthorn: Yearbook of the Dominican College, Eccles Street*, 1982, p. 20.
22 *Capuchin Annual*, 1959, p. 173.
23 Sheridan Papers.
24 'The Silenced Voice', Radio Documentary, RTE, 1958.
25 *Irish Press*, April 17, 1958.
26 *Capuchin Annual*, p. 182.
27 *The Lanthorn*, p. 210, 1944.
28 *ibid*, p. 211.
29 *The Bell*, No. 5, October-March, 1942/43, p. 115.
30 'A Song to Remember', May Piggott.
31 Nancy Cahir, County Limerick, 1988.
32 Sheridan Papers.
33 *ibid.*
34 *Freeman's Journal*, May 21, 1908.
35 *ibid*, June 2, 1908.
36 *ibid*, October 27, 1908.
37 *ibid*, December 5, 1908.
38 *ibid*, May 20, 1909.

Chapter 2

1 Sheridan Papers.
2 *Capuchin Annual*, 1959, p. 170.
3 Sheridan Papers.
4 *ibid*, Sheridan Papers.
5 *Chirk Castle*, The National Trust, p. 54.
6 *Pages From My Life*, Margherita Howard de Walden, p. 61.
7 *ibid*, p. 69.
8 Sheridan Papers.
9 *ibid.*
10 *ibid.*
11 *Thomas Beecham, An Independent Biography*, C. Reid, p. 136.
12 'The Silenced Voice', RTE, 1958.
13 Kathleen Joy Evans, 1988.
14 *Capuchin Annual*, 1959, p. 170.
15 Sheridan papers.
16 *Freeman's Journal*, October 5, 1918.
17 'The Silenced Voice', RTE, 1958.
18 *Emerald and Nancy*, D. Fielding, p. 39.
19 Sheridan Papers.
20 *ibid.*
21 *ibid.*
22 *ibid.*
23 *Ibid.*
24 *Capuchin Annual*, p. 178.
25 Sheridan Papers.
26 'The Silenced Voice', RTE, 1958.

Chapter 3

1 'The Silenced Voice', RTE, 1958.
2 *ibid.*
3 *ibid.*
4 *Gigli Memoirs*, p. 41.
5 'The Silenced Voice', RTE, 1958.
6 *ibid.*
7 *ibid.*
8 *ibid.*
9 *ibid.*
10 *The Irish Digest*, p. 9, 1940.
11 *ibid*, p. 10.
12 *ibid.*
13 *Il Messagero*, 4 February, 1918.

14 *ibid.*
15 *Rassegna Melodrammatica*, 15 February, 1918.
16 *ibid.*
17 *The Irish Digest*, p. 12.

Chapter 4

1 Sheridan Papers.
2 *ibid.*
3 *Two Centuries of Opera at Covent Garden*, H. Rosenthal, p. 398.
4 *Opera at Covent Garden: A Short History*, H. Rosenthal, p. 103.
5 *ibid.*
6 *Capuchin Annual*, 1959, p. 180.
7 *The Alchemy of Voice*, E. Herbert Caeseri, Ch. XVIII, p. 231.
8 Sheridan Papers.
9 *Daily Telegraph*, May 13, 1919.
10 Sheridan Papers.
11 *Daily Chronicle*, May 28, 1919.
12 *Morning Post*, May 28, 1919.
13 'The Silenced Voice', RTE, 1958.
14 *Evening Press*, April 17, 1958.
15 *Capuchin Annual*, 1959, p. 166.
16 *Daily Telegraph*, July 5, 1919.
17 *Daily Mail*, July 9, 1919.
18 *The Times*, July 9, 1919.
19 *Globe*, July 9, 1919.
20 *Corriere della Sera*, July 1919.
21 *Portraits of Greatness, Puccini*, p. 13.
22 *The Gramophone*, April 1944, p. 162.
23 *The Bell*, No. 5, October-March, 1942/3, p. 115.
24 Sheridan Papers.
25 *Corriere della Sera*, December 31, 1919.
26 *ibid.*
27 *La Gazzetta dei Teatri*, January 15, 1920.
28 'The Silenced Voice', RTE, 1958.
29 *Sole – Milano*, February 22, 1920.
30 *Corriere della Sera*, February 22, 1920.
31 Sheridan Papers.
32 *Ibid.*
33 *ibid.*
34 *ibid.*
35 *Freeman's Journal*, November 1922.
36 Sheridan – Private Recording (Marchese P. Maracreda).
37 *Il Mattino*, February 27-28, 1921.
38 *Capuchin Annual*, p. 168.
39. *ibid.*
40 Inscription on bust.
41 'I Hear You Calling Me' L. McCormack, p.100.
42 Sheridan Papers.
43 *ibid.*
44 *ibid.*

Chapter 5

1 Private Recording (Marchese P. Maracreda).
2 Toscanini, p. 142.
3 *The Opera Bedside Book*, H. Rosenthal (ed.), p. 246.
4 *Portraits of Greatness: Toscanini*, J. W. Freeman, W. Toscanini, p. 42.
5 'The Silenced Voice', RTE, 1958.
6 *Toscanini*, p. 37.
7 'The Silenced Voice', RTE, 1958.
8 *The Bell*, No. 5, October-March 1942-43, p. 116.
9 Kathleen Joy Evans.
10 Sheridan papers.
11 *Toscanini*, p. 39.
12 'The Silenced Voice', 1958.
13 *ibid.*
14 *Corriere della Sera*, January 8, 1922.
15 *Il Mattino*, January 11-12, 1922.
16 Sheridan papers.
17 *ibid.*
18 Private Recording (Marchese P. Maracreda).
19 EMI International Classical Division, London.
20 Kathleen Joy Evans.
21 Arthur Hammond.
22 Dott. G. Gualerzi, Turin.
23 Madame Renata Tebaldi, Milan.
24 'The Silenced Voice', 1958.
25 *The Bell*, p. 118.
26 *Evening Herald*, December 1, 1922.
27 *Freeman's Journal*, December 1, 1922.
28 *ibid.*
29 *ibid.*
30 *ibid.*
31 December 5, 1922.
32 *ibid.*
33 *ibid.*

Chapter 6

1 *Italy*, Mack Smith, p. 74.
2 *ibid*, p. 58.
3 *History of La Scala*, p. 292.
4 *Corriere della Sera*, April 27, 1923.
5 Sheridan Papers.
6 *Ibid.*
7 *Capuchin Annual*, 1959, p. 169.
8 Dame Eva Turner, 1988.
9 *The Gramophone*, April 1944, p. 163.
10 Sheridan Papers.
11 *Ibid.*
12 *Opera News*, 1952.
13 Arthur Hammond (1989).
14 *Irish Times*, June 30, 1951.
15 *L'Avvenire d'Italia*, September 1923.

16   *Cremona Nuova*, February 10, 1924.
17   *ibid.*
18   *Capuchin Annual*, 1959, p. 169.
19   Madame Renata Tebaldi.
20   *Corriere della Sera*, November 16, 1923.
21   *History of La Scala*, p. 296.
22   *Corriere della Sera*, May 15, 1924.
23   *ibid.*
24   *The Memoirs of Beniamino Gigli*, p. 97.
25   Kathleen Joy Evans (1988).
26   'The Silenced Voice', RTE 1958.
27   *The Memoirs of Beniamino Gigli*, p. 126.
28   *Il Popolo d'Italia*, February 2, 1926.
29   *The Alchemy of Voice*, p. 230.
30   *ibid.*
31   *ibid*, p. 231.
32   Sheridan Papers.
33   *Daily Sketch*, August 26, 1924.

33   *ibid.*
34   *ibid.*
35   *The Times*, June 29, 1926.
36   Sheridan Papers.
37   *ibid.*
38   *ibid.*
39   *ibid.*
40   *Two Centuries of Opera at Covent Garden*, p. 452.
41   Sheridan Papers.
42   *The Times*, June 2, 1928.
43   *The Field*, June 7, 1928.
44   'The Silenced Voice', RTE, 1958.
45   Kathleen Joy Evans (1988).
46   *The Star*, June 8, 1928.
47   *Sunday Times*, June 10, 1928.
48   *Evening News*, June 8, 1928.
49   *Daily News*, June 12, 1928.
50   *Ernest Newman: A Memoir by his Wife*, Vera Newman, (London, 1963), p. 82.
51   Sheridan Papers.

Chapter 7

1   *Daily Telegraph*, December 21, 1924.
2   *L'Avvenire d'Italia*, November 27, 1924.
3   *Rassegna Melodrammatica*, December 29, 1924.
4   *The Memoirs of Beniamino Gigli*, p. 137.
5   Sheridan Papers.
6   *Il Lavora*, December 29, 1924.
7   Archives, Royal Opera House, Covent Garden.
8   *Among the Covent Garden Stars*, J. O'Donnell, p. 135.
9   Archives, Royal Opera House, Covent Garden.
10   Sheridan papers.
11   *Ibid.*
12   *ibid.*
13   *ibid.*
14   *ibid.*
15   *Capuchin Annual*, 1959, p. 168.
16   *Daily Telegraph*, June 8, 1925.
17   *Evening Standard*, June 10, 1925.
18   *Daily News*, June 13, 1925.
19   *Daily Telegraph*, June 18, 1925.
20   *The Times*, June 17, 1925.
21   *Daily Telegraph*, June 18, 1925.
22   *ibid.*
23   *Herald Illustrated Sunday*, June 14, 1925.
24   *Daily Telegraph*, July 11, 1925.
25   *Il Piccolo della Sera di Trieste*, November 30, 1925.
26   *L'Abbonato*, December 30, 1925.
27   Sheridan Papers.
28   *Capuchin Annual*, 1959, p. 168.
29   Sheridan Papers.
30   *ibid.*
31   *ibid.*
32   *ibid.*

Chapter 8

1   Sheridan Papers.
2   *ibid.*
3   *Two Centuries of Opera at Covent Garden*, p. 460.
4   *Daily Telegraph*, June 19, 1929.
5   *The Times*, June 18, 1929.
6   *Daily Chronicle*, June 19, 1929.
7   'Good Evenin' Listeners'G. Smith, Dublin 1987, p. 67.
8   Sheridan Papers.
9   *ibid.*
10   *ibid.*
11   *ibid.*
12   *La Stampa*, January 27, 1930.
13   *Storio del Teatro Regio di Torino*, p. 145.
14   Sheridan Papers.
15   *ibid.*
16   *ibid.*
17   *ibid.*
18   *Daily Herald*, May 28, 1930.
19   *Daily Mirror*, May 27, 1930.
20   *Daily Telegraph*, May 31, 1930.
21   *Evening News*, May 31, 1930.
22   *Daily Telegraph*, June 17, 1930.
23   Sheridan Papers.
24   John Gualini, Milano, 1989.
25   EMI Archives, Hayes.
26   *ibid.*
27   *ibid.*
28   Sheridan Papers.
29   *ibid.*
30   *ibid.*
31   EMI Archives, Hayes.
32   Sheridan Papers.

33 *ibid.*
34 *ibid.*
35 'The Silenced Voice', RTE, 1958.
36 Sheridan Papers.
37 *ibid.*
38 *ibid.*
39 *ibid.*
40 *ibid.*
41 *ibid.*
42 *ibid.*
43 *ibid.*
44 Kathleen Joy Evans.
45 Endorsement for *The Science and Sensations of Vocal Tone*, E. Herbert Caeseri.
46 Sheridan Papers.
47 *ibid.*
48 Private Recording (Marchese P. Maracreda).
49 Kathleen Joy Evans.
50 Mimi Zuccari in DGOS Programme, Spring 1959.
51 John Gualini, Milano, 1989.
52 *ibid.*
53 *The Irish Times*, June 30, 1951.
54 Dott. Arnaldo Pertile, Padova, 1989.
55 Dr. Veronica Dunne, Dublin, 1989.
56 Dott. A. G. Viani, Dublin.
57 *The Lanthorn*, 1922, p. 54.
58 R. W. Lightbody, Belfast, 1988.
59 Sheridan Papers.
60 *The Alchemy of Voice*, p. 226.
61 Sheridan Papers.

Chapter 9

1 Derek Walshe, Dublin.
2 HMV Archives, Hayes.
3 Hotel Register, Renvyle Hotel, Co. Galway.
4 *A Sea Grey House*, J. A. Lidwell, p. 71.
5 *ibid*, p. 75.
6 Kathleen Joy Evans.
7 Oliver O'Brien.
8 Sheridan Papers.
9 Louise O'Brien, Dublin.
10 *Connaught Telegraph*, August 1939.
11 Mr. Jack Cahill, Castlebar, 1988.
12 Mr. M. J. Egan, Castlebar, 1988.
13 Sheridan Papers.
14 Mrs. Gwladys McCabe, Dublin 1989.
15 *ibid.*
16 Kathleen Joy Evans.
17 Mrs. Margaret Murphy, Dublin, 1988.
18 *ibid.*
19 Kathleen Joy Evans, Dublin.
20 *ibid.*
21 Cyril Cusack, Dun Laoghaire, 1988.
22 R. W. Lightbody, Belfast, 1988.
23 *ibid.*
24 *ibid.*
25 *ibid.*
26 Mrs. Gwladys McCabe.
27 *ibid.*
28 *The Bell*, 1942-43, p. 113.
29 *ibid.*
30 Kathleen Joy Evans, Dublin.
31 *Irish Times*, June 30, 1951.
32 Kathleen Joy Evans, Dublin.
33 *ibid.*
34 *ibid.*
35 *Sunday Chronicle*, March 10, 1946.
36 *ibid.*
37 EMI Archives, Hayes.
38 *ibid.*
39 *ibid.*
40 *ibid.*
41 Kathleen Joy Evans, Dublin.
42 *ibid.*
43 *ibid.*
44 *Sunday Chronicle*, March 19, 1946.
45 Mrs. Gwladys McCabe, Dublin.
46 Sheridan to Michael Cunneen, 1954.
47 Jeannie Reddin, Dublin, 1989.
48 *The Great Irish Tenor*, p. 90.
49 *ibid.*
50 *ibid*, p. 88.
51 R. W. Lightbody, Belfast, 1988.
52 Sheridan to M. Cunneen, 1954.
53 R. W. Lightbody, Belfast, 1988.
54 Dr. Veronica Dunne, Dublin, 1988.
55 DGOS Souvenir Programme, 1945.
56 *The Irish Times*, June 5, 1956.
57 Virginia Zeani-Lemeni, 1989.
58 *ibid.*
59 Mrs. Phyllis Sullivan (nee Boland) 1988.
60 *ibid.*
61 *ibid.*
62 Dr. Veronica Dunne, Dublin, 1988.
63 Kathleen Joy Evans, Dublin, 1988.
64 *The Lanthorn*, 1959.
65 *Evening Press*, April 17, 1958.
66 R. W. Lightbody, Belfast, 1988.

Chapter 10

1 *Capuchin Annual*, 1959, p. 126.
2 *ibid.*
3 *ibid.*
4 *ibid*, p. 185.
5 Fr. Leo Clifford, OFM, Dublin, 1988.
6 *ibid.*
7 *Capuchin Annual*, 1959, p. 168.
8 *ibid*, p. 177.
9 Hubert Valentine, Dublin, 1988.
10 *ibid.*
11 *ibid.*

12 *Capuchin Annual*, p. 184.
13 Fr. Leo Clifford.
14 *ibid.*
15 *ibid.*
16 *Capuchin Annual*, p. 185.
17 Fr. Leo Clifford.
18 Sheridan Papers.
19 *Sunday Press*, September 17, 1978.
20 *ibid.*
21 Sheridan Papers.
22 Fr. Leo Clifford.
23 *ibid.*
24 Sister Kathleen Power, Dublin, 1988.
25 Kathleen Joy Evans.
26 *The Lanthorn*, 1958, p. 35.
27 'A Tribute to Margaret Burke Sheridan', RTE, 1958.
28 Joe Lynch, Dublin, 1988.
29 *ibid.*
30 Fr. Leo Clifford.
31 Sheridan Papers.
32 Dr. Roderick Mansfield, Dublin, 1989.
33 *ibid.*
34 *ibid.*
35 'The Silenced Voice', RTE, 1958.
36 Mrs. Gwladys McCabe, Dublin, 1989.
37 Fr. Leo Clifford.
38 Cyril Cusack, Dublin, 1988.
39 'The Silenced Voice', 1958.
40 *Capuchin Annual*, p. 162.
41 *The Irish Times*, April 16, 1958.
42 *Capuchin Annual*, p. 167.
43 *Irish Independent*, April 17, 1958.
44 'The Silenced Voice', RTE, 1958.

APPENDIX 6

Bibliography

PRIMARY SOURCES

Ireland

1 Private papers of Margaret Burke Sheridan kindly made available by the Hon. Garech Browne.
2 Papers relating to Margaret Burke Sheridan kindly made available by Mrs. Pamela Manahan.
3 Papers relating to Margaret Burke Sheridan kindly made available by Mrs. Mildred O'Brien.
4 Convent of Mercy, Castlebar.
5 Public Record Office, Dublin: m.s. 4855, 4856.
6 Griffith Valuation – Mayo.
7 Registry of Wills.
8 Registry of Deeds – Dublin.
9 Registry of Births, Marriages and Deaths – Castlebar, Dublin.
10 Land Registry – Dublin.
11 National Library of Ireland, Dublin.
12 RTE Sound Archives, Dublin.
13 Trinity College Library, Dublin.
14 Central Library, Ilac Centre, Dublin.
15 Renvyle House Hotel, Co. Galway.
16 Dominican Convent, Dublin.
17 County Library, Castlebar.
18 Newspapers – various issues, 1870-1958: *Galway Vindicator, Tuam Herald, Connaught Telegraph, The Mail, Dublin Evening Mail, Freeman's Journal, Irish Times, Irish Independent, Irish Press, Evening Press, Evening Herald, Sunday Press, Sunday Independent, Sunday Chronicle, Cork Examiner.*
19 *The Capuchin Annual, 1989.*

England

1 Archives of the Royal Opera House, Covent Garden, London.
2 EMI Archives, Middlesex.
3 Royal Academy of Music, London.
4 Central Reference Library, London.
5 English Newspapers – various issues, 1918-1940: *The Times, Sunday Times, Graphic and Illustrated London News, Daily Telegraph, Daily News, Westminster Gazette, Daily Sketch, Sunday Chronicle, Daily Chronicle, Morning Post, Daily Mirror, Evening News, The Advertiser, The Globe, Evening Standard, Daily Express, Yorkshire Post, Manchester Guardian, Liverpool Daily Courier, Eve, The Lady's Pictorial, The Field, The Observer.*

Italy

1 Biblioteca Nazionale Centrale, Roma.
2 Biblioteca Comunale, Milano.
3 Biblioteca Comunale, Torino.
4 Costello Sforzesco, Archivo Fotografico, Milano.
5 Museo Teatrale alla Scala, Milano.
6 Ufficio Stampa Teatro di San Carlo, Napoli.
7 Ufficio Stampa Teatro Comunale, Firenze.
8 Ufficio Stampa Teatro Comunale, Bologna.
9 Ufficio Stampa Teatro Comunale, Cento.
10 Ufficio Stampa Teatro Comunale Ponchielli, Cremona.
11 Ufficio Stampa Teatro di Carlo Felice, Genova.
12 Ufficio Stampa Teatro Municipale, Piacenza.
13 Ufficio Stampa Teatro Grande, Brescia.
14 Ufficio Stampa Teatro Comunale, Giuseppe Verdi, Trieste.
15 Archivo Storico Musicale Teatro La Fenice, Venezia.
16 Archivo Storico Musicale Teatro di Regio, Torino.
17 Teatro dell' Opera, Roma.
18 Offices of: *Il Mattino*, Napoli; *Il Stampa*, Torino; *Il Messagero*, Roma.
19 Newspapers and periodicals, 1916-1940: *L'Abbonato, Il Mattino, Avanti, Corriere della Sera, La Stampa, Il Messagero, La Republica, Il Popolo d'Italia, Il Popolo Romano, L'Italia, Il Giornale d'Italia, Cremona Nuova, Gazzetta del Popolo, Il Resto del Carlino, L'Avvenire d'Italia, Musica d'Oggi, Revista Nationale di Musico, Nuova Revista, Rassegna Melodrammatica, Il Piccolo Della Sera di Trieste, Il Lavora, La Gazzetta dei Teatri, L'Arte, Gazzettino Azzurro di Rimini.*

Monaco

1 Société des Bains de Mer, Monte Carlo.

America

1 Papers relating to Margaret Sheridan kindly made available by Fr. Leo Clifford, New York.
2 Archives, Metropolitan Opera, New York.
3 Virginia Zeani Lemeni, Indiana.
4 New York Public Library (Music Division).

SECONDARY SOURCES

Adami, G. (ed), *Letters of Puccini* (London 1974).
Annario dell' Arte Lirica Italiano (1944-45) Milan.
Beecham, T., *A Mingled Chime* (London, 1944).
The Bell, Oct-March, 1942-43 (Dublin).
Blinkhorn, M., *Mussolini and Fascist Italy* (London 1984).
Bohème, La, *English National Opera Guide 14* (London 1982).
Bouquet, M. T., Gualerzi, V., Testa, A. *Teatro Regio di Torino*, vol. V (Torino 1988).
Brockway, W., Weinstock, H., *The World of Opera* (London 1963).
Burgh, U. H. Hussey de, *The Landowners of Ireland* (Dublin 1877).
Bussi, F., *Note Critiche Sulle Stagioni Liriche al Municipale Piacenza*.
The Capuchin Annual (Dublin 1959).
Carner, M., *Puccini: A Critical Biography* (London 1974).
Casini, C., *Il Teatro Di San Carlo Nel Novecento*.
Celletti, R., *Le Grandi Voci* (Rome 1964).
Chambers Biographical Dictionary (London 1984).
Caesari, E. Herbert, *The Alchemy of Voice* (London 1965).
Chisholm, A., *Nancy Cunard* (London 1979).
Chirk Castle The National Trust (Britain 1988).
Clark, M., *Modern Italy, 1871-1982* (London 1984).
Concise Dictionary of National Biography (1901-1950).
Cooper, D., *The Rainbow Comes and Goes* (London 1958).
Curcio, A., (ed) *Grande Enciclopedia della Musica Classica* (Vol IV).
Daly, A., *A Chronicle of Kenure House* (Dublin 1988).

Dublin Grand Opera Society, Spring 1959 Programme.
Dublin Historical Record, September 1986.
Enciclopedia della Musica (Ricordi Milan, 1964).
Fielding, D., *Emerald and Nancy: Lady Cunard and her Daughter* (London 1969).
Forlani, M. G., *Il Teatro Municipale di Piacenza, 1804-1984* (1985).
Frajese, V., *Dal Costanzi all' Opera*, Vol. iv, 1880-1960 (Roma 1978).
Frassoni, E., *Due Secoli di Lirica a Genova*, Vol. II (1980).
Freeman, J. W., Toscanini, W., *Toscanini: Portraits of Greatness* (New York, 1987).
Gaisberg, F. W., *Music on Record* (London 1946).
Gatti, C., *Il Teatro alla Scala 1778-1963* (1964).
Gishford, A. (ed), *Grand Opera* (London 1972).
Gramophone, The, April 1944.
Greenfeld, H., *Puccini: A Biography* (USA 1980).
HMV, *The Voice*, February 1927, 1928.
HMV, *Trade Catalogue*, 1927.
Hetherington, J., *Melba: A Biography* (London 1967).
Howard de Walden, M., *Pages From My Life* (London 1965).
Irish Digest, The, Vol. VIL, October 1940.
Irish, Genealogist The, Vol. 3, 1956-62.
Jacobs, A., Sadie, S., *The Pan Book of Opera* (London 1984).
Jellinek, G., *Callas: Portrait of a Prima Donna* (USA 1985).
Kutsch, K. J., Riemens, L., *A Concise Biographical Dictionary of Singers* (London, New York 1966).
Lanthorn, The Yearbook of the Dominican Convent, Eccles Street (issues 1944, 1958, 1982).
Ledbetter, G. T., *The Great Irish Tenor* (London 1977).
Lidwell, A., *Seagrey House*.
Lindsay, D., Washington, E. S., *Portrait of Britain Between the Exhibitions 1851-1951* (London 1952).
McCormack, L., *I Hear You Calling Me* (London 1950).
Marinelli, C., *Opere in Disco.*
Melba, N., *Melodies and Memories* (London 1962).
Moody, T. W., Martin, F. X., *The Course of Irish History* (Dublin 1967).
Narek, G. R., *Arturo Toscanini* (London 1975).

Newman, V., *Ernest Newman: A Memoir by his Wife* (London 1963).
O'Donnell, J., *Among The Covent Garden Stars* (London 1936).
Opera News, No. 13, 1950.
Parliamentary Companion (London 1909-1924).
Phaidon Book of Opera (London 1979).
Rasponi, L., *The Last of the Prima Donnas* (London 1984).
Roman, S., Carteri, R., Cerquetti, A., *The Meteors* (London 1986).
Royal Academy of Music Club Magazine, No. 5, January 1902.
Reid, C., *Thomas Beecham: An Independent Biography*.
Roscioni, C. M., *Il Teatro di San Carlo: La Cronologia, 1737-1987* (1988).
Rosenthal, H., *Two Centuries of Opera at Covent Garden* (London 1958).
Rosenthal, H., (ed), *The Opera Bedside Book* (London 1965).
Rosenthal, H., Warrack, J., *The Concise Oxford Dictionary of Opera* (London 1987).
Sadie, S., (ed), *The New Grove Dictionary of Music and Musicians* (London 1980).
Saint, Young, Clark, Crisp, Rosenthal, *A History of the Royal Opera House 1732-1982* (London 1982).
Santoro, E., *Il Teatro di Cremona, 1901-1972*, Vol. IV, (1972).
Seligman, V., *Puccini Among Friends* (London 1938).
Silone, D., *The Memoirs of Beniamino Gigli* (London 1957).
Smith, D., Mack, *Mussolini* (London 1987); *Italy – A Modern History* (Michigan 1959).
Smith, G., *Tommy O'Brien, 'Good Evenin' Listeners'* (Dublin 1987).
Tarozzi, G., *Puccini: Portraits of Greatness* (trans. J. W. Freeman) (New York 1985).
Thal, H. Van, *Ernest Newman: Treatment of Music* (London 1962).
Thom's Official Directory 1908-1918.
Tintori, G., *Duecento Anni di Teatro alla Scala* (1979).
Trezzini, L., *Due Secoli di Vita Musicale: Storia del Teatro Comunale di Bologna*, 1763-1966, Vol I, (1987).
Walshe, J. J., *Monte Carlo Opera* (London 1975).
Weaver, W., *Puccini: The Man and His Music* (1967).
Who Was Who, 1941-1960.

INDEX TO THE TEXT

ILLUSTRATIONS
Unless otherwise acknowledged, the illustrations are from the Sheridan collection, courtesy of the Hon. Garech Browne.

Cover: Gaeatano De Gennaro Portrait
(Courtesy: The Gaiety Theatre, Dublin)

We acknowledge permission for reproduction of the illustrations and other copyright items as cited in the photographic captions or elsewhere in the text, and where we have had difficulty making contact, the publishers would be grateful to hear from the copyright holders.